CAPTAIN
FRASER'S
VOYAGES

CAPTAIN FRASER'S VOYAGES

1865–1892

MARJORY GEE

STANFORD MARITIME
LONDON

Stanford Maritime Limited
Member Company of the George Philip Group
12 Long Acre   London WC2E 9LP

First published in Great Britain 1979
Copyright © Marjory B. Gee 1979
ISBN 0 540 07180 3

Set in 11/12 Garamond 156
Printed in Great Britain by
Ebenezer Baylis & Son Limited
The Trinity Press, Worcester, and London
Text design and jacket illustrated by Bruce Thomas

British Library Cataloguing in Publication Data

Fraser, Thomas Garry
    Captain Fraser's voyages, 1865–1892.
    1. Fraser, Thomas Garry   2. Seafaring life
    I. Title   II. Gee, Marjory
    910'.45   G540

    ISBN 0-540-07180-3

Dedicated to Harold and Nellie Bridges

CONTENTS

CONTENTS

INTRODUCTION

This is a record of a man's twenty-five voyages in sail that began a hundred years ago. Thomas Garry Fraser took his Master's Certificate in 1874 at the age of twenty-three and some forty years later wrote up his travels – for whom is not known.

About twelve years ago four worn Victorian notebooks, filled with close-written meticulous handwriting, were given to me by my Mother, having been found in her sister's effects. My Aunt's handwriting is on the inside cover of each notebook, saying they were written by Captain Fraser. I knew nothing more about the man: my only clue to discovering his identity was the connection with my Aunt.

I found that my Uncle, the Rev. Harold Bridges, BD had spent two years in the firm of W. Montgomery & Co., importers of minerals from South America, while waiting to go to College, and had hoped to go to India as a missionary. This, I discovered in time, must have appealed to Captain Fraser, who apparently took a great interest in my Uncle's future. They were friends until the Captain's death in 1934.

The notebooks were baffling to read from their minute handwriting. A naval architect friend, Mr John Perryman, went so far as to send them to the National Maritime Museum at Greenwich where they were copied and returned, together with a skeleton list of Captain Fraser's ships and the comment that they were worthy of publication. So finally I took the plunge and decided to transcribe

9

the manuscript so that it could be read more easily. As the accounts unfolded I followed the voyages in an atlas. Lloyd's confirmed the shipwreck of the *Doriga* in 1879, and the Royal National Life-Boat Institution records substantiated the loss of the *Maxwell* on Liverpool bar.

But what of the man? Who was he? How had his memoirs become the property of my Aunt? The search continued with rewarding results, and gradually flesh and blood were put on the bones of Captain Thomas Garry Fraser, 1850–1934.

He was born in Harrington, Cumberland in 1850 and went to sea in 1865, a boy dedicated to the sea and ships and ready to become a man as soon as possible. His love of his home County rings through his story. In the early nineteenth century the Cumberland coast was strung with busy shipbuilding towns clinging to the sea, with hills behind and beyond them the wild country of the Lake District. The communities were hard working and cut off from passing distractions. These towns, Whitehaven, Harrington, Workington and Maryport, were all industrial and building sturdy fine timber and iron ships for the China and other clipper trades. Many of the young boys' lives revolved around the romance and expectation of a seafaring life.

Like the rest, Thomas Fraser left home at fifteen, equipped with a good basic education and a firm Christian upbringing. When he began these memoirs in about 1915 he had a rich heritage to call upon, and I became enthralled with this man who was so sternly confident, and was able to convey a picture of Victorian life at sea 'before the mast' together with the standards and values of his profession and the business aspects of captaincy.

Perhaps the most rewarding part of the trail was a visit I made to Cumbria to Workington, Harrington and Maryport. Through the interest of a young relative of the family I had heard of someone who knew Captain Fraser in his latter years. This Captain Williamson still lived in Harrington, where his family had been closely connected with shipbuilding, and he took me to see the house where T.G.F. had lived in his later days, perched high on the top of the cliff at Harrington. I saw the grave in the Harrington churchyard and found the flavour of the place with its windswept coastline and plain stone houses above the harbour. Today much of the shipbuilding is gone and the busy yards at Workington have been levelled; steel works have taken pride of place.

Some strange coincidences have emerged during the years that I have been involved with this manuscript. Having just typed the account of the second voyage and read for the first time of Will Adams, obviously a hero of boys of that generation, I picked up a book in the library called *The Needle Watcher* by Richard Blacker, to find it was the story of Will Adams' years in Japan! Again, when trying to decipher a name that looked like 'Professor Lawson', I asked a Navigation Instructor at the Lowestoft College of Further Education if he could trace this man, who had been an Examiner in Navigation at Liverpool. He phoned me saying that there was a Professor Lawson but not conclusively the one I was looking for. Ten minutes later he phoned again, quite overwhelmed, saying that he had gone to the library to put a book back on the shelves and there beside the one he replaced was a little old book with the title *Norrie and Towson's Tables* by Professor John Thomas Towson, FRGS, Late Examiner in Navigation to the Marine Board at Liverpool.

I think that the best coincidence of all was the way I found Phoebe Mason, editor. She phoned our home to ask for an address that my husband might have and in his absence I found it for her and got to talking about transcribing the accounts, which produced the suggestion that I send her a copy. To my delight she too was confident that this slice of sea history was worthy of going into print.

Mr Fearon, another Harrington man who was Captain Fraser's First Mate, refused to leave him on the sinking *Doriga*, saying:

'What would they say in Cumberland if I went
home and said that I had deserted you?'

What do they say in Cumberland of one of their sons who left us this record of life and work at sea?

'East Keal', Romany Road,   Marjory Gee
Oulton Broad, Suffolk   1978

APPRENTICE BOUND

My First Voyage
COREA
1865–1866

LIVERPOOL – HONG KONG – FOO CHOW – LONDON

In the little seaport of Harrington, the boys of my generation were all for a sea life – several times a year we had a holiday when the launch took place of large ships designed for the East Indian, Cape Horn or Australian trades. The neighbouring towns of Whitehaven, Workington and Maryport were famous for the fine ships built there; all superb oak, teak, and greenheart built and copper fastened; no better built ships in the world. Ships, their passage and adventures were our common topics, and as many locally built ships were engaged in the China trade, the annual race with the season's tea from Foo Chow to London overshadowed the Derby, the Boat Race, and all other national competitions. At that time the age of fifteen was thought to be the proper time to begin a sea life, the reason given being that boys of that age were active, their limbs more pliable and adaptable to the monkey work of climbing and working aloft. There is truth in that reason, for two of my fellows who commenced their sea life at seventeen and eighteen respectively were killed by falling from aloft.

For several terms I was well grounded in the basis of the science of navigation at sea, and I thought the time would never come until I began my high adventure.

I was staying at Castlerigg Cottage, Keswick when the summons came, on the 12th May 1865. I had gone up by coach as the railway was not yet opened, but I had the pleasure of returning by the new railway, as the wife of the General Manager was a relative of my

13

friends and had come up to Keswick in a carriage attached to the ballast train. The next day I left home for Liverpool by the P.S. *Queen*, and was very sick – disgraced myself and damaged my neighbour's clothes at table! He was a nice man and made light of it and was very kind. His name was Mr Murray, on his way to the Australian diggings, and I heard of his death some years afterwards with regret. Little kindnesses are never forgotten.

On the 19th May 1865 I was bound apprentice to Messrs Bushby & Edwards of Liverpool and there joined my ship the *Corea*, a clipper of 581 tons registered loading for Hong Kong and Whampoa.

I was much disappointed, for I had imagined a frigate-built ship like the famous Blackwallers of Green, Wigram or Smith's lines. What I found was a yacht-like ship, pretty, graceful, but with nothing of the nobility of my imaginations. On the 22nd we left Princes Dock and towed to Point Lynas, and cast off the tug. Our ship's company was Captain, three mates, bosun, carpenter, sails, steward, cook, six apprentices, twelve ABs and two OSs. As second class passengers, four Birmingham artisans, their wives and seven children from fourteen years to a baby of six months. These skilled artisans were going to Hong Kong to start a Government Mint, and we were across the Bay of Biscay before I saw any of them on deck. They had a miserable time of it battened down in their narrow dark quarters – how different from the luxurious sea travelling of today [1915].

Down St George's Channel we had westerly gales with much rain and I was very seasick, cold and wretched; not allowed to lay up, the miserable wet watches on deck were changed for the close evil-smelling half deck. The smells of that time will never be forgotten. One ruffian of an elder apprentice amused himself by thrusting fat pork in my face (the next voyage I was big and hefty enough to wallop this bully). Since then I have had to sniff thousands of evil smells but none are to be compared to the seasick days of my first voyage. I can truthfully say that *at no time* of my misery did I wish to be ashore, or think of 'swallowing the anchor'.

On the sixth day out we wore ship off the Old Head of Kinsale [on the south coast of Ireland] and were stowing the mainsail, the night dark, stormy and forbidding. I was out on the lee yard when I heard a great shouting and disturbance on deck. When I got down one of the boys saw me and shouted 'Tom's here! Tom's here!'

Soon a crowd was round me and I learned the Captain was strongly upbraiding the officers for allowing me to go aloft in such weather, for a man had fallen overboard and it was thought to be me. On mustering all hands it was found the lost man was an AB named Steve. Nothing could be done, for no boat could live in such a sea.

I was now hearty and well, with a good appetite for the vile food of those days, and enjoyed every hour of sunshine, storm or rain.

We crossed the Bay, slipped down the coast of Portugal, passed Trafalgar's historic Cape [St Vincent] and got into the climate of the flying fish and nautilus. We passed inside of Madeira, close in to Funchal. The land with lovely foliage was beautiful and our passengers now full of life wanted the ship to be anchored there, but such luxuries were not for second class passengers of those days.

We now had pleasant times, the work was interesting, the ship with all studdingsails set overhauled everything, and as I was one of the signalmen and enjoyed the 'flag chatter' we boys did not have an idle time. The Captain believed in the sane adage 'keep young men well employed'. In our watch on deck, practical seamanship and sailmaking; in our watch below, navigation, trigonometry and observations; every fine night, 'stars', and when possible, lunars. Well and truly did our Captain do his duty towards us. I doubt if there could be found anywhere a more proficient body of officers and apprentices with the sextant, and working out practical navigational problems.

All through the fine trades weather we had dogwatch concerts. The wife of one of the passengers had a beautiful trained voice, several others had fair voices, and the doyen was a good violinist, so that all enjoyed these performances. Sometimes the Captain would give readings from the poets and prose writers. Dickens' Pickwick and Little Nell's wanderings were the favourites with the sailors. With all their faults I have a great love for those old sailors of the long voyage, and I hope their dream of a pleasant resting place after clearing Davy Jones' locker will be found for them.

This first voyage was the only one of my many voyages that I had a good view of Tenerife from base to summit, the whole of its twelve thousand feet in sight all day. We passed outside the Cape Verdes and fell in with the Doldrums soon after, with copious rainfall. Water tanks and casks were refilled, and crew and passengers had many washing days. Everything was washed and we had a clean ship and ship's company.

In those days the British shipowners fed their crews on the vilest offal. I never made a voyage on my apprenticeship without our getting served out rotten salt beef and pork. It was said that the Owners, being shipstore dealers as well as shipowners, made a practice of putting on board a portion of rejected stores, and as they stored their ships 'to a bean' the powers on board had to serve out this rotten stinking stuff. The crew would bring the wretched stuff aft and interview the Captain. The only redress they got was that it was used in the cabin and what was good enough for the cabin was good enough for them. Our sympathies were, of course, with the crew, for we had the same grub as them. They – and us – threw the wretched stuff overboard and were without meat. The biscuits, Liverpool pantiles, must have made many voyages, for they were maggotty and weevily. It was true the stinking beef and pork were taken to the cabin, but they were dumped out of the stern ports. In the cabin they lived on fowls and tinned soups and meats. Fortunately, at this time we caught bonito and shark and ate of those. The way crews were fed in those days was abominable and murderous.

About this time one of the Bates ships put into the Falklands, a great number of the crew dead from eating rotten salt pork. Some eight years after this Plimsoll commenced his agitation which has gradually led to the present state of comparative comfort. Shipowners of fifty years ago were the meanest of capitalists, and I often think whether the present members of many of our richest families and firms know that their fortunes were founded on the exploitation of sailors! In these merciful days, a relation of the way seamen were treated would not be credited. They were starved, robbed, gaoled and maltreated. In those days I wished to be a Captain so that I could have 'a pudding in the cupboard'. The starving of crews so moved me that when I was asked on my appointment as Captain about my salary, I said, 'That will show for itself what I am worth after a voyage', and asked, 'Can I feed the crew as I wish?' Mr Johnston said, 'You can', and his firm loyally gave me what I asked the twenty-seven years I served them; to me it is a pleasing fact that all my crews had in port and at sea plenty of well cooked wholesome food.

Before resuming my narrative I will just make a few remarks about my shipmates. There was no religious service. All the boys acted up to their religious training, and duly prayed nightly. Sunday reading was Bible, prayerbook and a volume of sermons; in the dogwatch, singing hymns in which the passengers joined. The forecastle held one simple devout Christian, an elderly Britisher. He was a power for good – a splendid seaman, always ready and willing, and took a delight in teaching us knots and splices. He was always happy and cheerful. It was a point of honour with even the most dissolute seaman never to speak obscenely or immorally in the hearing of us boys. Swearing was almost universal a habit. The most awful culprits were Yankees or men who had served in American ships, though their blasphemous utterances were spiced with a puritanical humour that somehow watered down the foul outbursts. On the whole sailors were good fellows. The most objectionable were the 'John nasty faces', fellows who were never content, always seeking and desiring trouble, sorry craftsmen, lazy loafers and shysters, men whose only fear was brute force, a good booting their best medicine.

I never could manage to wash my clothes. One of the men did that for me.

In the Doldrums a huge blue shark had attended the ship for several days, to the disturbance of the crew who were superstitious and believe the creature has an uncanny sense that tells it there is sickness on board, and that it is waiting to entomb the sufferer. So permission was asked and granted to fish for the 'scavenger'. A huge hook was baited with four pounds of fat pork and attached to a length of chain and manilla rope and thrown over. The dorsal fin disappeared, a ghostly shape, then for a time the water was churned as the monster flung himself about in wild efforts to free itself. Soon it weakened, was drawn to the ship's waist, bowlines slapped over its body and tied up to the rail, then it was treated with devilish cruelty. The climax was reached when the cook poured a kettle of boiling water into its mouth. As landsmen hate snakes, so do sailors abhor sharks. After ten days of the Doldrums we got a light air from the SSE which gradually freshened to the southeast trade wind.

The noon observation showed the ship to be ten miles north of the Equator. Orders were given to clear up decks and postpone work; Neptune would visit the ship at 2 p.m. when the ship would be on the 'Line'. For some time the men had been busy with great secrecy, and we boys had been chased away from the fore part of the ship. The 'Johnnie nasty faces' wore a look of expectancy and close privacy. At 2 p.m. a loud hail from over the bows; the Chief Mate replied – a messenger from the Sea God, fantastically garbed in imitation seaweed, announced that his master proposed visiting the ship to renew his acquaintance with his old, and initiate his young subjects, into the freedom and mysteries of the sea and also to collect customary fees and dues. A striking procession now came over the bows – maidens and sea dryads, Neptune and Procyon, who took their seats on a gun carriage. A noble pair, he with long wig and beard of white and hemp, she with long hair of white manilla and garbed in imitation seaweed. 'She' made a lovely Queen (a good-looking ordinary seaman to start with) attended by Trident Bearer, Barber and Assistants with their insignia and guards all properly attired. Neptune in a witty speech renewed his old acquaintanceship with the Captain and his old subjects, and was paid dues and fees by the lady passengers to mitigate in their favour the order of initiation. The neophytes were presented, then the roll call to prove that all were present and none hiding. The guards took up positions to prevent anyone escaping, and pandemonium reigned. The older ladies were let off with a sprinkling of salt water, the younger ones a little less gently. Ten male passengers and we other novices had to undergo the full ordeal. All took it in good part and the affair finished up with a concert and dance after we had cleaned ourselves of the thick of the Barber's lather. The taste of the shaving mixture comes to me now: a horrible concoction to which the tar-bucket, slushcask, hencoop and pigpen contributed. No one escaped, for the Barber's brush found a way into the mouths of the most determined and stubborn. The razor was a jagged piece of hoop iron (I can yet discern scars on my cheek). Then the sousing into the filthy mixture in the wash-deck tub, the rough humour of primitive sailors, now forever gone.

From the Equator we hurried down the Brazil coast, past the lonely Tristan da Cunha group where the descendants of soldiers who guarded Napoleon at St Helena live in rude comfort, plenty and freedom. A rapid rush for several weeks through the stormy Forties and a sight of the lonely islands of St Paul and Amsterdam [in the Indian Ocean], a lovely sail through the Southeast Trades (oh, the bliss of living after the cold discomfort of the Forties); my first view of a tropical island, a gorgeous vision of luxuriant foliage that will always remain one of my cherished remembrances (this was Christmas Island, a day's sail from Java). And then Java. The beautiful and romantic scenery, the luxurious sailing through these spice islands, the beauty of sea and sky, the prodigious wealth of foliage; the striking Krakatoa Island that was half destroyed and then added to by the terrible earthquake of 1883. The crowds of native boats who put off to barter from each little village, their crews yelling and shouting at the oars with sharp, savage tones, each boat loaded with tropical fruits, nuts, yams, sweet potatoes, fowls, ducks, monkeys, lovebirds, parrots, the lovely Java sparrow, and various strange beasts including the graceful little mouse deer. The men to me were veritable savages. The Javanese are a truculent-looking lot, their mouths and lips stained scarlet with betel nut.

We revelled in the good things – coconuts, pineapples, guavas, bananas and betel nut, the last a sweetmeat made of pineapple, sugar and coconut. After a two months' diet of putrid pork and salt horse, we gorged ourselves. All who have broken their teeth on Liverpool pantiles and eaten of the abominations supplied by the shipowner of that day will appreciate my grateful remembrances of my first introduction to the wanton plentifulness of a tropical land.

The Captain bartered for hundreds of little fowls, yams and sweet potatoes and we the crew were given several dinners of toothsome sea pie, that queen of sea dishes when fowls and yams and sea spuds and large capsicums are the ingredients. We also got turtle. I had a plate of soup by favour of the steward. Some of our 'nasty faces' cut the monkeys' painters: the animals took to the rigging. Their angry owners had to leave them; when hungry they were easily captured and became great pets and 'Johnny nasty face' sold them for drink at Hong Kong.

To our passengers the passage among the islands was a delightful break in the monotony of sea and sky. One of them had a narrow escape from providing a huge shark with a dinner. In these summer seas the ship glides along the glassy surface so quickly that apparently she is scarcely moving when really she is going five knots or more, unknown to the officers. A passenger named Pritchard, the Adonis of the party, tempted by the apparent calm, dived from the bows. When he rose he was on the quarter, the ship rapidly drawing away from him. He became terrified and exhausted himself by frantic screams. His wife and others added to the uproar. Luckily the Second Mate was a cool-headed fellow and in a few minutes he had a boat in the water, manned, and picked Pritchard up as he was sinking and one of the tiger sharks making for him. There was much joy when he was on board again and much satisfaction when an hour afterwards the would-be host, the shark, was captured and killed with the usual fiendish cruelty.

After passing Anjer we coasted along the beautiful Sumatra shore, trees to the water's edge and the Radjabasa Mountain in the distance on the starboard side. We had the famous thousand isles of the Java Sea, a fairy sea with balmy breezes and tropical azure sky. The earth has no more lovely spot. Wafted by gentle zephyrs, we passed through this enchanted sea and the Bangka Straits, past the many dangerous reefs that have wrecked so many fine ships. Amongst them the man-of-war that was taking the Earl of Elgin, first Ambassador to China, more than one hundred years ago. Many of the wrecks were visible – a pitiful sight.

We now entered the China Sea, daily passing groups of islands. In the far distance the mountain of Borneo was visible. From Borneo's shores the ferocious Sea Dyak pirates plied their merciless trade. I ought to have mentioned that before entering Sunda Strait we had mounted our eight-pounder brass cannon and had rifles, boarding pikes, ammunition and projectiles ready, and were prepared to deal with the Dyak gentry should they molest us. We passed their hunting ground scatheless.

Our Captain had a friend who owned the Distington Museum and he took every opportunity of collecting for him, so that when we were a safe distance from the haunts of the pirates he would have the gig provisioned and take the boys and the carpenter with his tools and leave the ship at daybreak for some distant island on the route. What glorious hours we spent on those island gems. We collected crustacea, corals of all hues, birds, land crabs and specimens of woods and shells. I cannot describe the wonderful things disclosed to us, looking through the limpid waters on the coral reef. The wild tangle of vegetation and flowers; orchids we knew nothing of, or we might have enriched Kew Gardens. Such a wealth of colour I have never again seen. For some days afterwards I was employed cleaning the bird skins and coating them with arsenical paste, preserving them for the taxidermist at home. With me was an ordinary seaman, a Manchester lad of eighteen years, a bully and a bad specimen of city gamin. He had fought and beaten several of the elder apprentices. Until now, not being in the same watch I had not come into contact with him (for I was the youngest on board and kept from quarrelling).

Sam took it into his head to strike me in the face with a wet skin. I retaliated, and then the Second Mate stopped further proceedings and Sam made use of an expression which rankled me. When the watch was up and officers and Captain at dinner, I went to the forecastle and bade him come out. Sam came up, sure of victory over the youngest boy and making use of vile language – but 'Brag is a good dog, but Holdfast is a better', and 'the best laid schemes o' mice and men gang aft agley'. After the most strenuous fight of my life, lasting half an hour, I was the victor and Sam for many days had a bruised and discoloured face, and there was a great improvement in his speech and manner. How men value pluck. That fight gave me respect from the men, and freed me from the bullying proclivities of the older apprentices.

Clear of the islands and reefs, we ran up the China Sea before the Southwest Monsoon, and one morning sighted the peaks of Hong Kong and Hainan. Soon we got a Chinese pilot on board. He cleverly worked up all day amongst the numerous islands and rocks, and brought us to anchor off Pedders Wharf, Hong Kong at 9 p.m. on 7th September 1865 after 107 days' passage.

Hong Kong is an island about twelve miles long and ten miles broad; a mountain approaching about two thousand feet high. When we anchored, the sight was very fine. Tier upon tier of lights far up the mountainside. Near us was one of Britain's 'wooden walls' with her three tiers of ports lighted, and hundreds of ships, junks and sampans, with their twinkling lights. A fairy scene. I longed for morning, was up at dawn and enjoyed the panorama. A lovely land-locked space of water twelve miles by three miles, covered with craft of all nations; countless junks, sampans and houseboats. The sun just peeping over the island and shining on the land of the great Mogul and Prester John. Then our decks were crowded with Chinamen and women nominally washerwomen, all with their little pidgin, hucksters with all sorts of curios and commodities. I was full of delightful wonderment, for this came up to all my Arabian Nights entertainments expectations. And then I was told to dress and go ashore with the Captain to take some precious packages to the consignees.

At that time the captains were made much of, entertained at the consignee's house all the time in port, and were honorary members of the best club. The passage ashore in the sampan was full of interest; they are about twenty feet long by eight feet broad, decked over, and the home of the sampan man, his wife and family, with two coops of fowls over the stern. Their wants are supplied by shop boats; the wife rarely goes ashore. Millions of China's population live in such boats.

I was quite dizzy when I stepped ashore, and bewildered. The constant stream of coolies with their burdens carried on a bamboo, the passing of sedan chairs, the strange cries of the innumerable street sellers and the strange costumes of the passing crowds was like gazing through a monster kaleidoscope. When I had delivered my charge I was presented with a dollar and told to return on board. On my way, and with the dollar burning a hole in my pocket, I came across a merchant with a barrowful of such beautiful fruit that I bought a dollar's worth, quite a large bagful to treat my fellow apprentices. I refrained from tasting them until I got in the sampan, when I eagerly put my teeth in a lovely red one and found it so nasty that I threw the lot in the water. Later I found they were tomatoes: it was many years after this before they were common in Europe. I had expected a delicious sweet plum! Oh, my poor dollar.

The next outstanding event was Liberty Day, the one holiday a sailor got in a twelve months' voyage. 'John nasty face' had spent his like a hog; drunkenness and debauchery ashore and shocking bad language on board until the drink was out of him. With what joy we went ashore: with what appetites we tackled the sailor's pet relish – ham and eggs – and got real good fruit. We ransacked the curio shops and bought for our homefolk what our purses could afford.

A few days afterwards we left in company with Green's clipper *Childers* for Foo Chow, to load tea for London. We had a stormy passage against the strength of the Northeast Monsoon and arrived off the River Min without mishap, when we took a pilot, an Englishman and a notorious consumer of brandy. He polished a bottle off before breakfast. He nearly cast the ship away on the White Dogs, dangerous rocks, but 'a miss is as good as a mile' and we entered the picturesque River Min which flows through a narrow gorge covered with hanging woods. The pilot knew his work, and by backing and filling worked up the nine miles to Pagoda Anchorage where we found the ships *Fiery Cross, Taeping, Belted Will* and *Dartmouth*. They welcomed us with a rousing salute.

I ought to have mentioned that in leaving Hong Kong we passed the wreck of our sister ship *Dunmail*, Commander Peter Thompson afterwards Principal Examiner, London. News came that the *Childers*, which left Hong Kong with us, was attacked by pirates when embayed in the Formosa Channel. All the crew with the exception of the carpenter were murdered; he saved himself by jumping overboard and clinging to the pintles of the rudder. After looting, they fired the ship. The glare attracted a gunboat who rescued the carpenter.

Foo Chow is famous for its bridge, over one thousand years old, and for its pagodas. A few days sufficed to load. The inside preparation for a tea cargo is nice to see. The whole skin is covered with beautiful designs of latticework; the smell of the tea chests was pleasurable to me. Nothing exceptional happened during our stay, but 'John nasty face' was delighted to learn that the swell and strict Captain of the *Fiery Cross* when walking under the balconies ashore was deluged by the Chinese ladies, emptying what belongs to the sewers on his head.

On leaving for London each ship gave us a salute of nine guns, which we returned. One of our guns was overcharged and jumped across the deck: no harm ensued. We dropped softly down the river and anchored at the mouth to await the Captain and a favourable chance to cross the bar. The Mate was enterprising, and instigated by the Pilot he lowered a boat and captured five fine goats. Christian morality! The poor Chinese farmer . . .

Now we had time to take stock. We found we were all robbed of our living space to swell the profits of the Owners and the perquisites of the Captain. The forecabin was full of the most expensive silks and teas; the bulkheads between the officers' rooms were taken down, making the passage to the after cabin. The officers had only their bunks and the space under. The after cabin transoms were full of boxes of silk and curios. The dining table a pile of tea chests, allowing only two to be seated. The bread tanks were taken from the lazarettes and lashed on deck; the small stores were reduced to a minimum and stowed in the steward's room. He had to sleep on the floor in the pantry. Paints, oils, ropes, and in our place the spare sails, with expert rolling and packing were got into the space left in the afterhatch. Coals in the longboat; salt provisions, tar pitch, stream cable and lumber of all sorts in the dark, dismal forecastle, robbing the men of all their floor space and harbouring filth inexpressible. The boats were filled with yams and vegetables, and the pigs and fowls and ducks with one wing cut had the run of the decks. The filth amongst the braces caused much bad talk, and the decks and booms were piled up with studding sail booms, sails and cordage. Hatches covered with hawsers, fenders and other ship's furniture. Only the gig available in case of sudden disaster. The biscuits were bad to start with: before we got home there were more maggots than biscuits. The flour was alive, and the black molasses full of cockroaches. These were the good old times! I only wish the wretched Owners are punished in Hades by having to live and eat as they compelled us to.

In a few days the Captain came with his papers from Foo Chow and we tripped anchor, with very hearty shanties for we were homeward bound, and were favoured with a fine monsoon and ran down the China Sea with all studding sails.

Approaching the reefs in the dark hours we anchored until daylight, then up through the narrows, threading our way among the thousand isles and sea of pleasant memories, and approached the Sunda Straits.

It was now the time of the Northwest Monsoon, a head wind with exceptional heavy squalls that gave little or no warning; awful thunderstorms that seemed capable of bursting creation, lightning that awed, and each yardarm was capped by the corpse candle of the old navigators, the 'corposant', those weird and ghastly balls of fire whose shadow sailors believed foretold death. The atmosphere was charged with electricity. The night was of Egyptian darkness, a most depressing time; we fought through having all hands on deck for forty hours.

On clearing the Straits we soon ran into the pleasant region of the Southeast Trades, where we had a pleasant sail of several thousands of miles to the Cape of Good Hope. We had plenty of work handling the studding sails, Jeremy Graves, and other fancy sails. I became an expert at handling the royal and top gallant studding sails, working them out of the tops. The watch appreciated the way I guided the sails clear of obstruction, thereby saving them many hours of the watch below. I was happy notwithstanding the lively grub, for I was also progressing in my navigational studies, which I liked very much.

We had some very tough 'nasty faces' among the crew and this part of the voyage was enlivened by some very furious fighting. The Captain believed in the old British way of settling disputes and allowed no interference with a fair fight. We mustered a very nasty dour Scotsman and a thorough blackguard of a County Tyrone man. Up to now they were afraid of each other, then something occurred that only a fight could settle and after a long struggle the Scotsman won. He got very cocky and flapped his wings too much, and made the mistake of striking a pasty-faced, pigeon-breasted Liverpool Irishman of no great size or weight – a quietly disposed chap and good seaman called Ryan. After a glorious fight Ryan knocked the Scotsman to pieces, for Ryan was a scientific boxer. No one dreamt of his prowess: everyone was delighted. Ryan, like the good fellow he was, took his victory very modestly and from that time peace reigned in the forecastle.

As we approached Madagascar the weather changed, and we had to face some smart gales. We made the African land north of Natal. In the Agulhas Current we swept close round the Cape of Good Hope in a sou'easter and had a good view of Table Mountain, the Lion's Rump and Lion's Head, and as sailors say, 'the girls had hold of the towrope' and 'hurrah for St Helena and home'.

On this run the ship's thorough cleaning was done. No afternoon watch; all hands toiled from morning to dark, tarring, holystoning, refitting standing rigging and painting. What a glorious appetite I had. The pease soup, salt horse, rancid pork, and travelling pantiles were a barmecide feast. Youth, ozone, health and contentment give happiness to a clean-minded boy. Most of the boys felt the same. Off St Helena we took in studding sails and backed the main yard and took on a supply of cabbages, watercress, potatoes, fruit and fish (thereby staving off scurvy), sent letters to be posted for home, squared away and set all studding sails, sailing in company with Green's trooper *Agamemnon* with a foot regiment from Calcutta, and the *Malabar* from Bombay with a cavalry regiment, both bound for Sheerness. We outsailed them in the Trades. On crossing the

Equator we met with stormy Northeast Trades, reducing our crank teaship to reefed topsails and foresail. We lost much time daily by veering away to pump ship, which was obligatory if the precious cargo was to be kept from damage. Strange the Owners had not enterprise enough to fit bilge pumps.

When we got north of the Trades we fell in with the brave coast winds that took us with studding sails set right to Beachy Head, which we sighted on a dark, windy, wet night, unexpectedly. The light was above us shining on deck. Then there was hubbub: halyards let go by the run, helm down, studding sail booms broken, sails lost, all the cables broken from their lashings and piled to leeward and the lee rail under water, as the ship went over by being brought to the wind with such a press of sails. This was near disaster – foolhardy and whisky prompted. A few hours cleared up the mess. We took the Pilot off Dungeness and anchored at the Nore for a tug. The *Agamemnon* and *Malabar* towed past us for Sheerness: we last saw them off St Helena.

That night we docked in the London Dock and were welcomed home by the ladies of Ratcliffe Highway, on Shadwell Bridge where the ship was detained. Their language was far from complimentary to the Mate for keeping the men. There are no such scenes now: the ladies of Ratcliffe are either more refined or the policemen more sensitive to profligation and lewd talk.

So endeth my first voyage.

THE SWEETEST SPOT ON EARTH

My Second Voyage
COREA
1866

LONDON – KANAGAWA – YOKOHAMA – LONDON

O'er the glad waters of the dark blue sea
Our thoughts are boundless and our souls are free
Far as the breeze can bear the billows foam
Survey our empire and behold our home

From the 18th March 1866 I had a pleasant holiday amongst my friends and had a good time at Keswick, though for some time after getting home I was much disturbed by horrid dreams; in them I was at sea, and I can recall the pleasurable thrilling relief when I awoke and found it be but the baseless fabric of a dream.

On the 6th May the summons came. It did not find me so light-hearted as I was on my first voyage. I found the few minutes waiting for the train at the home station most trying. They seemed hours. Once off, youth soon forgets, and we became interested in our journey and chatted of our coming voyage and what we would see in the jealously guarded kingdom of Japan, just opened to commerce by the warships of the United States. We had read of our countryman Will Adams, shipwrecked on the coast of Nippon in the seventeenth century. Having been spared out of all his shipmates, exalted to high honour and given a well-born wife, he was the founder of the Jap navy. He taught them shipbuilding and other Western arts, and his tomb is held in the greatest veneration. (Later

27

I visited it.) We had also read of the transactions of the Dutch who, by underhand dispicable means, by trampling on the Cross and decrying all other Christian peoples, kept for a hundred years the monopoly of a very lucrative trade. They had allotted to them an isthmus called Decima in lovely Nagasaki Harbour which I had the pleasure of visiting some years afterwards. Japan had great attractions for us also, for on our last voyage we had on board someone who had spent many years in a junk on the China coast, who spun yarns of his adventures smuggling opium and other things into Korean and Japanese ports, and there was the mystery of a civilization a thousand years older than the Norman Conquest of 1066.

We duly arrived at Euston and took cab for the West India Dock Road where we were boarded and lodged by a widow from Whitehaven, a Mrs Corkhill. She was Cumbrian enough to give us full and plenty, and she was motherly kind.

The ship was loading at South Dock and attracted much attention owing to the large advertising boards, with the then strange and unique announcement that the splendid clipper ship *Corea* was loading for Kanagawa and Yokohama. We found the officers and boys, with the addition of three extra apprentices, one each from our sister ships *Melbreck* and *Invincible*, and a first voyager Arthur Starsy, a Nottingham manufacturer's son fresh from Repton Grammar School. I may mention that Arthur only made this one voyage. Like many others he found the sea life did not come up to his anticipations, and that the climb to a Captainship was a rough hard fight – against the elements and controlling the roughest and most dissolute men of all colours and nations. A life of great personal discomfort and deprivation. He joined his father's firm and some years afterwards died of consumption, a malady that had killed all his family. Arthur was a nice boy and my particular chum.

Before sailing I went to the Metropolitan Tabernacle to hear Spurgeon. His ways were surprising to one only accustomed to the plain services of a village church. I liked his breezy tone, and the singing was grand; and from that time a volume of his sermons was a part of my sea kit.

On the 16th May we left dock and towed to the Downs, where we were detained for several days by strong westerly gales. At that time steam was in its infancy as propelling power, and the Downs contained over a hundred sail, from the noble Blackwaller to the Dutch *galliot* and French *chasse maree*. When the fair wind came there was such a singing of chanties, rattle of cables, and flapping of canvas as the numerous craft got under way, as amazed the Deal hovellers (local boatmen engaged in carrying out stores to sea). It was a beautiful and gallant sight that easterly dawn in May saw, all under way, the sun shining on their canvas; they fled like a flock of white pigeons, swept round the South Foreland, passed Dover with its hoary Castle and white cliffs, signalled Dungeness – I am sure the signal men would not be able to take half the numbers – and on to Beachy Head, now with all our studding sails set.

By this time our little Cumberland-built lass was in the van, in company with Green's high flyer the *Northfleet*. (This ship was sunk by collision off Deal a few years later with the loss of several hundreds of emigrants.) Also in the company was the famous Yankee clipper *Young America*. The mob were miles astern next morning, only a few sail in sight. At night we saw the effulgence of the Lizard lights in the sky, and bade adieu to England for a time.

We had only one passenger, a young Austrian going out to Japan on spec and to escape conscription. On account of his always saying 'So-so' to everything, he was dubbed 'Old So-so'. He was a great favourite with us boys, and spent his time in our quarters. We had a most agreeable ship's company (not one 'John nasty face' among the lot). London was always noted for the much better crew shipped there than at Liverpool, where packet rats and forties abounded.

We had a quick, pleasant and uneventful run to the Equator. This time we sailed inside the Cape Verde Islands, a scorious cindery group with green patches and a hybrid population. Having only one passenger to amuse, the ceremony on crossing the Equator was not enacted with the same histrionic display as the previous voyage. Old So-so got a good lathering, and though we had warned him not to, he could not resist answering 'So' to a question by Neptune's Barber, thereby getting a mouthful of Neptune's delectable shaving mixture. We ran through the Southeast Trades and into the brave west winds of the stormy Forties. Ran down over 100° of easting with heavy gales and high seas, narrowly escaping running into a large iceberg or rather ice island, for it was some miles long, and we pooped a huge sea which did much damage and caused much discomfort. We had a fine run through the Indian Ocean, and glided through the Java Straits amongst those lovely islands – mermaid seas. We revelled in the good things of Java, and more monkeys were stolen; up the China Sea; visited more uninhabited island, and got jewels for museum specimens. Passed the east side of Formosa, the most awful and forbidding land imaginable. Black precipices rose from the sea, six and seven thousand feet in height. Just imagine it – a horrible, awesome sight from a ship's deck half a mile off. The home of savages the Chinese could not conquer and whom the Japs, the present owners of Formosa, leave alone. The west of Formosa is a beautiful, fertile land. The east shores are swept by the Black Stream of Japan which runs from eight to nine knots per hour, compared to which our Gulf Stream is as the Thames to the Mississippi. This causes a startling phenomenon. Chow chow water, heavy breakers, like the sea breaking on a coral reef. It was to sail into a maelstrom, even for an experienced navigator in these seas, then not properly surveyed and charted. At night, passing through these vexed waters gave a weird uncanny picture nowhere else to be seen. The seas were bright with phosphorescence which gave a singular glow on the sails and faces of the crew, and a feeling as in the presence of death. We never got so used to the chow chow water as to breed contempt, for all hands rushed on deck when the roaring was heard. Everyone looked relieved when we had passed safely through.

We sailed close to the Loo Choo Islands (all my life I have had a desire to spend my days on such islands). I never passed an island in those days without a sinful wish that I might be cast away on one, and this feeling has not been confined to boyhood, for indeed with the prospect before us of a Lloyd George, fat Radical and uncoguid governed country, were I a young man I could make my way out to some simple, primitive, money-lacking land, content to be a vegetarian.

We passed many an active volcano; the long string of islands between Loo Choo and Japan are all volcanoes. I was drawing water and noticed a bed of coal shining under the ship. I called the officer's attention to it, and he promptly hove the ship aback and called the Captain. Fortunately the wind permitted returning in the direction we had entered and we hove to, sent a boat to sound and found a large reef with three fathoms shallowest sounding. A length further would have lost the ship. A sea life is made up of misses.

On arrival at Yokohama our Captain reported to the British Admiral, who sent out the *Serpent*, a survey ship, which located the reef as a very dangerous one some three square miles in extent. We arrived off Vries 120 days from London on September 18th – an excellent passage – and at daylight entered the Gulf of Yedo in company with the clipper *Chagge* and sailed up to Kanagawa Bay and anchored off the tiny European settlement of Yokohama. The British flagship three-decker *Conqueror*, two frigates and the surveying ship *Serpent*, the Yankee frigate *Hartford*, the corvette *Wyoming* and two French warships, with two merchant ships and very many large Jap junks at anchor. The Yankee *Hartford* was famous as the flagship of Admiral Farragut, when forcing the passage of the James River in the great Civil War. At this time the 9th Regiment (now the Norfolk Regiment) and a few companies of the French Marines were ashore to overawe the Japanese. What a force to bully the most fighting race on earth.

We were now in a land of mystery and wonder. This earth cannot now afford to the present or to the future generations the thrilling delight of moving amongst a strange civilization, amongst a people who were great in art and in war, when our ancestors' only dress was the skins of beasts and woad. The world is fast getting into a sameness that may please the Socialist and Utilitarian, but a world I do not admire, and I am glad that I have seen more beautiful things and dreamed more delightful dreams. We were so overwhelmed by the marvels around that I have not words to describe my sensations.

We were anchored seemingly in a huge lake surrounded by hills of from three to four hundred feet high, clothed with trees. Here and there the shore was flat and little villages peeped out, all thatched. In the distance the famous graceful sacred mountain of Fujiyama, snow crowned and distinctly visible in the clear air. The passage we entered by was hidden, and the continuation to Yedo shut out by a wooded promontory. The people were of never-failing interest. Two officers of *samurai* class were stationed on board; their heads were shaved making a V-shaped baldness, and on the crown the hair was worked into a short queue. No hair on the face. Kimono dress. Two swords, one long, the other short, to perform the ghastly Japanese rite of hari-kari (self-disembowelling). The lower orders in summer were nude, having only a bag and string. English ladies soon got used to seeing 'Nature unadorned'.

C
31

I have seen the wife of Sir Harry Parkes driving and flipping the naked coolies out of the way.

The towns were mines of never-ending delight. One museum, the temples, shops, teahouses and bathhouses – these last open to the world, where men, women, boys and girls, married and single, all naked, bathed, steamed and washed, unashamed with the innocent abandon of Eden. The Jap women have none of the timidity of Hindus and Chinese women in the presence of white men. The women are cheery little souls: always they greet you with their cheery '*Ohio*' (Good day). Their ways were not our ways. Morals judged from our standards they had none of. When I speak of our morals I mean fifty years ago when it was shocking for a woman to disclose a glimpse of her ankles. Now what does she hide? Different times – different manners!

Every Jap town possessed a *yoshiwarri*. As Roman Catholics placed their surplus daughters in convents, the Japs placed their daughters in those institutions. There was no thought of disgrace, and men of station often took their wives from there. Jap men are neither so honest nor so trustworthy in business as the Chinese. Perhaps the reason is that the business man is from the lower class, and not drawn from the *samurai* class.

I was in charge of the cutter that ferried the Captain to and from shore and went marketing. The cutter was rigged with Chinese sails. What glorious sails we had, Arthur, Jo and I. The Captain would say 'Won't be down for two hours', then over the bay we sailed to Kanagawa town. All the people were kind and hospitable and pressed on us their delightful tea and rice cakes. We had no fear, though only a short time ago they had murdered our Consul, Mr Richardson. We had also fun on the Yokohama side.

A Portuguese, Joe, had built himself a rough shanty on the beach, ostensibly to supply the sailors with hot coffee; really to provide rum and saki. We found the coffee and rolls very good when we were detained and missed our meals on board. In time Joe had no secrets from us, and we often held the skins (intestines) whilst he filled them with spirits. When Jack Tar came in the puddings were coiled round his body, and in that way great quantities of rum were conveyed on board in the Admiral's barge and the Captain's gig. For us he made excellent coffee, which was a comfort in our often long, wet waits, for captains had no consideration for our miseries.

Joe was not at all a bad chap. There was a simplicity about him that was childlike, and the sailors took advantage of Portuguese Joe. He was a good specimen of the beachcombers who people the beaches of tropical islands and towns, live their lives without care and enjoy the sun.

The way the Navy was hidebound by custom I can illustrate by the following episode. Merchant seamen of that day had a good-natured contempt for the naval men of that day. The Navy man was a specialist; he had his station. A man-of-war on board was good and smart at his special duties; on board a merchantman where to be of use he had to possess a general knowledge, he was next door to useless, so we had no use for him in our ships. A large party of bluejackets and Marines had been brought ashore to drill in the huge coppered launch of the flagship, First Lieutenant Lord Frederick Kerr (afterwards Admiral of the Fleet) in command, with two boatkeepers left in charge of the boat. Portuguese Joe's attractions were so powerful that these men neglected to note that the tide was leaving her. When a detachment of the shore party came down they asked our help, which we readily gave, and ran out their anchor with block and whip attached. Joe, one of our boys, was a real good chantyman and struck up 'Cheerily, boys, cheerily'. The sailors gave a mighty tug at the chorus and the launch was moving rapidly towards deep water. When Lieutenant Kerr and the rest of the party came on the scene he peremptorily stopped the chantying and ordered the Boatswain's Mate to call out 'One, two, three – haul.' Either the Jacks were sulky and would not use their strength or they had lost those vital minutes. 'For time and tide will not wait' even for a First Lieutenant with a handle to his name.

The launch stuck there all night, with a middy and six men in charge. They had a wet, cold vigil. The *Conqueror* had to send more boats to take them on board: in the meantime, under cover of darkness, many of the men visited Portuguese Joe's and by the time the boats arrived the majority were either hilarious or quarrelsome. Lord Lieutenant Kerr had one of the worst hours of his life. The punishment flag was flown by the *Conqueror* for several days afterwards. If the Lieutenant and his party had stayed away five minutes longer we would have had the launch afloat.

The market was a great attraction. Fish from a huge sixteen-foot shark to a sprat, and from green turtle to a periwinkle fish; beautiful and ugly fish. Nowhere in the world could such a diversity and profusion of fish be seen. Strange fruits, indigenous game of all kinds – deer, hare, rabbit, and beasts I did not know the name of. Beautiful copper and golden pheasants and many sorts of birds. Yams, cocoa, other vegetables, sweets, but none of our potatoes and abundance of grain. I attended market daily for our supplies, at 5.30 a.m.

I now come to the time of our never to be forgotten trip to the interior of Nippon and our visit to the famous bronze statue of Daibutsu, the largest in the world. (For the copper plate Statue of Liberty at New York is only a 'fake'.)

Our Captain, the Captain of the *Chagge*, Captain of *Burwood* and his son, Commander Bullock of the *Serpent*, two gentlemen from the Consulate, two stewards, Captain of the *Chagge*'s nephew, and myself. The last four being for culinary and navigational duties, and a Jap pilot. Our longboat was partly decked over to protect the provisions. We started with a fine wind early one morning, sailed down the Gulf, and reached a narrow embranchment and waited until high water. Then we crossed the bar and entered a channel not more than fifty feet wide and sailed up a mile or so, when a beautiful lake was entered, about the size of Ullswater. With several wooded isles, the shores and hills were covered with plantations of orange and saki apple trees, and a tree that grows a russet-coloured cross between an apple and a pear. They make delicious pies. Here and there groves of the beautiful camellia tree grow, to a height of forty to sixty feet; the flower is single. The majority of the trees in Japan are evergreen.

For a week our headquarters were in a large Japanese house, hired for a small sum. No furniture, the floor covered with padded matting making the most comfortable springy beds and seats. Boots are always removed before entering a Japanese house and soft grass slippers provided. The houses are built of wood, very lightly on account of the prevalence of earthquakes. The Japs squat on the floor and use a table one foot high. We had a dining table rigged up on the verandah, with seats. Our larder was well supplied; fowl of all sorts, game and fruits and saki. The stewards from the ships were Chinamen and well knew their work, and we boys pandered to our 'little Marys' and pitied our fellows on board, living on yams and tough buffalo beef.

We shot, fished, and ranged the country. Our seniors did not always take us with them. I should have liked to visit Daimoa's Castle as from what they said, it was wonderful. The people were kind to us: we repaid them by shooting their domestic fowls. This was amicably arranged by the seniors paying them handsomely.

The visit to Daibutsu was Number One Picnic. We went on ponies most of the way through paddy fields. All the country was highly cultivated with no waste land; all hand-tillage, the hills terraced and cultivated. A beautiful land, for which I deplore our Western Civilization with its Lloyd Georges, Keir Hardies, strikes and discontent manufacturers. Progress and discontent go hand in hand with Radical reformers. Japan had a happy civilization before the guns of America and Britain compelled them to have intercourse with white men. Strange if Japan is the yeast that will rise, the yellow and brown men to challenge our supremacy.

Daibutsu is marvellous. A stupendous bronze figure of a sitting god; the inside a temple, the shrine visited by the married women of Japan. Thousands were there during our stay of two days. The country was a succession of hills and valleys. The rice crop was ripe and this added to the beauty of the scenery. We enjoyed every minute of our stay and regretted having to leave. On returning to our headquarters on the lake, our Jap hosts were remunerated to their satisfaction. We stayed the night. My friend, the Captain of the *Beechwood*'s son, saw his old father (aged fifty-six) kissing one of the Musmees, and was wild and spoke to him. His father was much amused and told him it was but a Japanese custom.

Early next morning we took leave; all the village turned out and gave us a good sendoff. Their goodbyes never ceased till we passed out of sight, and we left one of the sweetest spots on earth with regret. After clearing the lake and river we had a toilsome job rowing the huge boat, owing to calms. About half way we got a good wind and reached our stable with the speed and vim of a horse returning home. Having now resumed the position of coxswain of the sailing cutter, I disgraced myself by dismasting her in a squall on one of our surreptitious trips to Kanagawa. I was disrated, and for punishment given the job of coaltarring the chain-work aloft, with dire threats of what would be done to me if I spotted the newly painted masts or clean decks. I cheerfully set to work, and in a week I finished to the satisfaction of the Chief Mate.

In the meantime my successor had succumbed to the attractions of the Jap town and kept the Captain waiting. For this heinous offence he was disrated and I reinstated. I managed to keep my job for the rest of our stay.

The ship only required some fifty tons to complete her loading when a great fire broke out in the European settlement and native town. All the stores and godowns were burned with their contents, the balance of our cargo being lost. Many hundreds of the denizens of the *yoshiwari* and native town were burnt to death. I saw many ghastly sights; in the European quarter most of the houses were destroyed, among them the British, American and French Consulates. It was decided the ship should sail minus the cargo burned, as it would take months to gather up cargo to replace it. We had engaged a deckload of ingenious Jap glasshouses containing rare flowering plants – arum lily, the japonica lily, and different sorts of chrysanthemum – I believe the first to be imported into Britain. They were consigned to the Marquis of Lothian from his son, Lieutenant Lord Frederick Kerr of the *Conqueror*. The glasshouses were so constructed that they watered themselves. We had the sight of lovely flowers all the passage. We also had as passenger Captain Clarke of the 9th Regiment, whose wife had eloped with a Hong Kong merchant (I do not wonder at her). He was going home for divorce proceedings. Also a paralysed Scotsman from the branch Hong Kong Bank, and two Jap pug dogs. After a very delightful stay of four months we tripped anchor, and with all studding sails set passed the man-o'-war and cleared the Gulf, and ran into the tail end of a typhoon which reduced us to bare poles for some days and drove us southeast near the Bonin Islands [Ogasawara-gunto], far out of our course. Heading for the China Sea we sighted a dismasted junk: as soon as they saw we were steering for them they cut away their rudder, thereby throwing themselves completely on our mercy. We hove to, lowered a boat, and towed the junk alongside. The crew were emaciated and by signs made out that for two days they had had neither food nor water and that they had ten days at sea being driven by the typhoon from the Loo Choo Islands. The junk had several large jars of saki on board, which were secured and the junk cast adrift. Every kindness was shown them and as it was impossible to land them in their own country we steered to a small island to the north of Lujon and gave them in charge of the Spanish

Governor and padre. We took on here a ton or two of yams and a quantity of fruit and fowls, and left having a narrow escape of shipwreck, for the ship struck a submerged reef that caused frequent attention to the pumps all the way home.

We had a rapid and prosperous run to the English Channel, when we met with heavy southerly gales and got embayed in Start Bay, the ship lying under close-reefed topsails, rail under water. Things were looking ominous when the Captain squared away and we came to anchor in Tor Bay. We were lucky for the *Friar Tuck* China clipper was lost that night on the Scillies. I stood on the rock at Brixham made famous by William of Orange and thought Devon was not as nice as Japan. Enjoyed a tuck out of fresh bread and butter and fish. The weather moderating, we hove up and ran to Dungeness, took a Pilot, and docked next day.

We learned that a new ship was almost ready for launching at Workington to which our Captain was appointed, and the Chief Mate and I were to go with him. So I bade *adieu* to my fellows. I never saw but one of them again: all either died aboard or were drowned.

The deep-sea sailor of the sailing ships is fast passing away. In a few years he will be as extinct as the dodo. It is a pity that his superstitions and foibles have not been collated. This voyage, I saw put into practice an ancient privilege they claim. That is, when the cook is charged with foulness and uncleanliness, in the practice of his art or in his person, the right to try him, and if found guilty, to punish him.

Our cook was a dapper little pleasant-faced American nigger above the average as a cook. His pet vanity was his long string of Christian names, 'William Frederick Augustus Charles George Washington Foreman'. As a cook he was above the average. One sweltering hot day, near the Equator, he was serving out pease soup for dinner for the awaiting ordinary seamen. He filled the mess lid and took it to the galley door. The ordinary seamen had run out on the bowsprit, to help getting inboard a large bonito. The cook was so interested in the struggle they were having to get the fish on deck that he kept the mess lid of hot soup in his hands. With the great heat, perspiration was streaming off him into the soup. The carpenter and sailmaker observed this, which took away their appetitite for the soup. When the men had finished their dinner they chaffed them so much about their dinner of soup with 'essence de Negro' that they became enraged and decided to deal with the cook by immemorial custom. He was tried, and by vote sentenced to undergo the prescribed punishment. He was seized, disembarrassed of his breeches, laid over the windlass end, and commencing with the youngest boy, all the deckhands gave him a slap on his posterior with the flat of the carpenter's saw. The cook was more hurt in his *amour propre* than on his person. In a few days he recovered his spirits and became a favourite. The Captain would not interfere; he said it was for the public good that the cook should be kept up to the mark in personal and cooking cleanliness.

MY FIRST GALES

My Third Voyage
CARRICKS
1867–1868

WORKINGTON – LIVERPOOL – CALCUTTA – MAURITIUS –
POINT DE GAULLE, CEYLON – LIVERPOOL

I joined the new ship as senior apprentice immediately she was launched, and learned how to splice wire rope, to fit rigging, mast a ship, send up masts and yards, and got an insight into the rigger's art that gave me a great pull over my fellows in after life. The *Carricks* was the last of the large and famous wood-built ships constructed in Cumberland, and she was a full-rigged ship with skysails and double topsail yards – a great improvement on the single topsails – a medium clipper of 2,000 tons burden.

On 2nd August 1867 she left Workington in tow for Liverpool to load salt for Calcutta. On the passage all sail was set and stretched, and the crew of runners were kept employed all the time, which they did not like; on arrival the dockmaster ordered the jib-boom to be housed further in and the runners struck. In a few hours they gave in – the only way they could get their run money. This was my first experience of that boomerang weapon, which more often hurts the strikers than the capitalists. Owing to their action the Captain would not engage any of the strikers for the voyage. I was sorry for there were many good Cumberland sailors among them.

On 28th August we sailed from Liverpool and had a fair, prosperous passage until after we entered the Bay of Bengal, when instead of having fine weather and smooth seas we had stormy seas, dark gloomy threatening skies and southerly gales. The ship ran up the Bay under a press of sail. We fell in with the Matlah Lightship; she was off her station [off the Sunderbunds] having dragged her anchor for miles. She made urgent signals: 'Stand off shore. Pilot brigs off their stations. Heavy cyclone rapidly approaching.'

In after life when I understood the ways of cyclones I was amazed at the reckless stupidity that in face of the many ominous signs steered the ship into the vortex of a destructive cyclone. We were in company with a steamer apparently doing her utmost to get off shore; our helm was put up, the wind now being northeast, and every endeavour was made to get away from the dangerous Sunderbunds before the cyclone was on us. We got the skysails and royal yards on deck. The wind increased rapidly and sail was reduced. The topsails were on the cap, in attempting to furl them we were driven several times from the yard. The men held back, then the officers went up. Several of us followed. I was well out on the yard when a furious gust tore the canvas from our hands and lifted the yard, knocking two men off, and I was blown like a rag into the topmast rigging, when a man grabbed me and hauled me into the top. I was bruised and dazed; shortly I recovered (another providential escape, the second time I was reported lost).

The wind was now blowing harder than I ever had experienced and the ship listed to a dangerous angle. To face the wind was impossible, for the sea was blown in a mass and would have choked you. The force of the wind was such that it pinned me to the rigging, so that I had the greatest difficulty in moving; being in the tropics, my dress had been shirt and pants, barefoot. The wind stripped off my shirt, and before I reached the deck I was shivering with cold. The thunderous roaring of the storm was appalling and I quite gave up hope of reaching the poop. However, I got there and found a few of the crew striving for shelter. It was impossible to hear anyone speak. Nothing could be done; primary nature was master, and man was powerless. There is nothing so appalling and awful as a tropical cyclone at sea. The phenomenon is nature's most awful power. To stay on deck was death and it was now the case of *sauve qui peut*. Everyone crept into shelter. For my part I was so worn out, having had no sleep for twenty hours and only a biscuit to eat, I fell asleep in the sailroom. When I awoke there was a strange calm. On going on deck I found blue skies and the sun just risen, a perfectly calm sea, and an absence of wind – what a change in a few hours.

The ship was a wreck – bulwarks gone from poop to forecastle, everything swept off the deck, boats gone and all livestock. Carpenter and two men missing, masts gone to the lower cap, such a mass of spars, wire rope, yards, canvas and cordage in an indescribable mass as was never before seen. The hull was very low in the water with such a list to starboard that the water was lapping the lee side of the main hatch coamings. The sea had found its way into the hold; many hundreds of tons of our salt cargo melted and we had a very narrow escape from foundering.

Our first proceeding was to man the pumps. The men struck up 'The Sailors' Grave' – the most lugubrious of songs, and most disheartening under the circumstances (sailors are really a mournful not a jolly lot). The Captain gave order for rum oh! and told them to strike up something lively; then we had the topical songs of the day. After nine hours of hard pumping we got a suck, went below and trimmed the ship upright. That night all hands slept, the two youngest boys keeping watch. Observations showed the ship to have drifted 120 miles to the SSW. Next day and the following all hands were employed cutting the wreck away. It was so pleated that it seemed that some giant skilful fingers had been at work. It was necessary to save all the lengths of spars, yards and rope to make some sort of jury rig and after several days of very hard work enough canvas could be spread to make the ship manageable. She was gradually worked up to the Sandheads [off the entrance to the Hooghly River] where a Calcutta Pilot was had. These men were very consequential and vain. This gentleman's first utterance was to complain that there was no awning. We rectified that. And it was amusing to see his airs, as his body servant bathed, washed and prinked him. He showed all the languor of the heroine in a cheap novel. This gentleman was the first namby-pamby creature that I had seen. Now the Bengal Pilot Service have a race of virile athletic men who climb the sides of rolling light tramp steamers with the agility of acrobats. These men are real and not sham Burro Sahibs.

On arriving at Saugor Island we found quite a fleet at anchor awaiting tugs [up the Hooghly]. One or two lame ducks were among them. In this cyclone the famous Blackwaller *St Vincent* finished her sea career and afterwards became a store hulk. The majority had sailed up the bay on the safe side of the cyclone. Great damage had been done among the shipping in Calcutta and in the track of the storm. Among others, a Pilot brig and *Aratoon Apcar* opium steamer and the *Thunder* were missing. The latter we had seen near the Matlah Lightship. Some months afterwards her wreck was found far in the Sunderbunds. (The Sunderbunds [Sundarbans] are an enormous tract of alluvial soil, formed by the debris from the many mouths of the Rivers Ganges and Brahamaputra; the home of the Royal Bengal tiger and other wild beasts, snakes and alligators, and the abode of perpetual fevers.)

In time, we got a tug and proceeded, the land only a line on the horizon, until we approached Diamond Harbour. Formerly this was the place of disembarkation for future nabobs and young ladies sent out on marriage spec. As the river narrowed the land was seen to be a vast low-lying plain highly cultivated and studded with villages, very comfortable looking with their groves of coconut trees.

We passed the one-time dreaded James and Mary River, the scenes of many ship tragedies, and anchored at Garden Reach under the King of Oude's palace. We listened with awe to the tales of his cruelties, and of his one thousand wives and harem women. The Mutiny was just about smothered at this time and there was no end to harrowing tales.

On the opposite side was the Botanical Gardens, containing the famous Banyan tree, said to be able to shelter a small army. When the tide served, the Mud Pilot took charge and dropped the ship up to the moorings at Princeps Ghant. Calcutta is not imposing from the river, as it is built on a low flat plain. Our moorings were abreast the Maidan, a large open space surrounding Fort William.

The cargo was rapidly discharged, and then the ship was moved above the great Hooghly Bridge, abreast the dockyard, for repairs. My knowledge of wire splicing was a great asset, and I was sent by boat daily to a rigging shed at Howrah to fit the new rigging. This was a pleasant change from the ship, and all my pocket money went for soft bread and bananas. When the ship was repaired, we dropped down to Kidderpore moorings and loaded a cargo of rice for Mauritius. I did not see much of Calcutta owing to the press of work, and distance from the city, during repairs. Then I had the usual attack of low fever and was ill from severe poisoned sores from mosquito bites.

Dangerous results rise from small causes. One of the boys had his leg amputated from a mosquito bite; the Captain and officers did not look after us as I looked after my boys. If taken in time, Frank would not have lost his leg and spoiled his career. We lost several men from cholera. The wonder is that the whole shipping population did not die from this cause, for our drinking and cooking water was pumped direct from the river. The Hooghly was a huge sewer flowing through a densely populated country – full of abomination. It was a daily occurrence for a bloated corrupted body of a native to foul our moorings, filling the air with a sickening stench, and a common sight to see an inflated body floating past, with a huge scavenging bird called the adjutant perched on it, feeding.

From the river's source to the sea, the Ganges is a holy river (the Hooghly one of the many mouths). Millions of people bathe in it daily, many lepers and others with disgusting skin diseases also. The ashes of the cremated Hindus are cast to Mother Ganges, as they lovingly call the river. The dying Hindu is carried on a stretcher to die on the bank of the river and drinks of the water, believing that so dying they escape reincarnation and attain Nirvana. No wonder that Calcutta was a sailors' grave forty and fifty years ago, though now sanitation and waterworks have made it the most healthy of all tropical cities, and there is a staff of river police who sink the bodies.

On Liberty Day we boys engaged a gharry and pilot and went to Seven Tanks, some miles from the city, a Rajah's place. He had a fine collection of Indian fauna – Royal Bengal tigers, leopards, cheetahs, jackals, monkeys, deer, birds and snakes, and in a large moat or pond the largest alligators I have seen. We paid the attendent a few pice to throw in frogs and the log-like beast showed lightning rapidity in snapping them up – that was awe-inspiring, and forever placed them among our detested *betes noires*, sharks and snakes.

On our return we visited the sight of the infamous Black Hole of Calcutta, now enclosed in the Post Office Compound. After a good meal we finished our golden day by listening to the Governor General's fine band in the Eden Gardens. During our stay Sir John Laurence, the most estimable and heroic of all the Mutiny heroes, was given a grand dinner by the Freemasons on his relinquishing the Governor Generalship. Our Captain was there and said it was a soul-stirring and affecting scene when Sir John made his farewell address.

Early in the New Year we dropped down to Garden Reach, where our 'Adonis' pilot took charge. In two days we discharged him at Sandheads and made a rapid and pleasant voyage to Port Louis in Mauritius.

On this passage my sense of humour cost my little Mary many gratifications. For steward, we had a mulatto from the Cape Verde Islands who was married to a white Liverpool woman. The cook was very jealous of the steward on this account, and told marvellous stories of his conquests of white women of high degree. The cook was a horribly ugly nigger, over six feet, broad humped shoulders, no hips, and so knock-kneed that when standing his feet were quite two feet apart, enormous knobbly feet and hands like a leg of mutton, yellow bloodshot eyes, a monkey's facial angle, a mouth ugly and full of black teeth, and bulbous eyes. His face was so hideous that it would raise envious feelings in the gargoyles of Notre Dame de Paris. His vanity and conceit were beyond endurance and he would yarn for hours about his amorous conquests of duchesses and countesses. I found it profitable for my stomach's delight to listen to his preposterous tales. One dog watch, sitting on the spars to leeward of the galley where he had regaled me with a dish of curry and a roll, for payment I lent him my ear . . .

He was a full-blooded Jamaica nigger, and like all the natives of that island had a fair education and was eloquent. He spun such a tale of his conquest of a 'fair Countess' – his visits to her palace and hairbreadth escapes from the jealous Earl, and the banquets, detailing the gold and silver table ware, the hothouse flowers, each dish and wine. (His imagination was so vivid that he slavered copiously when describing the dishes.) The lady was so enamoured with him that she often locked him in her boudoir, and brought his food and waited on him. One day the Earl forced his way into the Countess's private room, the nigger jumped out of the window, a distance of twenty feet, the Earl chased and fired at him, he turned on and overpowered the Earl and threw him in a pond, and only shipped as cook to escape his vengeance.

That night in our halfdeck, I was recounting the cook's tale to the great amusement of the boys while many unflattering and disgusted remarks were made about the cook's attractions and veracity. A dim shadow was seen to ascend the ladder, which proved to be the cook, who had heard all, and there were no more titbits for me. The foregoing is what is in the heart of a nigger. His dream is to possess a white woman, and I sympathize with the people of South Africa, the Southern States of America, and other black and white countries. Our Pharisees who decry their methods and fears should go and live with their black brother.

Our cargo was swarming with weevils. In our quarters (hammocks in the halfdeck) we swept from the floor several bucketfulls a day. Everything we ate or drank was full of them. In this tropical port we discharged our own cargo by hand. My cousin and I had to lift those heavy bags of rice (fed to us by two gangs, from 6 a.m. to 6 p.m.) four feet. No galley slaves were worked harder – it was worse than depicted by Dana in *Two Years Before the Mast*.

Some of the men struck for better bread, that is for bread free from maggots and weevils. They were taken before a magistrate, sent by him to gaol, and the biscuits were pronounced by the shore authorities as fit for food, but I spent my money and bartered my clothes for soft bread. Now the Government has passed an Act for the inspection of ships' stores, and enjoined such a liberal scale of provisions that there is great waste and extravagant profusion; and with the advent of steam, men are much better off and have none of the hardships of the sailing ship sailor of the long voyage. Shipowners of that day were cruel, grasping villains. We got plenty of sugar from the boys of the ship loading that dainty for home (called Blythe London grease soup ships from their glaring yellow paint), and we never troubled about breaking the eighth Commandment and so got strength to discharge the cargo.

On Liberty Day we went to Pamploma, and visited the tomb of Paul et Virginie and the strand where they were cast ashore. Their story is a classic of the eighteenth century. The Botanic Gardens situated here are very fine. I was much interested in the spice and nutmeg trees, sugar cane, and other tropical products, all here in the highest perfection. The country looked well, rising gradually to the range of mountains culminating in Peter Botte, a high peak. Mauritius is a fine island. The plantations are generally held by French Creoles whose language and laws obtain to this day. Their forefathers under Duplex had a narrow escape of occupying the position we now hold in India. They revere Duplex as French Canadians do Montcalm.

The cargo being now discharged and the ship ballasted, the Pilot came early to unmoor, when the ominous cyclone gun boomed its warning from the Meteorological Station, and then rapidly two more reports meaning 'Prepare for heavy cyclone'. We commenced to send down yards and top gallant masts. Then the tempest was on us and turning midday to blackest night, when no man could work from the weight of wind alone. The foremast was torn out of the ship, breaking at the deck partners and taking the main topmast with it, and though we were moored with two bower anchors ahead and astern, the ship was torn from her moorings and cast on a reef a mile distant, and fouled the *Marian* of Liverpool, whose Captain had died the day before the storm.

He had been a huge border Scotsman weighing over twenty-three stones. The undertaker was unable to get his coffin to the ship because of the hurricane. Owing to the nature of his disease and the rapid corruption that takes place in hot lands, his body had been removed from his room to a grating covering the rudder chains. As our ship bumped into the *Marian* the shock threw the body off the grating and burst it. The smell (as we were to leeward) was horrible! At daylight the body was drenched with disinfectants; the undertaker coming off with the casket, the crew of the *Marian* refused to assist him, so our Captain primed volunteers from our ship with brandy, and the gruesome task was effected. It took several days before all who took part in the coffining got over it.

The storm had passed as rapidly as it came. The destruction on shore and afloat affected every ship in the harbour and drove them ashore. One was totally wrecked; the *Edmund Graham*, a fine old Indiaman, a large French ship with coolies for the French West Indies. Chinese coolies had dysentery on board, but the sick were not allowed to be landed and they were dying daily. The dead were dumped outside the reef, among the sharks who did useful scavenging and prevented the bodies being cast ashore to breed pestilence. Several months were spent in repairing, and we had much sickness among our crew.

Here we got quit of the carpenter, shipped at Calcutta to replace the one lost in the cyclone. One of the strangest characters I have met: a middle-aged Scotsman with a gift of the gab, a most plausible man. Talk of and project work, but never do anything during the repairs. He was constantly drunk and made the most affecting prayers, beseeching 'the Almighty to take him to Himself' he would cry and pray for hours – we were all glad to see the last of him. In his place we got a good man, the carpenter of the wrecked *Edmund Graham*.

We left Mauritius without regret for Point de Galle, Ceylon. Our Captain was seriously ill with fever, with both legs paralysed. The Chief Mate's navigation was at fault and he anchored at Colombo instead of Point de Galle, so we had to pick anchor and beat round. We duly got there and I had a pleasant stay at the hotel, attending the Captain. The proprietor was descended from the old Dutch settlers of Ceylon. His family were very nice and I quite lost my heart to his little daughter, a dainty flower with nothing Dutch-built about her.

Ceylon deserves all the laudation lavished on it by past and present voyagers. One beautiful drive was unique, sheltered by coconut palms for miles and skirting the shore of the Bay. The scenery was a picture of soft luxurious dalliance with contentment; I could have spent all my life there and it has provided me with pleasant remembrances.

We were chartered at a very high rate to proceed to Akyab [Sittwe] in Burmah to load a cargo of rice for Liverpool. The passage across the Bay of Bengal was rapid: now was the time of the Southwest Monsoon. We safely entered the river, passing the wreck of the large wood ship *Theresa Tityars* lost a few days before on leaving with a full cargo. Our Captain, very ill, was taken to the consigner's bungalow. One of the boys went with him as attendant and I was given charge of the gig, attending to the ferrying to and from the ship. This being the rainy season, a properly thatched house was erected over the main hatch projecting over the side so that the rice could be taken on board from the lighters without damage, and the slow loading proceeded.

After we had been there some weeks, early one Sunday morning as I lay in my hammock under the boats I heard the Chief Mate and Second Mate talking as they took their morning coffee on the poop, and heard the Second Mate propose that the gun be loaded and he would have a shot at some large Brahminy kites[1] perched on the yards. Soon after, I heard a shot, and later surmised that the

---

[1] *Haliastur indus*, common scavengers and fishers in Asian harbours, which frequently perch in the rigging of ships.

Mate had loaded the gun in his room and, coming on deck, afraid that the Second Mate, an older and masterful man, would take the gun, held it with his finger on the trigger and in his excitement unconsciously pressed it, the gun going off. I heard the shot and a scream, ran up and found the Second Mate lying unconscious, his face from brow to chin completely shot off. I was ordered to go at once for the Doctor. On telling him of the injuries, he told me to bring him at once to the hospital, as he could do no good by coming off. We brought the poor man to hospital, but could do nothing to cover up his face, for to do so would choke him, and we had to take him on the roof of a gharry. I had the painful duty of holding him. When we got to hospital we found the Doctor with native dressers. After an examination he came to us and said there was no vital part injured. The eyes and the features were gone; he hoped to make a cure and would bring from his brow and neck skin to make a covering mask, and he would do for a doorkeeper!

I have wondered: did he talk in that way to ease our minds, or was he in earnest? To my imagination it was grotesquely horrible to propose the hideous monstrosity he proposed making as a door-keeper. I pictured the dread of the callers. . . However, as he was talking, the Second Mate had mercifully entered the next chamber and the agony was over. An inquest was held. The Chief Mate said the gun had gone off in the Second Mate's hands. No one asked questions, for the Chief Mate's agitation was painful to see, and a verdict of 'Death by misadventure' was registered. The burial was at once.

The Second Mate was a near relative of the Captain and myself; he had had a strange and adventurous life: given great abilities he had misused them, and was a source of grief and anxiety to his relatives. Brought up by his uncle to be a Doctor of Medicine, he had received a good education at Rossall and Queens. He had good parts and became a good classical scholar, and through his chequered career he kept a small Greek Testament and kept up his acquaintance with that language. When he was about twenty years of age he was studying under his relative, Doctor Johnstone, when his pec-cadillos compelled him to run away to sea. He rapidly got promotion, married, and was put in command of his brother-in-law's ship. On a voyage to Hobson's Bay [Melbourne] the discovery of gold in Australia was made; all his crew deserted and he followed, spending several years there, made and spent several small fortunes. He turned up at home and after several months with his family was given command of a West Indian trader the *Antilla* and made a good voyage. Unfortunately he arrived back at Liverpool when the offices were closed, went ashore with the ship's papers in his possession and could not be found for several days. This trick forever shut him off from getting a command in Liverpool. He went away for some years and was next heard of as a prisoner at Robben Island in Table Bay, having been captured in a slaver in the Mozambique Channel. He also fought in the American Civil War, where he lost a finger. He was a filibuster in Central America and Cuba, and engaged in gun-running. He was lost for years; then turned up again, when my father gave him a job as cashier and bookkeeper on the new dock construction. As usual, for some months his work and conduct were above reproach, then he broke out and left for parts unknown for a few years. When the *Carricks* was fitting out in Liverpool, the Captain had been prevailed on to take him in the only vacant berth, as boatswain, the Second Mate proving very unsatisfactory. He was discharged at Calcutta and the boatswain made Second Mate.

Drink was his *bête noire*. It was only in his cups that he related his adventures. When at sea he was a cheerful, pleasant and nice man, very clever with everything connected with a ship, and his medical knowledge was of great service during the time we had dysentry and fever on board. His misused life caused sorrow.

On finishing loading, it was decided that though the Captain was very ill he should return home in the ship as the route overland had so many broken connections and the weather would be so hot in the Red Sea that he would not survive it. So we sailed for home. The Dengue fever contracted in Mauritius troubled the crew, often for weeks not half of them doing duty. We arrived at Liverpool three days before Christmas, completing my third voyage and ending my hungry days of crew's food.

THIRD MATE AND BOATSWAIN

My Fourth Voyage
CARRICKS
1868–1869

LIVERPOOL – CALCUTTA – ST HELENA – SCILLY ISLANDS –
LE HAVRE – LIVERPOOL

The Captain was incapacitated from following his profession. In time he recovered his physical health, but his mental faculties never became normal, though he lived to a good old age. The Chief Mate, Anderson, a relative of the owners, was promoted to the command. Mr Llewellyn, a burly, lazy, black-eyed Welshman, was Chief Mate. Mr Braithwaite Second Mate, and I was made Third Mate and Boatswain, with a berth and board in the cabin.

After a short holiday of two weeks I joined the ship, then lying in the Princes Dock, Liverpool, loading salt for Calcutta. On leaving dock the weather was too strong to proceed to sea, and we lay at anchor in the river for several days. Mr Llewellyn had his bride on board during our enforced stay, and spent all his time with her, generally singing hymns. He belonged to a Calvinist Welsh Sect who had most comfortable beliefs. He was telling me of a shore adventure he had had in Calcutta when I was in hospital, and when I asked him how he reconciled his religious beliefs with his admitted many breaches of the seventh commandment, 'Oh,' he said, 'Christ shed his blood to save me and I am saved, no matter what sins are committed.'

The crew were a mixed lot including several blackguardly gaol-birds. They required a strong united afterguard to control them.

Unfortunately the Captain was not a strong man; he gave way to drink (killing himself with it next voyage). The Chief Mate was easy-going and lazy, occasionally blustering, with neither tact nor backbone. The Second Mate a smart sailor with a proper love of discipline and the pluck and will to ensure it; thanks to him the crew were kept in check. This was the only voyage I thoroughly hated, for the Second Mate and I had to constantly fight to maintain discipline, and I was thankful the voyage was a short one. A ship is hell without discipline.

The wind moderating, we were towed to sea. Off the Northwest Light we cast off the tug, set all sail and with a fresh north-east wind ran out of Channel across the Bay and into the Northeast Trades without a check. By this time the Captain had made many sorry exhibitions of himself. He was without resource within, had no taste for reading and no hobby, so was always at least semi-fuddled. He threw all decent traditions of a Master's bearing to his crew to the winds. Morning, noon and night, he had the Chief Mate and carpenter in the saloon playing cards, the Second Mate and I carrying on the work and controlling the crew, who were ready to be troublesome and said they had as much right as the carpenter to amusement in working hours. On crossing the Line, the ship was a saturation. The Captain decreed a holiday and sent several bottles of rum to the forecastle, so Neptune and his attendants were in high spirits and gave a good show. After the novices had been initiated they were given more rum and incited by the Captain; they became very rough and shaved the cook, steward, and others who should have been free from such insults. Then he egged them on to perform on the officers. The Chief Mate ran away and locked himself in his room; the Second Mate and I stood together amusing ourselves with belaying pins; the Captain, maudlin by this time, urged the half-drunken mob to put us to the indignity. We fought and broke the heads of all who attempted to handle us. This disgraceful scene went on for some time, and knives were drawn. We were not put to shame. Much bad and threatening language was used, and the punishment they had got kept them from again attacking us. Our determined stand sobered the Captain, who found that it was easier to start a fire than subdue it. In organized Society, the magistrates' dignity rests on the policeman, the Services, by similar physical force. On board a sailing ship on long voyage, with crews drawn from the most reckless, debased and dissolute of all countries, pluck, determination and an unchanging resolve to maintain discipline and resent insolence was necessary in a ship's officer. All merchant ship officers and captains know this, though some of them, to court popularity, relinquish control of such undisciplined men. The late Captain Toynbee of the *Gloriana* for his own ends would not punish a seaman. On one of his voyages to Calcutta the crew broached cargo and practically took charge of the ship for a while, yet on arrival he quickly paid them off with VG discharges. Captain Toynbee was after a Government job and it would spoil his chances with our armchair philanthropists to punish a poor sailor. He was made chief of the Meteorological Office.

In a British ship there is no fear of wanton cruelty being practised on the crew, for the force of public opinion is even stronger aboard ship than on shore.

At the southern edge of the Southeast Trades we sighted a barque who signalled 'Urgent need of assistance'. We closed her and hove to, and she lowered a boat and boarded us. The barque was of Danish nationality. Some hundreds of miles southwest of the Falkland Islands she had picked up a boatful of shipwrecked people, a portion of the crew and passengers of the *Blue Jacket*, one of the famous Blackwall Line of Australian clippers. Her Captain and Chief Mate were among the crew of the rescued boat. There was also a box containing four thousand ounces of gold. The Captain stated that fire broke out in the wool cargo; they fought it for several days, and at last had to abandon ship. Three boats were provisioned and the crew and passengers distributed, and in each boat a box of gold was put. They did not know what had become of the other boats; they had parted one stormy night. We gave them all the provisions they wanted, but could not send a supply of female clothing, so urgently required by the female passengers.

We were surprised that the Captain and Chief Mate were in the same boat and had given the Boatswain charge of the third boat when safety depended on experience.

For the remainder of the passage we were favoured with moderate weather and good winds and duly arrived at Calcutta. The rowdy blackguards of the crew were paid off; for some days they came alongside the ship, reviling the Captain and Chief Mate, who had to call on the police for protection.

There was much sickness in Calcutta during our stay, and with others I was taken to the Howrah Hospital. After getting better of fever I had to undergo an operation for fistula. In that hot climate wounds are difficult to heal, and I had much pain to bear from the strong acids used to kill mortification. When the ship was ready to leave I was taken on board. The doctors thought the change of climate would promote recovery: they were right, for I was attending to my duties before passing Mauritius.

In the hospital an English Roman Catholic priest was very good to me. He came daily and brightened me up, and visited all the sick. This gentleman was one of many priests, hospital nuns and laymen of his ancient faith whom I have met wherever there was poverty and sickness. I have great respect and love for them. Our Reformed churches may produce people as actively good, though I have never met such. Contrast the conduct of the paid Chaplain (Church of England). He gabbled over the service on Sunday morning in the great ward, and though I was in the hospital six weeks I never saw him speak to a patient, and many of his faith were dying daily.

One night in the hospital I had a horrible four or five hours. An epidemic of cholera had broken out, the wards were full. A bed was placed in my room to accommodate a patient, an Englishman brought in that evening. He was in great pain. The attendant gave him a sedative at 9 p.m. At about 10 p.m. I was awakened by his groans; I could not move to help him, nor could I get anyone to hear. At 2 a.m. he died, his body all crouched up and eyes wide open and his arms stretched out in the convulsive death agony. My bed was only four feet from his and I was but a boy of eighteen years. The dim light showed his distorted, discoloured face and I turned my back to him; this would not do, for my imagination pictured all sorts of wild horrible fancies, so I forced myself to face him, and waited until I attracted a sweeper at 5.30 a.m. The body was removed. For many years the remembrance of those gruesome hours were a shuddering horror.

At St Helena we anchored to land two of the crew in a dying state from dysentery. I was ashore all day, visited Longwood and the sights, and being very thirsty had a tumbler of what I thought was the *vin ordinaire* of France that we drank at Mauritius. It was alcoholic Cape brandy which went to my head and I fell asleep for an hour; the first and last time I have been affected by drink.

After my sleep I had a long ramble over the island. If people only knew of its delicious climate and many beauties, it would become a famous health resort; if the French or Germans owned it, it would become a Monte Carlo. The coloured inhibitants are of mixed blood, the descendants of coloured slaves and the garrison. Some of the young women are pretty. We took on board two ABs in place of those left in hospital, and one distressed British subject; also watercress, fruit, fish and delicious white cabbage.

In the Horse Latitudes, that is from 28° to 33° north, we fell in with a Spanish barque from Cuba with refugees, bound to Cadiz. Sixty-two days out (we were only a little longer from Calcutta), they were short of provisions, so we gave them a little, and the Captain took from them some demijohns of rum, which some of us thought a shameful thing to do.

The passage to the 'chops of the Channel' was accomplished in good time; there we met with strong easterly gales and after battling with them for two days, on short allowance of water, it was decided to run for the Scilly Islands to fill our water tanks while we could. We anchored off Hugh Town on St Mary's Island. The islands are well worth a visit, the inhabitants unconventional. They had secured enough tea to last them for years from the wreck of the clipper *Friar Tuck* in the gale that had compelled the *Corea* to shelter in Tor Bay the year before. The wind becoming favourable, we sailed for Le Havre and arrived safely. At that time the authorities did not allow fires on board in dock, so the officers and apprentices were lodged at hotels. The one we were sent to was kept by an American, and frequented by the Yankee packet ship officers. There was a great trade with cotton and other produce carried on by regular lines of American sailing ships. The United States had possession of the 'Trident' then, and would have retained it but for the advent of iron and steel for ship construction. They maintained discipline.

My apprenticeship having expired, I left for Liverpool in the Cunard S.S. *British Queen* and travelled with the emigrants for the sake of economy, had an experience I would not follow, arrived at Liverpool and received my indentures. In settling up Mr Edwards, a partner, asked me for a half-penny to balance my account. I suppose this was strict business. It seemed to me sordid meanness, considering the very small sum I received for my four years' service.

SECOND MATE
My Fifth Voyage
COREA
1869–1870

LONDON – HONG KONG – WHAMPOA – MACAO –
ST HELENA – LONDON

After a short stay at home I returned to Liverpool for the purpose of going up for my examination for Second Mate. Mr Ion was then the expert who defined for candidates the methods of the Board. After an interview he directed me to make an application, putting in my service documents, to be examined the next Board day. On my way to the examination rooms I passed down Pitt Street and was accosted by a man, his wife and four children. From their physique they were of the most degenerate of our population; it would have been hard to find another such wretched group. They were ill-clad, cold and very hungry. Nearby was a small shop which displayed in the window a large yellow ware dish of potted herrings and several loaves of bread. I arranged with the very kindly woman shopkeeper to allow them to eat in the shop and provide milk, plates and other requisites. The thanks and tears of the poor things was most embarrassing, and I have always thought this small action was repaid me a thousandfold, for I passed my examination on that and the succeeding day, without one check and with commendation. The examiners were Professor Towson, author of *Towson's Tables*, *Great Circle Sailing* and other practical works for the use of nautical men, and for seamanship, Captain McLord; both nice gentlemen, the latter noted for his shrewd, searching questions.

I called on Bushby & Edwards and was told by them they would notify me in a few weeks the ship I had to join, and then went home after, to me, an eventful week. In due time I was notified to join the *Corea* (my first ship), then lying in the East India Dock in London, loading for Hong Kong and Whampoa. The Captain had such a name for strictness that he was known as 'Bully Can' and my people tried hard to dissuade me from going with him. I have never been afraid of any man and it was my resolve and nature to do my duty. With a disciplinarian I felt that I would be content and happy. The want of discipline in the *Carricks* was demoralizing and hateful. In due course I joined, and found the Captain to be a sturdy middle-aged gentlemen with a face that told the poorest physiognomist that he was a man who knew what he wanted, and would have it: a bad man to cross. He told me to take charge. He had not appointed a Chief Mate yet; he was off to the Derby and the next day was going to Scotland for a week. By the time he got back, with the help of a very unwilling shipkeeper the ship was got into order and the decks coated with varnish. The cargo came down slowly, for the stevedores only worked when a full day's work was in the shed. On Whit Monday I went to Greenwich Fair and had a ride on a donkey at Blackheath, and a late whitebait dinner at the Ship Inn.

In due time the Chief Mate was appointed. A tall Scotsman who was always railing at what he called his bad luck, contrasting himself with others. The fault was in himself – whisky, conceit and laziness was his bane, and I feared with our fiery and imperious Captain he would have a sorry time. He was very slack and dilatory in his duties, which I saw the Captain noticed.

On the day I shipped 'on the Articles' at Tower Hill I went to the London Tavern and had a good dinner, and so long as I was an officer I celebrated that event the same way.

On the day the ship left the dock for the basin, the Chief Mate was not down to take charge at 5 a.m. I took her down, getting into the basin at 8 a.m.; there was no sign of the Mate. The Captain ordered me not to allow the Mate on board if he came down; he would engage another, and send him to join at Gravesend. At 9 a.m. the Mate came down with plenty of whisky inside. He attempted to board. I told him my orders. He was for forcing his way. I kindly resisted and he got a fall which quietened him. I then landed his effects. We left the dock for Gravesend. I had to get the long jib-booms out and rigged, backstays set up that had been cast adrift for convenience in loading, the mainsail and jibs bent, and top studding sail booms aloft. In short, to have the ship ready to proceed from Gravesend under sail as necessary. The scallywags of a ship's crew always endeavour to shirk the first day's hard work by shamming drunkenness. I was determined none should shirk this time. The apprentices, petty officers and a few decent men I told off to bend the mainsail, set up the backstays and secure the spars under the Third Mate. The rowdies I kept to get out the anchors and rig out the jib-booms, etc; when the boom was set a Welshman attempted to go down into the forecastle and I stopped him. When my back was turned he got into the scuttle hatch and with an insolent gesture defied me. I dragged him out and locked the door. Then there was a row. By the weight of numbers I was driven with my back to the foremast. I was armed with a heaver (a piece of hardwood used for heaving up earrings) which I found a very useful weapon, when Mr Mumford, a fine old Trinity House Pilot, came to my aid with a stick, and very soon peace reigned. The ship was ready for sea when the anchor was dropped at Gravesend. The Pilot must have reported the affair to the Captain for from that time the Captain's behaviour to me was all I could desire. I have the strongest feelings of affection and respect for his memory; he was a disciplinarian but a just and good man who did his duty and extracted from all others theirs.

The new Chief Mate (Watson) was a cockney and a snob; a cheery lion as vain as a peacock. By his account his father was a Chancery lawyer with a huge practice and a large income, possessor of a large country house and estate and a town house in Portland Street, W. For hours he would relate his doings in the hunting field, his skill at shooting and his conquests in the drawing room. By his account, he must have surpassed the 'Admirable Crichton'. A coachman, butler, gardener, grooms and footmen figured largely in his tales; also his mother's and sisters' 'lady's maids', the tutor and governess not left out. He had a photograph of a lovely girl in Court costume whom he averred was his half-sister Lillah in her presentation robes. I found myself apologising to him for our humble ship and modest fare (I never doubted his account). He said he didn't mind roughing it, he took the berth to oblige the agents who were clients of his governor's. On completion of this voyage he asked me to his father's house, and took me there in a cab. He must have forgotten the stories he told, for with trepidation I went to visit for the first time such magnificence. Instead of driving through the City towards the aristocratic West End, I saw we turned eastward after passing the Minories. The ship was in the London Dock; we had taken a cab on Tower Hill and after travelling halfway down Commercial Road we entered a mean side street, Portland Street E., all small houses of one design of which one was our destination. His mother and sisters were very nice and they made me heartily welcome to 'high tea' of which soused mackerel was the prominent feature.

The room was about twelve by nine feet and the only servitor an untidy girl. I could not look at Watson, I felt so ashamed for him. He was quite unperturbed, however, and talked of imaginary adventures that he said had occurred on the voyage. His mother and sisters believed, and beamed. I was glad he didn't ask me to confirm his stories. His father was an attorney's clerk. Watson was dismissed on his arrival home and I heard of his death a few years later.

We left Gravesend in tow; off the Foreland got a fair wind, set sail, discharged the Pilot, and with on the whole favourable winds, reached the Trades. The passage to Java Head was uneventful; the crew were kept in hand, the Captain took great interest in their food, and when the usual casks of beef and pork were found bad he did not force it on the crew. The casks were headed up, pitched and stowed in the forepeak; on arrival home they were dispatched to the Owners. In Hong Kong beef and pork were purchased at a high price. Never again were rotten stores sent to the *Corea* while Captain Can was in command. I was nineteen years of age and four of the apprentices were older and gave me some trouble to subdue. Afterwards we got on well, with the exception of an Irish lad of twenty-one from Cork. He was bad: a drunkard and treacherous. 'A good Irishman is better than the best – a bad one worse than the worst.' They have more lovable and more hateful qualities than any other race.

I was glad to see again the lovely scenery of Java, Sumatra and Borneo. The charm of these beautiful seas can never pall. That famous sailor-novelist Joseph Conrad has depicted the beauties of this region with the skill of a Milton. This is where the rich and leisured should do their yachting.

Having left London late in June, on entering the China Sea we found the Southwest Monsoon scant and variable. In pursuit of better winds the ship had been kept to the eastward of the surveyed route. One night I was awakened by a great shock and rumbling. The ship was on a reef. She bumped over it. On sounding the pump well it was found she was leaking badly, and from then until the ship was got into the Whampoa drydock we had the hardest of all work, continual pumping. On arrival at Hong Kong the cargo was rapidly discharged, then the ship was towed to Whampoa drydock when it was found that the forefoot and thirty feet of false keelson had gone and several planks had been damaged. The Chinese carpenters are skilful and made an excellent job of the repairs. Owing to the damage, forecastle hands had not been discharged at Hong Kong, and several of them with the carpenter had been stationed in the drydock to prevent the Chinamen from stealing the copper sheathing and nails. I regret to say that our carpenter was detected stealing some sheets of the metal: the Captain fined him heavily.

After the carpenter's conviction, copper was still missing. The Captain made a surprise visit to the forecastle and found the Welsh A.B., Watkins, in possession of spirits – presumptive evidence that he had sold copper. In fact, later we found that, in conjunction with the Irish apprentice O'Hean, he had stolen considerably. The Captain took possession of the spirits and destroyed them. The Welshman resented this action and threatened to attack him. I heard the disturbance and rushed in, butting the Welshman and frustrating his attack. We had a smart scrimmage from which I emerged victor, thanks to a little knowledge of the art of wrestling and the great factor that 'thrice aroused is he whose course is just.'

On leaving drydock we anchored in midstream a mile from the town. The Chinese are such smart thieves, and so expert, that ships to preserve their underwater bottoms being stripped of their metal sheathing have to suffer blackmail by being compelled to hire two sampans with their crews, to protect the ship from these robbers. One sampan attached to the jib-boom, the other to the rudder. No vessel who had this safeguard was molested.

The town of Whampoa is not attractive. It was a stinking receptacle for thieves, loose women, all kinds of horrible diseases, rampant smallpox and poisonous spirits.

The Captain was the guest of the merchants at Canton during our stay and made occasional visits to the ship. He gave strict orders to the Chief Mate not to allow any of the crew to visit the town, which under the circumstances was a wise and reasonable order. On Sundays, it was agreed that the Chief Mate took the mornings, which he spent ship visiting, and I the afternoons. I took the boat, and with the boys rowed far up the irrigation canals among the gardens. The Chinese are the cleverest and most careful gardeners, the prolific richness and order of their gardens being beyond anything I have seen. I had plenty of pice with which to barter, and brought back the boat loaded with fruit and succulent vegetables.

One Sunday, on returning from one of these jaunts, I was told the Mate had permitted some eight of our worst men and O'Hean the Irish apprentice to go ashore: he had not the moral courage to withstand their importunities. He told me they had solemnly promised not to go to the town. They did not return that night nor until breakfast time the next morning. When they came aboard Mr Watson allowed them to pass on deck without reproving them. I was so annoyed that I told him that if he did not rate them I would. After my experience of slackening discipline on board the *Carricks*, I was determined that there should be nothing of the sort where I was an officer. He was afraid of them, so I tackled the leader, a bad Englishman and like all bullies a coward. I taught him he could not play such pranks with impunity.

In port it was my duty to carry on ship's work. The Mate attended solely to the days. I told off hands for aloft to cross the topgallant and royal yards, keeping on deck the majority to man the capstans and heave up the yards. The yards were crossed and I was examining the gear with one of our best men, a handsome Peruvian about twenty-five years old. In examining the ropes we changed positions a few inches. Those inches saved my life and cost him his, for a large double block came from the main crosstrees and split his head, part of it with blood and brains falling on my breast. The block was deliberately thrown by the aforementioned forecastle bully to kill me. O'Hean, the apprentice, stated he saw him unhook the block, take deliberate aim and throw it. Only the slight shifting of position made the Peruvian the victim instead of me.

At the inquest O'Hean denied having said the above, and a verdict of misadventure was returned. Both O'Hean and the murderer were shunned for the rest of the voyage. The latter got many beatings from those whom before he had lorded over. From this time, whenever the Captain saw me standing under men aloft, he anxiously called me away, saying some of them would kill me. I was not afraid, for few men will commit deliberate murder, though I got many treacherous knocks on dark stormy nights – some of which I made the striker pay dearly for.

Early one morning we left Whampoa for Macao, the Portuguese settlement near the western mouth of the Canton River, to complete loading. Macao is an interesting and very dirty city with plenty of priests and nuns in evidence. The Portuguese have had a footing there for nearly four hundred years. The stinks killed my curiosity, and I returned on board with the official I had been sent for. In a few days the loading was finished. The Captain returned from Hong Kong with two seamen to replace our wastage, and brought news of the loss of the clipper *Serica* on the Paracels, a dangerous reef a few hundred miles SSW from Hong Kong on the homeward route. Only one of the crew was saved; he was picked up from floating wreckage sixteen hours after the ship had been battered to pieces. The *Serica* left Whampoa the day before us, bound for London via Hong Kong.

With the Northeast Monsoon at half a gale, we reached the entrance to Bangka Straits in eight days. These straits are between Bangka Island and Sumatra, and gave very pretty sailing between wooded banks. Not many years before, the Strait was infested by Malay pirates and was the scene of many horrible massacres. I very much preferred the route between the islands of Billiton [Belitung] and Bangka; though it was obstructed with reefs, it was shorter and gave less anchor work and furling of sails. Entering the Java Sea, we soon cleared the Sunda Straits and had a pleasant run across the Indian Ocean, round the Cape and to St Helena, where we took aboard the usual welcome garden stuff, and from there had a rapid passage to London, completing the voyage in a little over eight months.

A NEW LIFE?

My Sixth Voyage
COREA
1870

LONDON – HONG KONG – WHAMPOA – MACAO – LONDON

This was my second voyage as Second Mate of the *Corea*. I hoped it would be a quick one for I wanted less than three months' service to enable me to go up for the First Mate's Certificate. After a short visit home I returned to London and found my ship lying at the jetty in London Dock loading for Hong Kong. The Chief Mate was Mr Braithwaite, ex Second Mate of the *Carricks*.

The day after I joined I witnessed an amusing contest between a bargee and the Mate of a Yankee packet ship lying nearby. At that time steam had not ousted the famous lines of packet ships running between New York and the principal European ports; these fine old ships were threshing their way between New York and London, officered and manned by the toughest, most daring and reckless of seamen. It was the proudest boast of sailors to have been in those ships, for the Yankee Captains and officers were a law to themselves, and the crews were driven by brute force to an astounding smartness. This packet was the *General Slocum*, freshly painted. A barge was being shifted, as is customary, by one man who moved her along by the help of a boathook, hooking anything he could get hold of. When the *General Slocum* came within his reach he hooked on to her, at every dig scratching and defacing the paint. This annoyed the Mate, for his chief pride is to keep his ship in spick and span order. The Yankee yelled his remonstrances using the most vituperative language, reflecting on the bargee's ancestry, country and the character of his mother, to all of which he did not reply. He kept on his digs: it seemed to me he dug more viciously when his detractor used a particularly offensive epithet. The Yankee became even more clamorous and brutally abusive, with high and strange oaths to come down in the barge and immolate him.

By this time the barge had arrived abreast the ship's gangway. The bargee made fast to the gangway, and speaking for the first time and without show of temper, said, 'You need not trouble yourself to come down Mr Mate. I'm coming up to you.'

He sprang up the ship's side, and although the Mate was a typical powerful Yankee buck, in the course of half an hour the bargee gave him a thorough good thrashing, apparently keeping his surprisingly calm temper. All our stevedores and the dock employees had suspended work, climbing the rigging and other points of vantage to get a good view. They threatened to go over in a body should anyone attack the bargee or should the Mate use any other weapon than his fists, and cheered every shrewd hit so loudly that crowds gathered. Absolute fair play was maintained, and the victor was cheered all through his journey.

We left dock on a lovely May morning in charge of our old Pilot, Mr Mufford. He had the Trinity licence from Dock to the Isle of Wight, one of few issued. His dress was black frock coat and silk hat. On board he changed to a reefer and cap. He earned both the Mud Pilot's and the Sea Pilot's remuneration, and died a few years afterwards leaving the respectable fortune of £20,000. His only son, First Mate of the *Invincible* (sister ship to the *Corea*), a few months after this was bitten by a dog when sailing through the Sunda Straits and died a sad death from hydrophobia.

We anchored off Deal, close to a Maryport barque the *Mary Marie*. (I saw this barque nearly twenty years afterwards – she had just been bought by a Mr Montgomery of London.) The weather improving, we tripped anchor in company with the *Mary Marie* who kept with us until we had cleared the Channel, when we drew away from her. It was a rare thing for a ship to keep in company so long with the *Corea*. The outward journey was uneventful, excepting for a fight I had with the carpenter, a strong built Cumbrian twenty-eight years of age. He was a good workman who had been spoiled by sailing in a loosely disciplined ship, and resented the officers' overlooking. Mr Braithwaite, First Mate, had trouble with him one Sunday morning when he flatly refused to assist in washing decks. This was a rule of the ship: all the petty officers were informed of the rule before they signed articles. Mr Braithwaite, the First Mate, informed the Captain of this refractory conduct, but he for some reason did not wish to interfere. He ordered me to enforce the rules next Sunday morning when it was my 4 a.m. watch.

At 5 a.m. I sent the Third Mate to rouse him. He flatly refused, and did his best to persuade the sailmaker to do likewise. Sails would not listen to him. I then stepped in and gave him the option of turning out at once or I would cut his hammock strings and let him down by the run. He dared me – and came down with a run and bang. Picked himself up and came on, threatening me; thought better of it and submitted at once to the routine. A few weeks afterwards the carpenter had apparently nursed his wrath, for he still kept in his sulky stupid humour, and he and I came into contact . . .

In the China Sea we were painting ship, a job everyone takes a hand in. He was painting very carelessly and badly. I took his brush, saying, 'Do paint this way. You are spoiling the job.' I handed him the brush, he threw it on the white holystoned deck: I picked it up and wiped his face with it. There was the making of a disturbance which the Captain quelled. I soon saw that a quarrel between the carpenter and myself had been engineered, for when the Captain and Mate had gone to breakfast the carpenter came bouncing on deck in fighting rig, crying to me, 'Now I'll fight thee!'

This was a big proposition. The man weighed over twelve stones, a full-grown and mature man, with his frame and muscles hardened by his vocation. In a scientific combat I had not the slightest chance. In a rough and tumble melee I could have held my own; I was a stripling, nineteen years old and not exceeding ten stones in weight. It would never do for me to refuse, either. To show the white feather would be unbearable. A challenge to an officer to fight any other member of the crew would have been treated with derision and dealt with differently. Yet if I had refused the carpenter's challenge I would have lost prestige and authority: I must fight him. My plan of battle was made up in a second. The carpenter was dancing around me in the approved style of the stage boxer. The crew were watching, sure that I was going to get a trouncing: I represented authority, which was to them hateful. I saw that they went on with their work, then rushed at my opponent, ducked under his guard, butted my head into his stomach while protecting my face with my bony arms and calmly waited whilst he pumped his wind out by thumping my arms. When I heard him panting and winded, I rose like a shot and delivered heavy blows at his face, blinding and bleeding him. From his breathless condition his blows had no force. His futile thumping when I was in 'chancery' had tired him; he drew away, dazed and discomfited. Again I pursued the same tactics, getting in many blows and giving him no time to recover, and the fight was won. The Mate came on the scene and my opponent made that an excuse for retiring. His face for many days was an object lesson to all who 'kicked against the pricks', and many wondered at my victory. I did not get off scatheless, though no one knew it. For some days afterwards I lost consciousness for a few seconds. Fortunately I never fell down, and until I was better I did not go aloft. I have always hated fighting and quarrelling, yet I am a firm believer in Sheridan's advice to his son – 'Always be ready with your pistol.' And Shakespeare's – 'Beware of entering into a quarrel, but when in bear yourself so that your adversary beware of you.'

After this episode we had a quiet and pleasant passage, arriving at Hong Kong on the ninety-sixth day from the Downs.

While lying there, a wicked typhoon passed over the island doing much damage afloat and ashore. Many thousands of lives were lost in its track. Our ship was well prepared, having topgallantmasts and yards on deck, leaving nothing for the wind to get hold of, and though we had two anchors and all the cables out we dragged until the stream anchor with second hawser was put out, which brought her up in Kowloon Bay.

A huge British warship had also dragged; her cables were fouled. So after the typhoon had passed, yet still blowing a hard gale, a boat from her ran a hawser to our after bitts, making fast without permission. The executive officer used much strong language which was returned to him with interest. Service men were very imperious and arrogant in those days.

I had several pleasant trips ashore, and was surprised to see the many improvements all over the island. The cemetery in Happy Valley is an ideal resting place after Life's fitful fevers. Having discharged our cargo, we took in several 'dhopps' of tea, and left for Whampoa to complete our loading for London.

At Whampoa I was glad to renew my friendship with Mr Le Croix and his wife and daughter. A French officer of Marines when the French troops occupied the island of Hainan, he had married a native lady and left the service. Shortly afterwards he joined the Chinese Army, serving under 'Gordru' in the Border War.[1] For the last five years he held a good position in the Chinese Imperial Customs. He had only one child, Marie Celeste Le Croix, whose pet name was Chinese. She was a remarkably pretty girl of sixteen; Captain Can said her beauty would create a sensation in London, Paris or Vienna. She was of medium height, with an oval face, large lustrous brown eyes with long silky lashes, a creamy white complexion with the roses showing in her cheeks. Her expression gentle, bright and intellectual. She spoke and wrote three languages, played and sang sweetly, and was gentle, amiable and lovable.

I spent all my spare time at the Le Croix house and met many Mandarins and Europeans in the Chinese Service there. I was offered the position of First Lieutenant on a Mandarin gunboat doing duty on the Pearl River for the suppression of piracy. There were many tempting reasons for acceptance of the offer: good pay, assurance of promotion, a romantic life of adventure, and freedom from having to fight every insolent, bumptious blackguard to maintain order and authority.

But my Captain would not listen to my request to be discharged. So I deserted a few days before the ship had to sail, and was duly installed aboard the gunboat, which at once moved up the river to a creek on the inland side of Canton City. Several days later, when I thought the *Corea* was far away (the tailor was fitting on my new uniforms) a sampan came alongside, and the Consul, Chaplain and Captain Can stepped aboard. After a long conflab, I was persuaded by *force majeure* to return to the *Corea*.

Captain Can was very good about my escapade. He put me on honour not to desert again, and said smilingly, 'Why should you earn your fortune pleasantly in the Chinese Service? You must go home to your mother and sail for mean British shipowners!' He also said, 'Stay with me until you get your Certificate and then I will

---

[1] 'Gordru' was a local nickname for Charles George Gordon, when a mandarin and lieutenant-colonel in the Chinese Service in 1862–5. He commanded a force of four thousand Chinese, officered by Europeans, against the T'ai P'ins rebels, and was deeply respected by his men.

further your interests out here.' My friends came to think that the best way. I parted from them with hope, though with a very sore heart.

We had a quick and prosperous passage home and arrived once more alongside the tea warehouse top of London Docks, after another smart voyage of eight months and ten days.

CHIEF MATE, TO CANTON

My Seventh Voyage
COREA
1870–1871

HONG KONG – CANTON – WHAMPOA – MACAO – LONDON

I left London for home, stayed a few days, then left for Liverpool to sit for my First Mate's Certificate, for which I had prepared myself during the voyage. Mr Can advised me to put in my papers at once and go up for examination the first Board Day, which I did, and passed without a hitch. I was then in my twenty-first year.

I called on Bushby & Edwards. Both partners congratulated me on so rapidly getting my First Mate's Certificate, and appointed me to the *Corea* in that capacity, then wanted me to take one pound a month less than the previous Chief Mate, on the plea that I was so young. I declined with much heat, saying that it was a mean thing after my services to offer less pay to me than they would pay a stranger: 'If those are your terms, I decline the appointment, though I am sorry to leave the ship.' Mr Bushby said, 'I should think you are.' I replied, 'Don't make a mistake. There is nothing desirable in your ship or firm. It is Captain Can I regret leaving.' He tried hard to persuade me, saying what all mean people say when enforcing a contemptible thing: he was doing it on principle. Pity he is not living in these times, when 'Jack is as good as his master', if not better. Such employers as Bushby & Edwards made possible the strained relations now existing between Capital and Labour.

I went home. Mr Bushby wrote to my Uncle to use his influence to get me to accept his terms, who however replied that he thoroughly approved of the position I took. Captain Can wrote, 'Never mind Bushby. Come and you shall have what you ask.' So I went to London and found the ship in the East India Dock on the berth for Hong Kong. I had plenty to do, for Bushby & Edwards would not employ a ship's clerk when they had a Chief Mate by the ship.

I left my lodgings at 5 a.m. daily and seldom got back until 8 p.m. The cargo was such a mixed one with so many different measurements that it took me long after work was finished to make up my books, which I had to give the broker's clerk at 10 a.m. daily, and there was no half holiday on Saturdays. I had only Sundays to see London, which had always had the greatest fascination for me.

The Second Mate was a Welshman named Griffiths who really had more virtues and good points than his countrymen are credited with. He was my shipmate during my service as Chief Mate. We completed our cargo, and in charge of our old Pilot we cleared the river and had a spanking run down the Channel and to the trade winds – nothing out of the normal round until we were in the China Sea, when a seaman went mad and a sad death and burial took place.

The man who went mad had strong suicidal and homicidal tendencies: he had to be put in a straitjacket and tied up. He was an anxiety, and it was a great relief when we landed him at Hong Kong. His practices and antics convinced me of the truth of Darwin's theories. The death of one of our men was sad and awful to all of us who believed in God our Saviour and the Life Eternal. The man was taken suddenly ill, and failed rapidly. He suffered from many diseases brought on by his manner of life. He was a mystery; an educated man with cleanly personal habits, neat in his dress and with that trick of speech we ascribe to our higher classes. He destroyed every scrap of paper that could give a clue to his identity, and gave his clothes and effects to his shipmates the day before he died. A few hours before the end he asked to see the Captain and told him that he had been a Lieutenant in the British Navy. He had to leave – he had broken most of the Commandments – he had lived a life the world would call infamous – he had enjoyed every minute of his life, regretted nothing, knew he was dying and was glad of it, for he had no wish to live, now that his powers of enjoyment had left him. He believed neither in God nor Devil: there was no resurrection. He told the Captain it would be a mockery to hold a service over his remains, and that he wished as soon as possible after death to be dumped overside and let the sharks entomb him. His wishes were carried out. Many of us were horrified and saddened.

We dropped anchor off Peddars Wharf, Hong Kong, a passage of 101 days from London Docks. I had the pleasure of turning out the cargo I had tallied in, not only in good order in accordance with the manifest but without any claim against the ship: such a happening Captain Can never had before. This added to my reputation and pleased me much.

Leaving for Whampoa, we detected that our Chinese Pilot was making himself stupid with opium smoking, so the ship had to be brought to anchor until he was in a fit state to navigate through the many dangerous shoals. After making a thorough search of his luggage and person, even unpleating his pigtail for opium, we locked him in a room to sleep off the effects. In the early morning he was made to drink quantities of strong coffee. When he was master of himself, we hove up, set sail and worked up the river past the Boca Tigris (Tiger's Mouth – the narrowest part of Pearl River, defended by strong Chinese forts) and came to anchor off Whampoa. I was warmly welcomed by the Le Croix family.

After the ship was ready for the cargo of tea and silk, the merchants sent word that cargo would not be sent for a week, so the Captain was good enough to say he would stay on board (the European crew with the exception of the petty officers and apprentices had been paid off at Hong Kong) and I could take my long desired trip to Canton City with the Le Croix and stay there a day or two if I wished. Mr Le Croix hired a 'flower boat' or large roomy craft, fitted up after the style of the Upper Thames houseboats, laid in a stock of provisions and we started on a delightful adventure.

Canton then had a population of nearly two million of which over two hundred thousand lived on boats on the river, having no other home. The flower boats were hired by rich Chinamen, who gave rare dinners and entertainments there. The river was their pleasure ground. There was also a large population of Magdalenes and robbers living in boats. Canton is quite seventy miles from the sea, over twenty from the anchorage at Whampoa. The Pearl River has two distinct channels, called the East and West Rivers. Canton was the first Chinese port opened to European commerce; the river is there as broad as the Thames at Gravesend. The European merchants live in a protected area well outside the city and very seldom venture in the city. The Consuls strongly object to any of their countrymen visiting the city, for the populace hate Europeans.

Mr Le Croix directed our boat to near a retired landing place. That evening we did not land: it was dangerous to be in the city at night time. There were many fanatical rogues who would murder a *fanqui* (foreign devil) at sight.

The scene around us as night fell was very strange and pretty. All the craft were lighted by innumerable paper lanterns of many colours, and distance lent enchantment to the sights and sounds. Close to, Chinese music is not grateful to English ears; in our boat after dinner Marie Celeste sang sweetly to the accompaniment of a guitar and we had a pleasant evening. Two villainous looking guards were hired for protection from robbers during the night, and we all enjoyed a good night's sleep. Next morning we had a real Chinese meal. It was good, and I was advised not to enquire what some of the dishes were made from, to be content the food was pleasant and wholesome, though differing from English prejudices. The tea and preserves were delightful.

We went ashore at 10 a.m. I had a rather long red beard which in one so young was a matter of some astonishment to the crowds of Cantonese, for only very old men have beards amongst them. We were followed by crowds of silent folk, which gave me a creepy feeling. Very narrow streets with peculiar, but not offensive smell, open shops, the number of people all moving silently in their paper-soled shoes. The transport of merchandise is effected by coolies with long bamboos, the packages slung from each end. Sedan chairs and strange one-wheeled vehicles are for the carriage of the well-to-do people. In no other country have I seen such numbers of deformed and diseased folk; some of them were too horrible to describe. Many of them inhumanly wicked looking: they seemed devils incarnate. Our missionaries have a tremendous task to uproot the hellish depravity of thousands of years. The Chinese submerged will take some salvage.

We went into the market and saw many things sold for food that we hold in abhorrence: rats, cats, hairless fat dogs that look like suckling pigs except for their pug-faced heads, sea slugs, birdsnests, ugly fish and all sorts of creeping things. I told my friends that I would have no more Chinese breakfasts, and they were amused and said that Europeans did not make use of all the good things that nature provided.

I enjoyed the shops and saw many beautiful carvings, metal-work and all the processes of silk manufacture from the coccoon to the finished piece. We had lunch in a Chinese eating house; the Le Croix advised me what to eat so my prejudices were not offended. Indeed there was a diversity of cakes and fruit so that of them alone I could have satisfied myself.

We visited the famous Temple of the One Hundred Gods, a collection of the most horrid grotesque caricatures of humanity. Such Gods to worship – the artists who carved them knew how to depict devilish wickedness. I only saw one amiable God. When we left the temple, the crowd following us had greatly increased. Some of them commenced crying, '*Fanqui*!' so Mr Le Croix advised getting back to our floating home before they became dangerous. They followed us to the landing place, pressing us closely and getting impudent. Mr Le Croix spoke to them in Chinese and we got clear by throwing a handful of small coin: whilst they scrambled for the money we got aboard. All the Consuls give notice that they will not be responsible for the lives of their countrymen who venture into the city, and the Europeans live in a protected area well outside the walls of Canton. There is generally a British river gunboat at anchor opposite the Consulate.

Next morning the ladies were left in the boat. We were going to visit a friend of Mr Le Croix, a Mandarin with a high position in the city, and see the gaols and execution grounds. We had tea with the Mandarin, who spoke a little English. He took us to see malefactors undergoing punishment – horrible torture. One row of thirty had their heads and wrists in stocks, their toes only touching the ground. Their faces were smeared with syrup and flies, gnats and mosquitoes battened on their poor faces. That and the fiery hot sun drove them mad: such horrible torture I was sickened. Other forms of torture are indescribable; even Torquemada the Grand Inquisitor never dreamed of such hellish torture as practised by the Chinese. I was taken to the execution ground and saw sixteen pirates decapitated. The victims were apathetic and sat silently smoking until the heads-man called on them. They knelt down and the headsman with one cut parted the head from the body. It was like a bad dream: I could not believe what my eyes saw was real. Life is very cheap in China.

May God prosper the Missionaries. I did not eat that night and had horrible dreams.

A very pretty bridal procession passed our boat that evening. Next morning the Chinese Commander of the gunboat that I had been second in command of for a few days paid us a visit. I told him that I was coming out to join his Service when I had passed all the examinations. He was kind and sent lots of presents, as did the Mandarin we visited. We bade adieu to Canton and reached Whampoa in the evening, quite satisfied that I did not again want to see such horrors.

In a few days we completed our Canton cargo and left for Macao to finish. The Le Croix came with us to Boca Tigris, the last time I saw them for death and fate intervened.

Three days afterwards we sailed from Macao for London. We had a pleasant uneventful passage, again making the voyage under nine months. I had three months' sea service before I could sit for the Captain's Certificate, so I had to make another voyage as Chief Mate.

VOYAGE ROUND THE WORLD
My Eighth Voyage
COREA
1872–1873
LONDON – ADELAIDE – NEWCASTLE – NAGASAKI – YOKOHAMA – NEW YORK

The *Corea* was too late in the season for the favourable monsoon in the China Sea, so she was chartered at a high rate to load for Adelaide, South Australia from there proceeding to Newcastle, New South Wales to load a cargo of coal for the British Naval Agents at Nagasaki in Japan. It had been proved that little more time was taken by this route than by going direct to the Far East when the unfavourable Northeast Monsoon was blowing in the China Sea. The profit was doubled by having two cargoes. We did not relish the idea of a coal cargo in our pretty ship, but now the Suez Canal is opened, I expect that sailing ships will get only rough cargoes.

I had a short visit home for the ship was only two weeks discharging and getting the drydock overhaul. When I rejoined, she had taken her loading berth in the East India Dock. She was quickly loaded, and we left dock on a bright June morning, had a pleasant run down Channel, meeting with adverse winds in the Bay of Biscay. On approaching the Portuguese coast the wind drew from the north, which soon took up into the Northeast Trades. The crew were all natives of the British Isles, mostly men who had sailed on the coast of Australia and been tempted by high wages to take a run home. They intended to desert at Adelaide. These men required driving: they did not intend giving any more work than was forced from them. After passing the Canary Islands I came on deck at midnight, the weather was delightful, the wind of that degree of four that kept the sails asleep, not a tremor in them, the ship slipping along about seven knots, the rippling of the water making a musical lulling lullaby. After mustering the watch, which I did in a perfunctory way, I took a walk round the decks to see that each sail was well set, then called the boys on the poop and with my sextant instructed them in the art of taking star observations. The night was an ideal one with a clear horizon; whilst busy I noticed the ship was being steered very carelessly. I went to the steersman and chided him, thinking that the charm of such a perfect night had seduced his mind from his work and made him dreamy. When steady on course, I returned to the sextant and the boys. Again the ship was off her course. I called to the helmsman to be careful; he muttered something and did worse than ever, bringing the studding sails aback. I ran to the wheel and hove it up. The man was cheeky and stupid and I had to pull him from the wheel. He attacked me and got worsted. The Captain and Second Mate, roused up by the row, came on deck. They examined the man and decided there was nothing the matter with him and he resumed his trick at the wheel. (I heard, as the skylight was open, the Captain say to the Second Mate, 'Mr Fraser is too ready with his fists.') This annoyed me. Very soon I had my revenge, for standing to leeward of . . . I was choked with an overpowering smell of rum, and then the Third Mate reported that something was the matter with the lookout man. At once it dawned on me that the crew had broached cargo. On going forward I found the lookout dazed and stupid from drink. The watch on deck was drunk. The watch below drunk. All mixed together, like overfed swine.

With the Third Mate, I dragged a specimen along the deck and rattled him down the cabin stairs into the saloon and asked the Captain if I had been 'too hasty'. He grasped the situation at once, and gave orders to call the petty officers. In the meantime I went down the forecastle and started to get the drunken brutes on deck. The Captain came armed to the scuttle hatch and called on me to come up until I had more force. Shortly I got them all on deck, handcuffed and lashed them all round the poop and quarterdeck, then went and made a thorough examination. I found the men's chests and bags and bunks full of all sorts of Crosse & Blackwell's condiments and tinned comestibles, currants, raisins, nuts, tins of fancy biscuits, lime juice bottles full of rum, candles and lots of goods that could have been no use to them. They had gone down the hatch leading to the store holds in the forepeak, cut through the bulkhead, and tunnelled through bales of cloth, etc. for fully fifty feet until they came to tins and puncheons of rum. I found a piece of candle stuck on the cask close to the bunghole: it was marvellous the fumes had not burst into flames when extracting the rum. Within ten feet of the rum was a wooden magazine containing twenty tons of explosives and gunpowder. There can be no doubt that many missing ships have been lost with all on board by the reckless thieving of the crew. We had a providential escape and the severe punishment meted out was well deserved. We waited for no landlubber's law but gave the punishment suited to the crime. Every precaution had been taken to stow the spirits and beer so that the crew could not get at it: unknown to us one of the sailors had worked with the stevedores in London and noted where the rum was stowed. Hence the dangerous engineering feat to get at it.

When I made my report even the most amiable was angry, and each and all of them got a well deserved dutting and were kept in the painful position we had lashed them in until we, with great labour, had returned what goods we could to their respective cases and had taken sufficient coals from the peak to serve the passage, bolted the hatch, caulked and payed it. I undertook to make an examination of the hatch and bulkhead every watch until arrival to prevent further outrage, although I was convinced that not one of the eighteen culprits would attempt another adventure. I was hard at work for eighteen hours and slept soundly when all was secured. It was providential that these happenings took place in the serene latitude of the Trade Winds.

From this time until the arrival at Adelaide (a quick passage of seventy-one days from London) the crew were kept hard at work and were too weary in their watch below to hatch mischief. The ship was got into spick and span order, and the three days we laid at anchor outside the port was sufficient to tar down and paint masts and yards inside and outside to the bands. I doubt if any ship ever entered Adelaide harbour from an oversea voyage in such good condition.

The Captain informed me privately that he did not intend to prosecute the men for their reckless robbery and destruction, not from humanitarian motives but because all the consignees of the cargo, some sixty or seventy, would make claims, just or unjust, and cause law delays. The men had been punished and could never forget the lesson. On arrival at Adelaide Wharf they all ran as if the devil was after them with a hot poker, and were taken in and hidden by the many lawless ruffians abounding in the Colonies at that time.

We had a set of good loyal, plucky, petty officers and boys who deserved reward for their extra work and loyalty. On arrival home the owners turned a deaf ear to the Captain's request that their conduct should be adequately rewarded.

Port Adelaide was then a small town and all business was transacted at the City, a beautiful spot seven miles inland. The buildings were artistic with parks and gardens laid out and a picturesque position. I much enjoyed my visit there on two Sundays.

A few days after we got to the Wharf, the Glasgow ship *Roslyn Castle* arrived from New York. The crew on the passage also had broached cargo; in the mêlée that ensued, one of them cut the Chief Mate's face open from mouth to eyebrow. After the Captain had stitched up his dreadful wound, the Mate was so enraged that he went to the place the man who had defaced him was confined, knocked him down, turned him over, and with the knife that had so cruelly cut him, made a deep cross on each of the man's buttocks, then took a handful of coal dust from a bunker there and rubbed it in the deep cuts, making an indelible mark.

When the case was tried, the man as the aggressor got six months' hard labour. He would have had a number of years but for the Mate's taking the law into his own hands. The Judge censured the Mate, though he allowed he had grievous provocation. I thought the Mate had done right, for the use of the knife is hateful.

One night the Mate of the *Roslyn Castle* roused me up. He told me that the Captain of the barque *Tonjoy* had been brutally murdered by several members of his crew and wanted me to go off to the ship with him. The *Tonjoy* was lying at the Semaphore Anchorage. Her Captain I had met several times; he was a nice gentlemanly man about thirty years old and on his first voyage as Captain. The son of a Royal Navy Captain of Coastguards in Ireland, he had with him several young men, sons of Coastguards under his father. Three of these young fellows deserted. High wages, opportunities and the attractions of seductive women were the enticement. The authorities captured these runaways and they were kept in limbo until the ship was ready to leave, when they were put on board. They refused to work. The Captain spoke gently to them, told them that he could not pay them off, nor allow them to leave for there was much difficulty in getting substitutes and the wages demanded exorbitant. His duty compelled him to keep them to their agreement. He came ashore where I met him at the Customs House, and he told me of his brothers and said he expected they would listen to reason when he returned to the ship in the evening. I bade him goodbye, saying we should meet in Newcastle, as we would leave for there shortly. When we got on board the sight of the Captain's body was sad and amazing. The handsome young man's face was battered and kicked into a revolting pulpy, sickening mass. It appears that the three men asked to see the Captain on his return. They demanded to leave the ship. He spoke gently: they attacked him with iron belaying pins, killing him and sadly defacing him with kicks and blows.

During the attack the Chief Mate locked himself in his room; the Second Mate ran and hid himself. It is sickening even at this day to write of such despicable conduct, and they were British. We expressed ourselves very strongly to them – such dastards. When we landed with the body of the Captain, there was a large crowd of roughs and rowdies and I heard one say 'Another b . . . Skipper the less.' I think of Adelaide in the words of Heber: 'Where every prospect pleases and only man is vile.'

In due course the murderers were condemned to death, afterwards reprieved on the sentimental plea that capital punishment had never been inflicted in South Australia! Many people were indignant at such misplaced leniency. Democracies are inconsistent.

After discharging, we took on board 700 tons of copper slag for Newcastle, N.S.W. The yards on the mizzen and the royal yards were sent on deck to make the ship easier to work with a reduced crew. It was difficult to get men at any wages. The Captain was up in the City closing up his business when a Pilot came aboard and handed me a note from him directing me to proceed to the outer anchorage at once, as several writs were out to detain the ship until claims for short delivery and damaged cargo were settled. At that time the writs of the different Colonies were ineffective outside their own boundaries. We cast off and proceeded down the Gut, striking heavily as it was nearly low water. We reached the Semaphore

Castlerigg Cottage in Keswick, where Thomas Garry Fraser stayed as a boy, and from which he departed for his first voyage as apprentice.

The launch of the *Patterdale* in 1871 attracted thousands of spectators. She was over 1200 tons, and one of the finest ships built by the Whitehaven Shipbuilding Co., which in 1869 had taken over the old Brocklebank yard, established in 1782. Despite this picture of maritime industry, by 1889 the firm had been liquidated, and Cumbrian shipbuilding in general was in sharp decline. (*Graphic*)

Williamson's famous covered yard at Harrington (1870). The visiting ladies are inside one of the empty bays. This yard was considered unusual; most Cumbrian shipbuilding was out of doors, as can be seen in the pictures of Whitehaven and Maryport. The *Parthia*, 1022 tons, was launched in 1864, and was one of the larger ships built there. The *Doriga*, also iron but rather smaller (678 tons), was built at the same yard two years later, and was Fraser's first command.

Old Quay and entrance to South Harbour, Whitehaven, from a painting by George Nelson *circa* 1896. Although these sailing ships are smaller than the clippers on which Fraser sailed, the steam tug is typical of the period. The paddles made for excellent manoeuvrability in close quarters, and such tugs were used for towing and docking much larger ships.

The outer breakwater of Whitehaven harbour at high water. The shipyard in the foreground also appears on the back of the jacket of this book, just visible on the shore outside the uncompleted breakwater. By 1890 when this photograph was taken both shipbuilding and the fortunes of the harbour had declined; larger vessels turned to the enclosed non-tidal docks at Liverpool.

The Maryport yard of Ritson's, with the barque *Southerfield* ready for launching in 1881. Maryport was another of the coastal towns that built and manned ships, and from her harbour sent cargoes of coal and iron ore round the world.

Workington docks, showing a variety of types of ship, and coal hurries for loading. The *Corea*, 581 tons, and *Carricks*, 916 tons, both wooden ships, were built here by Fell's yard in the period in the mid-1880s when Cumbrian ports such as this were prospering and expanding.

The port of Liverpool in 1859. This lithograph shows the already very extensive dock facilities and the immense amount of shipping using the estuary. The view is to the northwest, looking out towards the Liverpool bar. Birkenhead docks and shipyards are visible on the left bank, and New Brighton is on the point beyond. Outside the estuary, confined channels led through shoals and banks in the approaches. Though marked by buoys and lightships, they were narrow and hazardous for large sailing ships and towing was normal. A lifeboat was stationed at New Brighton, and is mentioned in the last chapter.

A portion of a page in the Princes Dock Master's Register recording the arrival of the 'new ship' *Carricks* in 1867 in ballast from Workington, to load for Calcutta. Her Master, Captain J. Garry, was a relative of Fraser and the Second Mate. After contracting a tropical fever he was permanently incapacitated and retired ashore. Fraser was senior apprentice on this eventful voyage, and fortunate in not contracting the same fever, which afflicted the crew on the homeward voyage. (The above lithograph and register are reproduced by kind permission of the Mersey Docks & Harbour Co.)

The aftermath of a cyclone and the wrecked opium steamer *Thunder*. She had been sighted by the *Carricks* off the approaches to Calcutta, before all ships were warned to stand off because of an approaching storm.

The Hooghly River in Calcutta, with numerous foreign merchantmen at anchor. The effects of the cyclone are visible: upper yards are down, and in some cases topmasts broken off; lower yards are damaged. In midstream, in the gap between the stump of the foremast of the wrecked *Thunder* in the foreground and the stern of a ship anchored off her bow, the mast and gaff of a smaller vessel sunk in the roads still stands above water.

A painting of Macao in 1847, showing warehouses and a fascinating selection of native and foreign craft.
A Chinese family on a 'chop' on the Canton River, with foreign ships in the background. (Coloured lithograph, *circa* 1860)
The anchorage at Queenstown (Cork). (Coloured lithograph, *circa* 1840)

Foo Chow, with the tea clippers *Serica*, under sail in the centre, and *Lahloo*, second from right. The wooden clipper *Serica* was built in 1863, took part in the great race from Foo Chow to London in 1866 with the *Aeriel, Taeping* and *Fiery Cross*, and was mentioned by Fraser as having been wrecked off the Philippines in 1869 or 1870.

Whampoa, from Dane's Island. The etching dates from a slightly earlier period and shows the merchant ships which pre-dated fast clippers of the type Fraser sailed on. (T. Allen, 1830s).

Anchorage and in an hour the Captain came off with six drunken specimens of the beachcombing fraternity in place of our eighteen seamen: he could get no more. We at once hove up anchor and proceeded to get out of South Australian jurisdiction, paying all claims, just and unjust, with the foretopsail. The weather was bad and stormy, though the wind was favourable. We had an anxious and dirty night in the backstairs passage (between Kangaroo Island and the Main). It was well we had such a fine band of fellows as our apprentices and petty officers, for our drunken beachcombing contingent were little good excepting to growl, grumble and swear. One old rascal was such a persistent swearer that his language got on my nerves and I was forced to handle him. The old reprobate had been Captain of a fine ship in the Indian trade. He had done everything an honest man should not do. Captain Can knew him well. He was then such a swell that his cognomen was 'Beau Hitchcock'. Afterwards we had peace and much hard work, without the aggravation of bad talk and back talk.

Arriving at Newcastle, the runners were paid off and the Captain told me to get the copper slag discharged and take in stiffening. He then went to enjoy the gaieties of Sydney for three weeks. What a sorry time I had. All were in an unamiable mood; the slag was dreadful stuff to handle, making the hands sore, several so bad that I had to engage two men from shore. I agreed to give them 10 shillings per day and their food, work 6 a.m. to 6 p.m. They commenced at 6 a.m. and worked to nearly 3 p.m. when I saw them put their coats on. I asked 'What is the matter?' One replied, 'Well, Mr Mate, we have decided if we can't earn our living excepting by such nigger work as this, we'll go ashore and hang ourselves.' I said, 'You'll get no money for what you have done,' and he replied, 'We'll make you a present of it, Mr Mate. We've had enough of this ship.'

I could get no more men from shore, so commandeered our fat and pompous steward for a couple of hours in the afternoon. This man was one of those fellows who have much to say of their former superior position, that ill fortune or vice has sent to sea. He toadied to the Captain, and it suited him. With much patience our troubles were surmounted, and when the Captain returned from Sydney the stiffening coals were aboard, and the ship awaiting her turn to go under the tips where she would get loaded in twenty-four hours.

Instead of commendation, his greeting was, 'Why have you painted the ship inside? You might as well throw the paint away.' I said, 'The ship has not been painted, only washed and cleaned.' After my worries and troubles in getting so much work done with so few hands, I felt sore and bruised at such treatment and got provoked when I heard the steward relating to the Captain my methods of getting the work done. I went in to him, and in the Captain's presence slapped the steward well. I then told the Captain I would leave the ship for he had left me to do with few hands more work than any ship in the harbour had done with their full crews, and that I had to demand more work from the apprentices and petty officers than my conscience approved of, etc. This talk made him more amiable, and he frankly made a generous acknowledgment of the work done and gave the petty officers and boys a day's holiday, which pleased them and gratified me. A week afterwards the steward robbed the Captain of ten pounds and deserted.

Our turn to go under the tips came at last, and as was the custom we moved under bedecked with flags. Everyone was tired of Newcastle. When lying at the town's wharf, the body of a woman was brought to the steps under the stern and left there for over an hour. The body was almost naked, and the ribald and disgusting remarks made by the crowd, and their heartless levity, have left an indelible feeling of dislike for the Australian proletariat. Our men who deserted at Adelaide and the rumours from there to here had spread such adverse reports concerning our ship among seafarers that we could not pick up a crew at Newcastle, so the Captain had gone to Sydney where he met with no better luck for a time. The ship was loaded and doubled off (there were only two buoys at 'Horseshoe' at this time). I got a wire to meet the Sydney steamer on Sunday morning and found the Captain with a full crew of Malayans and three Chinese, steward, cook and assistant – the shipwrecked crew of a Danish ship. To protect them from the crimps I put everything in the forecastle for their comfort and convenience, and personally kept watch over them all day, and at night locked them up and kept double watch, for the boarding masters and crimps were trying their utmost to steal them from us; some astute member of the fraternity got a warrant out for keeping the Malays in false and forcible imprisonment. In all young countries the law lends itself to help rogues. The Captain got wind of this and we left in a hurry. When turning the bend towing to the Nobbies, a boat was making frantic endeavours to overtake us. It contained the marshall with the warrant for me. The Pilot was going to stop for him: he was told to mind his business which was to get the ship outside the bar. He could say with truth he was prevented by force! We cleared the bar, set all sail, dismissed the Pilot and circumvented the harpies!

The passage to Japan was made to the westward of New Caledonia, passing between the New Hebrides and the Bismarck Archipelago and through the Caroline Islands. The Captain did not stop off at any of the islands as we had a crew of Malays, a treacherous race with piratical traditions, and in all the savage South Sea Islands were many desperate men, escaped convicts from New Caledonia and Australia who would stop at no crime for the pleasure of looting a ship.

Earth has nothing more lovely than these island gems of the Pacific. Many are of volcanic origin with lofty hills, tree crowned. The coral atolls had a beauty of their own. The foliage and blue sea, misty foam of the breaking seas, white coral shores and calm emerald-hued basins inside the reefs presented a picture indescribable by mere words.

We passed through Van Diemen's Straits between a very active volcano and Cape Satano on Kinshui [Kyūshū?] and entered Nagasaki harbour at dawn. The harbour is entirely land-locked and has the appearance of an inland lake surrounded by hills five to six hundred feet high, well cultivated. The wind failed at the entrance and we were towed to our anchorage abreast the British Consulate by hundreds of oar-propelled boats. The Malay serang attempted to stab with his kris. He was punished by the Consul, and the rest of the Malays were discharged and sent home. The three Chinese cooks and steward stayed with us until the voyage ended in London.

The coal cargo was discharged by hundreds of women who passed it from the hold in hand baskets. They worked well, and were quite as well conducted as our pitbrow girls. A cargo of Japanese coal was loaded here for Yokohama by the same women. The freight earned for this cargo was more than is now paid a steamer from Australia to London.

Nagasaki is a beautiful and interesting town with a pretty hinterland. I visited Deshima, the historic Dutch entrepôt situated on a small peninsula at the head of the harbour. Three centuries of occupation had left very little Dutch architectural remains. I noted with regret that American occidentalism had besmirched the people in the town, and that many of the charming and polite mannerisms were changed to rude Americanisms.

However, in my trips to the country I found the same hospitable courtesy I had so much admired in the people of Kanagawa six years before. There is little notable architecture in Nagasaki; the buildings are principally of wood, and flimsy, owing to the frequent earthquakes.

There being no European seamen to be had, a crew of Japanese were engaged and no better men would I wish to have. We were towed by boats to the mouth of the harbour, and getting a breeze set sail and had a most tempestuous passage, this being the hurricane season. The Black Stream of Japan runs with force on the eastern shores of Nippon; the stream is the track of the typhoons at this season when thunder, lightning, storms and especially heavy squalls are the constant experience of navigators.

We arrived at Yokohama in a snowstorm. Soon after a Japanese naval officer came aboard and gave notice that no Japanese subjects were allowed to engage themselves for overseas voyages: locally, yes. We parted with our Japs with regret.

The coals were discharged into a hulk. I chose to work on Sundays and holidays, even on Christmas Day, to get the dirty stuff out. Then a gang of Japs soon had the ship sweet clean and polished, fit to take the cargo of fine teas and silks to New York. I found many objectionable changes since my former visit, and much regretted that Western civilization was sweeping away all that was quaint romantic and beautiful in the oriental world. The cities of the earth seemed destined to be as dreadful as Pittsburg and Manchester.

Yokohama always had a large quota of foreign men-of-war. The Admirals made it their headquarters, preferring this land of milk and honey to the unhealthy stinking Chinese ports, and other rich globe-trotters had also found it out. The town had grown considerably; many hotels, clubs and banks had been built, and European merchants had built themselves spacious offices, godowns and residences. The Manager of the branch of the Hong Kong & Shanghai Bank opened here was John Hodgson, who had served a clerk's apprenticeship with the Owners of the *Corea*, Bushby & Edwards. My uncle had brought him out to China ten years before and got him a post in the 'Compton d'escompte de Paris'. After passing some years in this Bank in Hong Kong, he joined the Hong Kong & Shanghai Bank. All the years he spent in Hong Kong he lived as a guest on board the Bushby & Edwards ships. Captain Can had been exceptionally kind to him. Hodgson was an arrant snob; his promotion had given him an enormous swelled head. Four weeks the *Corea* had been in port and he had never looked near the ship nor sought out the Captain, though he was a member of the same Club and Masonic Lodge. One Saturday afternoon Hodgson came aboard bringing two large cases which he informed me contained valuable presents for Mr Bushby, the Owner. I told him that I could not take the cases without the Captain's authority, and advised him to go ashore and find the Captain. I was not at all cordial, and when he excused himself for being so long in calling, I reminded him of the proverb 'He that excuses – accuses.' He came back in an hour saying he could not find the Captain, and entreated me to take the cases on board for safety as the Custom House was closed, and the contents, valuable bronzes and Satsuma vases, would have to be left in the boat all night, which was a risk he was afraid to take. I consented to take them on board for the night and without prejudice. About 1 a.m. my room was banged open. A very angry Captain demanded why I 'had taken Hodgson's cases on board without authority?' I explained. It was no use, he would not be pacified. So I got angry, roused up all hands, put a boat in the water with the Third Mate and four hands, and went ashore to the Hong Kong & Shanghai Bank premises. I battered the door until I had aroused the street and Hodgson. I gave him my mind and told him that if he had not a boat alongside by 6 a.m. to take the cases I would dump them in the Bay. He was there at 6 a.m. and got them. I was vexed with the Captain and would not go to breakfast with him. Shortly afterwards he explained Hodgson's conduct to me, and I sympathized with him: Hodgson was a paltry snob who had found money in his pocket and lost his head. On arrival, Mr Bushby asked me why I would not take his cases. I told him for sufficient reason that I knew no authority but the Captain's, and that Hodgson was an arrant fool.

We had great difficulty in getting a crew. At last the crimps got together the bad foreigners of Japan, the jails and hospitals were scoured, and we mustered four sailors drummed out of the American

Navy, two mariners, deserters from the French Navy, a Negro prize fighter (stony broke), a blackguardly Yankee Mate and Second Mate, both kicked out of a whaler, six rascals from the different Consular gaols – one a murderer. There was also a notorious scoundrel up before the American Consul for some crime, who stated he was shipped in the *Corea*. On that account he was let off. This appeared in the little paper printed in English. The Captain saw it and ordered me to turn the fellow out when the crimp brought him. I turned him out, the crimp objected in the usual manner, we had a squabble, and with the help of the Third Mate he was thrown in the boat. He had a lot to say of what he would do if he saw me ashore – so I went ashore and asked him to do it. He went home. We picked up a substitute of sorts for the fellow sent ashore, and I doubt if any ship had so much evil humanity aboard. Japan was rid of many bad men and I had the prospect of a lively time before reaching New York.

We took the Malucca Straits passage [between Malaya and Sumatra], and I was heartily glad to get into the open ocean, for it was weary work with the hot sun and nightly squalls of wind and rain among the dangerous reefs and rocks. The men had so far behaved decently. They were mostly poor seamen, but with our splendid apprentices and petty officer, the meanest sort of sea labourer if willing would suffice. Mr Griffiths, the Second Mate, was an excellent sailor and I liked him. He had the great fault of needlessly irritating and threatening the men, and when faced, backing down when he should have made good his threatenings. Dealing with rough and primitive men, tact is as necessary as force. I had taken in my watch all the toughest of the crowd. The Second Mate had in his watch the Negro prize fighter, who I thought was the best of the lot and who, if handled properly, would never have given occasion for offence.

In the Indian Ocean near noon, the Captain and I were taking the sun when the Third Mate told me that the Negro had attacked the Second Mate. I told the Captain and ran for'ard; I saw the Negro strike the Second Mate. I handed my sextant to the cook, picked up a heaver and struck at the Negro's shins, the most vulnerable part of a Negro. I did not hit him hard enough. He took out his knife and slashed at me, cutting my shirt and grazing my side rather badly. I ran from him until abreast the main hatch, he close upon me with his knife. I threw myself down before him and over me he fell, the knife flying out of his hand. I jumped on him and he threw me off, making a shuttlecock of me for some time. I tackled him with a handspike and with the help of the Third Mate made him impotent. The Yankee ex Mate and others interfered: they got a good trouncing, for the Second Mate proved he only wanted a leader to be worthy of his Welsh ancestry. The rest were kept in check by the apprentices, carpenter and sailmaker. We had a good half hour's strenuous fighting. This was a dangerous affray, and the Captain should have been there with a revolver. The mutiny was quelled. The Negro had three ribs broken and severe contusions; the Yankee ex Mate a black eye; several others were marked, the Second Mate a bruised face, the Third Mate a bitten hand and swollen jaw, and I had a long narrow knife cut on my side, a bruised body and a shirt bloody and destroyed. Small damages for conquering in such a serious fight. While the steward was dressing my wounds the Captain came in beaming, saying 'Well, you fixed them finally, Mr Fraser!' I was vexed and said, 'It was a mutiny, Sir. You ought to have been there, armed.' However, he was fifty-five years and shaky on his pins . . . only, the moral force of his revolver might have been useful. It was a fight to a finish and ensured peace for the rest of the voyage. The Captain ordered me not to allow the Negro to lay up. I bandaged his broken ribs and gave him easy sitting work until he was better. His training as a prize fighter stood him in good stead, for in three weeks he was well. He asked to be shifted from the Second Mate's watch into mine, and six weeks after, running before a stronge breeze, the foretopmast studding sail was carried away. To save time and work I always ran out on the boom to reeve the tack, making a footrope of the head of the lower studding sail. I was on the foreyard to do so when the great active Negro ran up the rigging, passing me and taking the tack, saying 'No, Mr Mate, you shan't do that while I am aboard,' as he went on the swaying boom. I called to him 'Come back you silly man – I am only ten stone, you are thirteen stone and will break the boom and go overboard!' He went out.

This action proved him to be a good man with no revengeful feelings against me. I suppose his sports training had given him some of the instincts of a gentleman, and he thought that I had only done my duty in protecting the Second Mate, whom he disliked.

Our murderer was a young Frenchman with a face like the Liverpool Sack Murderer, Ball – a dangerous man. One of the boys told me he overheard the sailmaker warning him that did he offer to draw a knife on anyone he would kill him. This fellow had treacherously killed his Captain. As there was no witness, the French Consul, to save the expense of deporting him to France, had kept him in nominal confinement until our requirements led to a gaol delivery.

We sustained rigging damage rounding the Cape of Good Hope and had hard and severe work repairing. The men worked fairly well, a few of them worthy of praise, and the ship was got into excellent order. We hove to off St Helena, took on fresh vegetables and sent letters to be posted for home. Communicated with Ascension Island, crossed the Equator, and after a short spell of Doldrum weather got the Northeast Trades.

The Second Mate had dismissed his watch without noting the favourable trend of the wind; orders were given to trim yards, rig out all studding sail booms, and set the sail. The watch was called out again and as I went forward I met the Yankee ex Mate with his pot of coffee. I told him to join his watch in setting the studding sails. He threw his pot of coffee on the deck. I picked up the tin and well tapped his head with it. This fellow was a bad egg: only his cowardice kept him from being actively dangerous.

The sequel to this was the revenge he took in New York, using the Negro and the vile murderer and the shyster lawyers who battened on sailors' woes, imaginary and otherwise. (Though the United States had no jurisdiction over foreign ships, the state laws were often prostituted by venal officials.) The winds were favourable and the weather serene in the month of June. We got a New York Pilot far out and sailed up to Sandy Hook where a tug was engaged.

New York harbour is beautiful. The air was clear and the scenery on both sides temptingly attractive after our long voyage. The ship was docked on the East River and then beset with boarding masters and crimps who took possession of our consignment of bad humanity.

A few days after arrival, I was busy examining the stacks of discharged tea chests piled on the wharf. The previous day we had discovered an ingenious way of robbing the tea. The wharfs were of wood built on trestles. The thieves came under the wharf in a boat where a confederate, pretending to fish underneath from the wharf, marked where the tea was stacked. The thieves climbed up the trestles with an auger, bored a hole through the wharf planking and through the tea chest, and the tea ran into the bags they had brought with them. Fortunately we discovered the device before much was stolen, and I had all the apprentices patrolling the wharf to stop any further proceedings on behalf of the would-be thieves.

Six men came down the wharf and asked if I was the Chief Mate. I replied, 'Yes.' He then enquired for the Second and Third Mates. I pointed them out. He thrust a blue paper in my hand and rushed off to the Second and Third Mates. My paper was a sworn statement of the Negro backed by the ex Mate and the murderer: a warrant for my arrest had been issued by one of the venal judges of New York. I put the paper into my pocket when Mr Hogan, the Master Stevedore, requested me to step on board and view some tea chests stowed near the mainmast which showed signs of damage. I was going towards him when a hand was rudely placed on my shoulder, jerking me back. I naturally struck at the man; he whipped out a revolver and fired at me. Mr Hogan struck up his arm so no harm was done. Several of the other men overpowered and handcuffed me.

Mr Hogan advised me to submit, and he and the Captain of a fine New York ship, the *St John Smith*, talked to and somewhat appeased the marshall, from whose nose ran a large quantity of blood. I am sure my blow was a blessing in disguise to him for he looked apoplectic. I was taken handcuffed and guarded by four policemen through New York streets. The Second and Third Mates were guarded by a man each, but their wrists were not encircled by steel bracelets. They must have thought me a terrible fellow. With the crowd following us there was quite a sensation. I was taken into the Marshall's house; I thought this was like the ancient Fleet Prison practice, as illustrated by Thackeray in *Vanity Fair*, when Colonel Rawston was confined for debt. The Second and Third Mates were put in the House of Detention and I was placed in a parlour. By and by, the door was opened an inch or two and I saw bright eyes looking at me and heard much giggling. One said, 'I am going to speak to him – he doesn't look a tough.' I said, 'Do come in. I'll promise not to bite you.' So three young women came in and chatted away. They all wanted to know why I 'had slatted their

Poppa over the nose.' Then one brought in tea, which I partook with them. Now and again one of the Marshall's assistants looked in, and seemed satisfied I was so well guarded by his chief's daughters.

I asked him why I was kept here: he said Lawyer Smith was in another room waiting for Captain Can, who was waiting at the British Consulate. This lawyer Smith was a notorious rascal whose only practice was aiding seamen to bring manufactured charges against ships' officers. He made an enormous income, for besides squeezing the Masters and Officers he pocketed the seamen's wages. In our case the United States had no jurisdiction. The offence alleged was stated to have taken place on board a British ship on the high seas in the Indian Ocean, two months or more ago. The law of England only had jurisdiction. This was well known to lawyer Smith and the magistrate who signed the warrant.

Smith's method was to get a Precinct Judge, i.e. a New York magistrate, to sign a warrant to arrest the victim, then his black-mailing expertness squeezed the dollars out of the flies, for by using the legal methods of the State the victims could be kept in gaol several months before being brought to trial, if the affair went so far as that. The magistrate, after hearing the case, would say 'in jurisdiction'. Smith would then move to take the case before the Federal Courts, that is, the United States Courts, who only have administration when foreigners are concerned, and then the case would be dismissed with no compensation for the sufferers. The British Consul would do nothing to help their countrymen. It appeared to us that their sole policy was on no account to embarrass the United States. If the case had been brought in England it would have proved that the Negro wantonly attacked the Second Mate, aided and abetted by the rest. I, as the Chief Officer, had gone to the Second Mate's aid. My scarred side would have proved the serious nature of the Negro's attack which I had to repel, and the strong methods I had had to employ to prevent him killing me. The case would have been dismissed, and the Negro and others abetting would have to meet a charge of assault and mutiny. I have been prolix in explaining the situation so you will understand the out-come of the case, and how we were sheared by the Yankee sharps.

After a detention of three hours I heard my Captain making a tremendous row. He was saying that he would never call himself an

Englishman again. The Consul General would give him no help: he had told the Consul that he was afraid of the adjectival Yankees, that he was taking Britain's pay and not doing his duty, and many other home truths! It took all the staff of the Consulate to put him out. I could hear a smooth silky voice making soothing remarks (this was lawyer Smith). Then I heard Captain say, 'I want my Mate. The other two you can keep. The Mate never had a row on his own account. All his trouble was in fighting their battles.' Then I heard him enquire how much bail was wanted to get me out. Smith replied, 'Fifteen hundred dollars, and you'll never see it again. Pay the Negro's and ex Mate's wages to me; the Mate pay the marshall $180 for the damage he did his face and feelings, and $50 more for the expense of arresting him, the Second Mate pay $100 and the Third Mate pay $50.'

I called out, 'Pay nothing for me. I'll go to gaol.' I felt a martyr; the Captain stormed and protested. Smith's silky voice kept on, 'I want him: you want your Mate. I've got an option on him. Yes, I know we've got no jurisdiction when it comes to court, but you cannot force me to go there until I want to. Your Consul won't help you: guess your Government is skeered of us. Better pay up, Captain – if you want your Mate you'll have to pay up. If you don't, we'll give you the bad time of your life by suing you on all sorts of charges. Now Sir, be sensible: I've got you covered.'

After a long wrangle, the Captain paid. It was the only way. His ship and her valuable cargo could not be left without officers. The Negro and the Yankee ex Mate did not get one cent of their wages. All went into lawyer Smith's pockets.

On arrival home, the owners would not pay a farthing though they had saved the wages of the crew from London to Adelaide, thence to Newcastle, and from Yokohama home – many hundreds of pounds. The Captain offered to pay for me. This I refused; so after this long voyage I had to send home for money to pay my fare from London home. Bushby & Edwards were very mean and in after life I noted they did not prosper.

After discharging our tea and silk, the ship was shifted over the river to Brooklyn to load a cargo of oil cakes for London at a high rate of freight. The ship had made much money on the voyage and had been run at small expense. When at Brooklyn, I went to hear the Reverend Henry Ward Beecher, then at the height of his fame, and that reflected from his sister, the creator of *Uncle Tom's Cabin*. I thought he was too theatrical for the pulpit, and for fervour and eloquence was not to be compared to the Vicar or Rector of Gravesend I had heard in Stepney Church before leaving London. The Captain took me to Barnum's Circus, which I much enjoyed; also to the Opera, which I did not care for. Classical music is I think an acquired taste. I also had some glimpses of the underlife of the Bowery in company with Scott, one of the *Brocklebank*'s mates. We ventured into a place we should have kept out of, and got swindled out of ten dollars each. We brought a few of the petty officers of both ships and recovered five dollars each by our sailmaker taking a chair and threatening to smash a large glass case and contents worth thousands of dollars. It is marvellous we didn't get shot. All's well that ends well: the sweet little cherub that sits aloft and looks after sailors, befriended us. The policeman on the beat told us we had been in one of the worst dives in the city. We never repeated our adventure. Curiosity and danger are attractive to youth.

There is only one church in New York of historical interest to Britons and that is Trinity Church on Broadway. It is very like one of our London City churches. Amongst others, there is a monument to Lieutenant General Montgomery, a revolutionary soldier killed in the War of 1812 when leading the Yankees' attack on Canada.

Having completed our loading, we left for London with a crew of West Indians. This gang were a means of gain to me for they taught me patience and tact. We had favourable weather and painted the ship. South of the Banks of Newfoundland in 41° north in misty weather we fell in with two large icebergs apparently aground. The Captain did not like their company in foggy weather and steered south for some hours. The proximity of icebergs gives the same feeling of awe as entering a huge gothic cathedral.

Without further incident we made London. There I bade goodbye to my faithful shipmates. Captain Can was much moved when I bade him *adieu*.

My father had died a few months before, and left his affairs in great confusion. I spent a few sad days at home, and then left for Liverpool and sat for the Master's Certificate, secured it, and was home a week from the day I left. I was twenty-three years of age and quite ready to tackle the Master's job.

CAPTAIN FRASER:
AGE TWENTY-THREE YEARS

My Ninth Voyage
DORIGA
1873–1874

GREENOCK – COQUIMBO – IQUIQUE – LIVERPOOL

Having now all the necessary certificates, it was my intention now to proceed to China and accept the position in the Hong Kong and Canton Service that had been promised to me, when I had a letter from Captain Can to say that he was leaving at once for Manila to take charge of the *Carricks* (stranded on a reef in the Philippine Sea and now lying in Manila Bay; her Captain had been tried by Naval Court and his Certificate cancelled) and had recommended me for the command of the *Corea*. A few days afterwards Mr Bushby wrote asking me if I could explain how the damage was caused to the *Corea*'s bottom: on drydocking extensive damage was found, and Captain Can had not reported anything that could have caused the damage. I wrote referring him to my logbook, where an entry stating that the ship had struck the rocky bottom on leaving Adelaide would be found. Shortly a legal document embodying the entry was sent me for my signature on oath, which I duly signed having been sworn by Harry Fletcher, Magistrate of Workington, who at the time was superintending the building of his new house, 'Stoneleigh'.

In the meantime I had a letter from Captain John Can, brother of my old Captain, to drop Bushbys and apply at once to Johnston Churchill & Co. of Rumford Place, Liverpool for the command of the *Doriga*, an iron vessel they had just bought. I did by wire, was requested to call on them and was appointed by Mr Johnston to the command. When the question of my pay was mentioned, I said, 'Never mind my pay, that will be proved by my work: can I feed the crew as I wish?' Mr Johnston said at once, 'You can', and for the twenty-seven years I was with the firm they gave me all the stores I asked for and my crews were well fed on the best of provisions.

At this time the sensational agitation headed by Samuel Plimsoll, M.P. for Derby, was at its height. His book had had a tremendous circulation and the scenes in Parliament when he made serious charges against the shipowners in general and Sir Edward Bates of Liverpool in particular had attracted world-wide attention, and made magistrates and Consuls very wary in punishing seamen for breaches of agreement. The seamen in their ignorance, and misled by the universal sympathy for the way they were fed and exploited, and the loud cry of 'coffin ships', assured a licence and conduct that was most trying and vexacious to the Masters and officers who had to do with them.

At this time it was a common thing for crews after signing on to refuse to go to sea, and dozens of ships were forced to put back or into the nearest port on some frivolous pretence: they invariably were unpunished.

My first command, the *Doriga*, was an iron barque of 678 tons registered built by Williamson of Harrington for G. H. Fletcher then sold to Spaniards. She was now six years old and had been neglected. She was loading at Greenock for Coquimbo [Chile], and when I tried to engage a crew I found there was a seaman's strike in force at the Clyde ports. I shipped a Chief Mate, Second Mate, carpenter, sailmaker, steward and cook there, and went to Liverpool to get the seamen and signed on a rough scratch crew of all nationalities. These men got a month's advance wages paid on leaving Liverpool and intended to desert at Greenock.

I wired for the ship to be taken to anchorage in Greenock Bay and arranged with a tug to meet S.S. *Bear*, in which we travelled from Liverpool, and transported them to the ship. Next morning we sailed, cast off the tug and dismissed the Pilot off Ailsa Craig, and proceeded with a southeast breeze, taking the North Channel. At 10 p.m. the wind flew to the WSW and I was compelled to run for Lamlash anchorage [Isle of Arran] for shelter.

We anchored about 1 p.m. On going on deck at 8 a.m. I found the head gear adrift and the officers had made no attempt to put things right, though I had told them I would proceed as soon as the wind got a point of northing in it. Got the crew to work. In the afternoon six of them refused work. I got them in the cabin one by one and forced my wretched officers to handcuff them. I primed the rest of the crew with rum, hove up, gave a tug five pounds to hold on until sail was made, and then sail was set and anchors were taken inboard for I was determined I would cast the ship away before I would be forced by the crew to put back, for it would be said I was too young for command. Fortunately the ship had a good donkey engine and the work was rapidly performed, and at 5 p.m. we passed the Mull of Kintyre going twelve knots with a northwest gale.

Next morning at 9 a.m. *Sultan* was astern and the malcontents on promise of good behaviour were released from their bonds. If the Mates had been worth their salt, the lesson given at the outset would have served and the conduct of the crew would have been normal.

I was the youngest of all on board. The Chief Mate, a poor feckless body, had been Master of a brig; the Second Mate, a Nova Scotian who must have stolen some man's certificate, for he made no shape as an officer and I found him many times neglecting his duties. Under these circumstances I seldom slept, night or day, and managed to get the ship into some order. The Spaniards had left her in a disgraceful state. When south of the Equator, the skylight being open I heard the Mate chide a man for disgraceful steering. The man made use of a very dirty expression, such a one that has cost many men their lives. The Mate did not resent it. I rushed on deck and asked the Mate why he allowed a man to speak so to him. Then I tackled the man and gave him a 'harelip'. This fellow stuck to the ship for the voyage and behaved himself... (On arrival home he came down with his father and blackmailed me on account of the harelip I had given him, and as I could not depend on the Mate's evidence I paid two pounds sooner than appear at the Police Court.)

During this passage I had an anxious time. Discipline was kept by constant personal supervision: it was a great strain. It was marvellous how I kept up, though on deck part of every night watch and all day. I had little help from the officers; the Chief Mate was a poor feckless creature with no backbone, afraid of the rowdy black-guards amongst the crew; the Second Mate a cringeing deceitful fellow: both officers despised by the crew. Sailors like to have real men over them. The carpenter was a dissolute Scotsman who had unmanned himself by drink and vice. The only really decent fellow was the steward, who was on his first voyage. He was the son of a Glasgow baker and had come to sea to avoid the disgrace and penalties attached to unlawful paternity.

I worked the crew well and dared them to refuse duty. They thought I wished to entrap them by refusing, and of course never gave me the opportunity of logging them for that offence, which was just what I wanted. Off the Cape, a great hulking Liverpool rigger pretended to fall: he made a great outcry. On examining him I felt what seemed to be a fractured rib. I had him taken into the spare room in the cabin and gave him every care and attention. Three days afterwards four men had taken him to the w.c. and brought him back. He was making great outcries and groanings. Something in his cries did not sound true: I slipped off my boots and stole quietly down the companion and saw the fellow jump like an acrobat out of the top bunk, pick up a piece of tobacco he had dropped, and spring back. I went to him, pulled him out of the bunk and took the bandages off, turned him on deck to work, and told the crew of their malingering shipmate. The fracture I had felt was an ancient one: no doubt the fellow had played the same game before. We were in 60° south; the cold was severe and the work hard and unpleasant. This shirker was a Liverpool Englishman.

The crew ascribed their good food to the Board of Trade and 'Sam Plimsoll'. I commenced my career as Master with good, generous and kind intentions towards the crew, and was soon taught that kindness to them was ascribed to weakness, and tended to licence. For the future, I fed them well, nursed them in sickness, and extracted from them good service to the ship and respectful and decent behaviour.

We arrived at Coquimbo after a good passage of eighty-one days, the best of the year. When I returned on board after transacting the usual business, the crew came aft demanding to see me. The wages were high and their plot was to trump up charges and get the Consul to discharge them. On my asking, 'What do you want?' they replied, 'We want justice. We are afraid to go in the ship. Our lives are in danger by the mad way you carry sail and we demand to see the Consul.' I replied, 'You are a sorry lot of sea lawyers. The Act says that I am bound to let you see the Consul or magistrate *before* the ship *leaves* port, and I will do so after you have worked out the cargo. I quite understand your game, which is to get off working the cargo and to try and get your wages.'

Next morning at 5 a.m. the Mate reported that the crew had all gone ashore. Of course he and the Second Mate knew all about it. The mooring Pilot, an Irishman named Doyle, was also a boarding master for sailors and in the conspiracy, and sent the boat which took them ashore, so with this coalition and Mr Sam Plimsoll's agitation effect on my judges, there looked like looming a pretty struggle.

I called on the Consul, Alexander Golland, afterwards knighted and Consul at Cuba during the war, a poor creature who could never deserve the position and honours given him. I reported that fourteen of my crew had absented themselves without leave and requested his help to get them back to their duties. 'Oh,' he said rudely, 'nothing of the sort. The men have been to see me and make serious charges against you, and I have appointed a Naval Court to be held at 1 p.m. to enquire into all their allegations.' I said, 'Indeed, then, you are the greatest and most powerful man on earth for you can over-ride the Queen and the Lords and Commons of Britain. These men are lawbreakers. They have deserted their ship. Put them on board and then I will listen to you.' He tried to bluster: found that was no use. Then he entreated me to attend the Court and I consented. The Court consisted of the Consul, President, the Commander and First Lieutenant of H.M.S. *Supply*, and the English Doctor.

The men made charges, I cross-examined. They contradicted themselves and each other, and then they charged the Second Mate with being in a conspiracy to murder me and seize the ship and land on the coast of Brazil. They implicated the Chief Mate: he stoutly denied being privy to the conspiracy. Their hearts failed them. The skulking rigger told a piteous tale of his fractured rib. The Doctor said there had been a fracture. I asked him, 'Was the fracture a recent one or was it done many years since?' The Doctor could not say. I then told what I had seen. The hero of the harelip showed his beauty spot. I called on the Mate, who related the course of his getting it, and he was told it served him right. I then narrated the events of the voyage: told of the conduct of the officers, which I charitably ascribed to cowardice; proved by the men present that they had been well fed and well treated when they did their work, and the Doctor who had been on board said that the ship was the cleanest he had visited at Coquimbo. I also mentioned the Consul's ill-advised and high-handed proceedings, which were unlawful as I ought to have been the prosecutor not the defendant.

The naval officers whispered together for a few minutes then the Commander said that they 'could find no fault in my treatment of the crew. The man with the harelip had brought the punishment on himself; the rigger was a malingerer; I was the best and only judge as to the carrying of the sail; the proof of my abilities as a navigator was that I had made the quickest passage of the year, without loss of spar or sail. The men must return to their duties at once. They would each be fined the statutory amount for absence without leave.'

The officers came and shook hands with me; the Commander said I was a young hero and advised me to get quit of the blackguards, and as I accompanied them to the door invited me cordially to visit their ship.

On returning to the Consul's room for my hat, the crew were attacking the Consul. He called on me for help. I refused, and told him to put them on board and I would manage them. I left, called at the agent's office with the Mate, and when returning opposite the Consul's office was attacked by several of the crew. A Spaniard struck me with a weapon. The Consul locked his door and told me I must call on the Chilean authorities for help. The Mate ran away, and then I was left to fight with the crowd. I told the Consul what I thought of him: no man could have seen one man set on by a dozen without giving help. I held onto the Spaniard and when the vigilantes came on the scene handed him to them and caught another one. These two were the only ones who really struck me. I saw them into the gaol and then went to search for the others. Six of them had gone aboard. I went on board and the Second Mate had the effrontery to come to the tea table, after the charges the men made against him. I threw a cup at him and have not seen him since.

After tea I was walking the poop with a Welsh skipper who wanted to sell slops to the crew, when two of the men came and hailed the ship from the wharf to send a boat. I told them to swim off: no boat would be sent. By and by they succeeded in getting on board and came aft threatening what they would do to me. One a black Irishman, the other a wastrel who had been kicked out of the British Navy. They attempted to mount the poop when I struck one in the eye and kicked the other in the face. Then I whipped out my revolver and chased them along the decks and into the forecastle. They took the ladder away so that I could not get down. I fired a few shots down and watched for an hour or so; then I was persuaded to go aft. Next morning those two and the rigger had cleared off. The remainder had to discharge the cargo.

I went to Valparaiso to charter the ship. On my return I noticed that the Mate, the carpenter and a few others were the worse for drink. I allowed three glasses each per day when discharging cargo. I did not expect the Mate would take it. At once the rum cask was brought on deck: I took a hammer and knocked in the head and let the stuff run overboard. I never took rum in any of my ships after this. I gave them cocoa, coffee and tea, which was better for them.

The Mate was very little use. He was usually ashore taking the weights of the cargo discharged. One evening I was ill and sent him ashore to order the ballast and requested him not to keep the boat waiting, to come right back. Instead of doing so, it was 2 a.m. when he returned, slightly intoxicated. I tried to keep calm, but when he got cheeky gave him the thrashing of his life. Next morning I gave him money so that he could make a complaint to the Consul. He knew better than to go and told people his bruised face was the result of falling against the ladder when coming on board. (On arrival home I found that he had never posted several letters to the Owners I had entrusted him with.) The wretched coward had found out that if he had done his duty and upheld his position he would have been happy and respected.

All these worries caused me to be troubled with insomnia. There was no one I could talk to. The Welsh skippers who traded to the port on the Swansea copper ore run were a dissipated lot who spent their time in low pursuits. I got very depressed, and even contemplated suicide. I would draw fifty or a hundred dollars in silver and pretend to stumble on stepping from the boat to the ship's ladder: the weight of the silver would keep me down, and the affair would be put down to pure accident. I shudder now when I think of my feelings at that time. I had only my loyalty to my trust and my duty to God to help me. I have had many trials and disappointments in life, but none when I suffered so much mental agony and was so much alone. I was very young and proud, and the things I had to face and fight loomed large and out of proportion.

After this time of mental darkness came the dawn. An old school fellow was Chief Mate of the S.S. *Quayarian*, a Chilean steamer trading on the coast. He looked me up and his companionship drove away the black dog of depression, and he gave me two fine fellows to act as Second Mate and boatswain. The Second Mate had no certificates. He was a handsome Scotsman of twenty-eight years named Campbell, very well educated, and had served in Yankee ships in that capacity. He proved a tower of strength and from his advent we had discipline and good work. For the first time I now felt that I was a Captain and not a boatswain, and never again was I possessed by the devil of depression.

Having now leisure to look about, I visited Guyacan and La Serena. The former is peopled by a colony of Welsh copper smelters. The change of country has not improved them; they have adopted the manners and way of living of the lawless natives and lead a swinish life. La Serena, so called from its serene and equable climate (I think it is the most favoured spot on earth), is a city of rest. Down the principal street, which is very broad, run two streams with rows of beautiful trees bordering them. The town is a very ancient one and as yet many inhabitants of pure Castilian blood live there. To the north of Coquimbo stretches the desert of Atacama as far as Arica.

Having finished discharging, we took in ballast and a quantity of hay and grain for Iquiqui. The first day we attempted to get out, the wind failed and we came to anchor on the Serena beach. With the land breeze we got under way in the evening and had a narrow escape of shipwreck as a strong current carried the ship alongside a large rock. We got out boats and with the help of two fishing boats got back to our first anchorage. The ships in the harbour gave no help – though they were all ready for a salvage job should I have requested help. The next day we got away. When well outside, the two men who were taken out of gaol were released from confinement and Mr Campbell found means of making them work. It was summer sailing along the coasts of Chile and Peru. At dawn one morning we had a magnificient view of the Andes, snow-capped above the clouds. We arrived at Iquiqui and the two prison birds attempted to desert by floating ashore on a hatch. The surf is deceptive: one was drowned, the other one got off. I did not trouble to get him captured.

Iquiqui was then a stinking town of wood houses and godowns. Nothing to see but sand; no amusements, plenty of vice and gambling. I went ashore only on business and got plenty of amusement fishing and trying to get the ship in order. Having taken all the nitrate of soda the merchant had for us here, he ordered us to Caleta to finish. This place was twenty miles to the northward, so we had little trouble in getting there.

The port was a small bay behind rocks, where the nitrate was brought from the mines on muleback for shipment. There was only a few wood shanties for the use of the Captain of the Port and clerks overseeing the shipments. Three barques were lying there: the *Black Watch*, to whose Captain I owe a debt of gratitude, the *Rose of Devon*, whose Captain was a poltroon; the other ship I forget the name of. My carpenter had become insane and I had him sent to the asylum at Iquiqui. I arranged with two Austrians who were working ashore to take the run home; the Captain of the Port witnessed the agreement. As the *Rose of Devon* and my ship would finish loading ten or twelve days before the steamer called on her passage to Iquiqui, and as we had to get to Iquiqui to finish ship's business and clear out, the Captain of the *Rose of Devon* agreed to join me in hiring four Greeks to row us the twenty miles to Iquiqui and back. When the time came he refused to go, saying he was not going to be murdered by Greeks, and no persuasion could get him to change though his ship would lay idle for twelve days. He was a drunken man, so I suppose he would spend the time as he liked best.

I went, the Captain of the *Black Watch* lending me his fine rowing gig. I knew that I was perfectly safe on the passage down for then I had no money with me. Coming back, I would have several hundred dollars to pay my disbursements. The Greeks knew this. We pulled down one night arriving about 6 a.m. I pulled alongside a ship and waited until 8 a.m. when I went ashore and found that my agent, who was also the British Vice Consul, was in bed sick and that several vessels loaded had waited for him to get up and clear them out. I found myself in his bedroom and told him that if I was not cleared out by 4 p.m. I would sail without papers and he could explain to the merchants and authorities as he well could.

He got up, cleared the ship and transacted all other business. At 4 p.m. I was ready to return to my ship. I was taking ten sacks of potatoes in the boat, that I had arranged to form a barricade between the rowers and myself. They could only attack me singly, and I was prepared for eventualities. The Consul and others had warned me that a Captain had been murdered under similar circumstances and the murderers had got away. We started at 6 p.m. I was detained by having to get two doctors' certificates certifying that the carpenter was insane owing to his own acts. At 10 p.m. we were more than half way; our slow progress was owing to an adverse current. The bow oarsman stopped rowing and spoke in his own language to his fellows: I immediately whipped out my revolver and covered the stroke oarsman. The fellow in the bow demanded my bag of dollars, the second and third seconded him. The stroke was covered and told that the slightest threatening movement on his part would mean a bullet in his body.

For a time it was stalemate. Then I showed them that I had two revolvers and that they were powerless to attack me with any chance of success. They sullenly gave way, and it was after 1 a.m. when we got alongside the *Black Watch*. The good Captain was overjoyed to see me, and said that he and the Port Captain had reproached themselves for allowing me to go. I told him my tale, and the Captain of the Port was sent for, heard the story and took the four to the calaboose. I paid him the money I had agreed to pay the Greeks: he would keep the money and the would-be villains would be punished that way.

At this time every ship had much trouble with the crew. Plimsoll's agitation had caused much unrest and given rise to absurd expectations. The Board Schools would educate the coming generation so that future reformers would not cause men through ignorance to act in ways that gave infinite worry to shipmasters and ended disastrously for themselves.

The Captain of the Port placed on board the two Austrians I had engaged before I went to Iquiqui to clear out, etc. They had each been living with a Peruvian woman and refused to keep their agreement; also, two refractory men who had been kept in the calaboose during our stay in this port: as the four refused to work they were placed in confinement. The three vessels in port sent a boat's crew to assist in getting the anchor and setting sail, for our vessel was shorthanded. Having cleared the port, the ship was hove to, anchors taken on board and lashed, and all sails set; then the assisting boats' crews and Captains left, the foreyards were filled, and we started on our homeward passage with a crew, including the four in confinement, eight short of the outward complement. Next morning the four men returned to their duties and I had no more bother with the crew, who had plenty of work and a sufficiency of good food.

In latitude 40° south the foretopgallant was lost in an exceptionally severe white squall. We had no carpenter and few tools, yet with constant work in three days a spare spar was converted into a new mast and all was again '*a tout*'.

Rounding Cape Horn we had a succession of heavy gales with snow and frost. We passed a dangerous iceberg south of the Diego Ramirez Islands, and in hauling up suddenly to clear it heavy seas swept on board, doing damage and washing the watch from the braces. One of them sustained a fracture of the thigh. When the ship had cleared the iceberg and was on her course once again, I attended to the injured man. The fracture was a clean one; I placed small splinters from the medicine chest over the break and then had two splints made, one from above the thigh to the ankle and the other from the groin to the ankle. Both were well padded. Then I had a bed cut and lined with leather, with a wide rubber tube, and cut the bunk boards to take the tube into a large tub fitted underneath, and had his body washed and clean clothes put on him, for we would have tempestuous weather for a month and during that time with our small crew, no one could be spared to attend him. The man was made as comfortable as possible. A month afterwards he could get around on crutches and was soon able to walk. On arrival home he had a very slight limp which would pass away. He was one of our bad men; on account of his misfortune I did not prosecute him, and paid him his full wages. We made a fair passage to Liverpool and went in the Stanley Dock. The Mate was discharged without a recommendation. Mr Campbell I wished to retain, and paid the fees for his tuition as Second Mate at [the Nautical] Academy. Within a week the poor fellow came to me saying the vagabond wanderlust was too strong in him, that he could not steady himself to study and regretted leaving and disappointing me. He was going off to America to join a whaler and offered to repay me;

this, of course, I refused, and bade goodbye to one of the most interesting and mysterious characters I have met.

Messrs Duncan Fox & Co. of Valparaiso, who chartered the ship from the West Coast house, gave me a letter of gratuity. This sum had to be paid by their head house in Liverpool when the cargo was delivered. I thought so little of it that I had forgotten its existence. I had placed it in the ship's Register box. Mr Johnston had found it there and told his clerk to take me round to Duncan Fox & Co.'s office and collect it. We went round and were kept waiting for some time in a large outer office tenanted by a number of clerks, when a very red-faced man who I found out was Mr Duncan, the senior of the firm, came to me and in the rudest and most insolent manner said, as he threw down the gratuity letter, 'What do you mean by blackmailing me in this manner? Does your owner not pay you sufficiently that you come to me?' He poured out such a string of invective and insult that my breath was taken away. His clerks were grinning and much amused at my discomfiture.

'That letter was sent to me by your Valparaiso house without any solicitation on my part. It is you who are all the things you accuse me of being, for you are not only false but dishonest in repudiating the act of your Valparaiso house.' Then I let myself go. I gave him the tonguelashing I would give a bad sailor, until he slunk away like a whipped cur and made a sorry exhibition of himself for his clerks to laugh at.

When Mr Johnston was told of Mr Duncan's conduct, he said, 'You have as much right to the gratuity as I have for the freight.' He wrote a cheque out for the amount and gave it to me and then went off to interview Mr Duncan. When he returned he was all smiles; he had got the money, and said, 'Duncan has told me all you said to him. I hope that I will never annoy you and cause you to speak so to me.' I said that Mr Duncan deserved all that I said to him. Mr Johnston smiled. At that time the most snobbish and arrogant men were to be found amongst the brokers and merchants of Liverpool.

In settling up for the voyage, I asked Mr Johnston, 'Have I given you every satisfaction?' He replied, 'You have.' 'Have I sailed the ship as well and as economically as your experienced masters?' to which he also replied that I had.

I thanked him, and said should I not do so to tell me, for I would not sail anyone's ship on sufferance. Mr Johnston said, 'We have given you your first command. We will pay you well, and hope you will never leave us.' I said I never would as long as I gave satisfaction. This was very pleasing to me, and though I had undergone bitter sorrow on this my first voyage as Captain, yet I now felt Mr Johnston's kind words had repaid.

A SHETLAND CREW
My Tenth Voyage
DORIGA
1875–1876

LIVERPOOL – VALPARAISO – SAN ANTONIO – LIVERPOOL

The Owners purchased a cargo of coals on ship's account which was loaded in the Bromley Moor Dock and we soon left port, cast off the tug after passing the bar and with a southerly gale reached over to the coast of Ireland, where we dodged about until the wind westered, when we cleared the Channel and fought our way to the pleasant latitudes of the Trade Winds. I had a decent crew. The First Mate was a Shetland man twenty-nine years of age. The Second Mate, named Dixon, was a native of Carlisle, a member of the spinning family who had large works there, afterward insolvent. The crew were Shetlanders, I think all relatives of the Mate, and several apprentices.

We had a pleasant passage to the Horn where we met with some stormy weather. I expected from the Shetlanders much more endurance of cold and hard weather than from men born in warmer climates, but was disappointed, for they swathed themselves in clothes and moved like snails. After a hard battle we won round and arrived at Valparaiso eighty-four days from Liverpool. The cargo was sold through agents to the Chilean Government for the Navy.

The head of the firm of agents and merchants by whom the cargo was sold told me the ship would get paid on the quantity per bill of lading. The broker of the Chilean Government required the weights of coal put forward by him as having been delivered to be vouched for. Of course he said a firm like theirs could not do such a thing and intimated that I could do so. I said at once that my soul and honour was as precious to me as theirs to them: I would not do such a thing. My reply discomfited him; the ship got paid the bill of lading quantity and the Chilean Government paid their broker for more coal than would sink the *Doriga*'s decks under water – who signed the vouchers?

The Chilean naval commanders sent hundreds of men on board to discharge the coals as they were in a hurry for it. This was fortunate for us for we were soon rid of the dirt and confusion. I chartered to load a cargo of wheat at San Antonio, an open anchorage on the coast south of Valparaiso. After ballasting we proceeded, arriving safely. There was no other ship at the anchorage. A fine new vessel loaded with wheat, in trying to get out, had struck the rocks and sunk in deep water a day before our arrival.

We had a very pleasant time loading as fruit, game and food generally was very cheap. I bought plump partridges for ten cents each and live sheep for five shillings. I had several pleasant picnics; the shipper's agent was a Scotsman married to a Chilean lady and they had several daughters. These with several farmers and their families formed a good company. We all went on horseback to the Maipo River where a camp was formed amidst lovely surroundings. Live sheep and every sort of provender had been brought, and the cooking was excellent. The principal dish was most appetising: in a large iron circular pot were put mutton, partridges, rabbits, pigeons, sweet potatoes, capsicums, chillies, salt, maize flour and country wine. The result after many hours of cooking would make a London Alderman think the City feasts were not the last words in gastronomy.

We sailed, congratulating ourselves that instead of the stinking desolation of the nitrate ports, our experience had been so delightful. We had a favourable passage round Cape Horn and all went well with us until we were involved with a hurricane or *pampero*, south of the Rio de la Plata. The storm was very violent, and although reduced to a mizzen staysail and two lower topsails the ship was thrown on her beam ends, shifting the cargo. She lay with the lee yardarms in the water. I directed the Mate to take hands and cut away the main topsail; the mizzen staysail halyards were fortunately on the weather side and were let go. The sail blew away. It looked so bad and death seemed so imminent that I made myself fast to the weather rigging so that when the ship went completely over I should not struggle. When the main topsail was cut away the ship paid off before the wind, and by carefully bringing the immersed side to the wind the cargo was brought back and the ship uprighted. After securing the cargo as well as we could, the main pumps were found to be broken. The ship was as tight as a bottle or that would have proved disastrous. Several days afterwards complaints were made about the drinking water having an unpleasant taste and smell, and on examination it was found that when the ship had been thrown on her beam ends the wheat cargo had broken the casing and ran into the fresh water tanks through the sounding pipes. This was indeed a grievous disaster. In a few days the water stank like a sewer and our stomachs revolted. By making strong coffee we could manage to swallow sufficient to starve off distressful thirst.

I wanted to avoid putting into the Brazil ports for it was the yellow fever season, and decided to steer into the rainy zones near the Equator. I had, as I thought, a reserve of pure fresh water in a tank used for supplying the donkey engine. This tank was in the 'tween decks and had several inches of water in it, the pump pipe being that distance from the bottom. Several of us began to suffer from sickness and colic and I directed the Second Mate to get a few bottles filled from this tank. He returned and told me that there was no water in this tank – it was swabbed out dry. I was much perturbed and could not imagine how the water had disappeared; I could not think that it would have evaporated. Then I learned through the cook that the First Mate and his watch, all Shetland relatives, had used this water whilst the rest of us had struggled along with the loathsome stinking water. It was mean of Mr Sharp: I expected him to have had a higher conception of his duty, for I told him of my fears that the water might prove poisonous and my intentions. It came to my mind then what an old shipmaster said to me in Liverpool, when I told him I was taking a Mate and all his relatives as a crew. He said, 'Look out or they will take the ship from you.'

I spoke to the Mate when he was surrounded by his watch, asking him who gave him authority to use that water, and why he had done so, when he knew I was reserving it for sickness. He did not reply respectfully: I saw he was going to be insolent and I repressed myself, as it did not suit my dignity to squabble with the Mate before the crew. That afternoon, when he was resting in his bunk, I took one of the long cavalry swords from the armoury in my room, and went into his room and closed the door. 'Now,' I said, 'you dared to speak disrespectfully to me when surrounded by your relatives, and would have been insolent had I not had the tact to stop you; now you must ask my pardon for your conduct. You should be an example of obedience.' I flourished the sword, feinting to prick him and making a savage face. The fear and horror in his face was stimulating, for I was not really angry but only wanted to impress on him that I could not be 'bearded with impunity'. He abjectly made a sufficient apology, and said the water at first had been taken without his sanction. So I logged his relatives and fined them three days' pay each. Mr Sharp never again gave me cause for complaint, though he always locked his room door after my visit with the sword. We found the rain region, pumped out the stinking water and refilled. The first shower was nectar.

We duly arrived in Liverpool having been 103 days on the passage. On the whole Mr Sharp had been a good officer, and I got him a berth with a fellow townsman who would not take his relatives. Mr Dixon, the Second, would be the next Chief Mate.

SOUTH AMERICAN VOYAGE

My Eleventh Voyage
DORIGA
1877

LIVERPOOL – MONTEVIDEO – BUENOS AIRES –
ENSENADA – VALPARAISO – CONCEPTION BAY –
TOMÉ – PENCO – TALCAHUANO – DUBLIN – LIVERPOOL

On this voyage the ship was chartered to load a general cargo for the River Plate ports, which was a pleasant change. We left dock on a Saturday morning and anchored in the river for a few hours to take on board gunpowder and other explosives, and sailed on the evening tide. The weather was bad, a southwest gale brewing. I dismissed the tug at the Northwest Lightship and retained the Pilot, thinking to land him at Point Lynas. The stores, to save a day's interest on their cost, had been dumped on board the day we left dock and been put into the saloon, and the bread, sugar and other heavy packages were piled under the after hatch. We were off Point Lynas before all was secured, and the wind had backed to the southeast, blowing hard. The Pilot boats had run for shelter and the Pilot could not be got rid of. Under lowered topsails and staysails we rapidly cleared St George's Channel, and were fortunate in getting a Waterford [Ireland] fishing boat to land the Pilot. He was disappointed, for he had hoped to have a trip to Madeira and escape part of the winter.

With fresh easterly winds, the cold and discomfort of an English winter were left behind and we had warm and pleasant weather until we got to the mouth of the Plate, when we experienced a heavy local storm which blew two lower topsails away and laid the lee rails under water for some hours. After sunset the weather cleared up. We bent fresh topsails and arrived at Montevideo next day and learned that the 'pamperos' had done extensive damage, and numbers of cargo barges been sunk making a scarcity which delayed discharging of the ships.

At this port the crimps were diligently plying their vocation and enticing seamen to desert. It came to my knowledge that they were to bring a boat under the bows to get some of our men. We kept a strictly secret watch, and one night detected a boat approaching with muffled oars. We crept forward and got on the forecastle head, but not in time to prevent a man dropping into the boat. I hailed the boat, and threatened to fire if they did not come alongside: they rowed away. I fired several shots and thought they had got away. An hour afterwards the boatswain of H.M.S. *Scout* brought our man aboard. He had been thrown by the crimps into the corvette's boat hanging astern. The crimps were deadly scared; one of my shots had slightly wounded one of them. Next day I called and thanked the Commander of the *Scout* and took my man to the British Consul. The Consul commended my action in shooting and said he would back me up if I had killed one of the pests. He advised me not to stay ashore in the evenings as the fraternity were lawless, desperate men who thought nothing of killing. As for the man, he wanted to put him in gaol. I would not consent, for it would cost the ship two dollars a day and the punishment was nil. So I took him back. No one else tried to desert.

After discharging the Montevideo portion of the cargo, we sailed for Buenos Aires to enter at the Argentine Customs. Montevideo then was a typical Spanish American town with a large cathedral containing many chapels with tawdry decorations and paintings. One was dedicated to a Negro saint. The music and singing was bad. The congregation was composed principally of people of mixed blood, from butter colour through all the shades of black. The surrounding country had nothing attractive about it.

We anchored several miles from Buenos Aires and I was taken ashore in a large sailing boat that plied for hire. One of the occupants was the Captain of a German steamer, who came well provisioned with a basket of German beer which he kept drinking all the way. The boat anchored fifty yards from the shore and a horse and cart came alongside in which the journey was completed. After entering the ship and depositing the articles with the British Consul, I interviewed several Pilots regarding piloting to Ensenda. Their demands were so exorbitant, and as the pilotage was not then compulsory, I determined to find my way there without their expensive help. So when we started I arranged a simple code of signals with the Second Mate. He with four rowers took the gig and went ahead two or three hundred yards, sounding; when he got less than six fathoms the oars were elevated. The ship was manoeuvred uneventfully and brought safely to Ensenada pier, much to the chagrin of the pilotage fraternity.

We completed discharging and loaded a quantity of tallow, jerked beef and *maté* for Valparaiso. While here a Nova Scotian brigantine came to the wharf; one of the crew died of yellow fever. If this had been known to the authorities both ships would have had to spend a long time in quarantine. With bribery and corruption we got the man buried. I really think the priests were more rapacious than the Custom House officers.

The land about Ensenada was a level plain much more monotonous than the sea. Our passage to Valparaiso was a quick one, twenty-five days, and we quickly discharged the cargo and chartered to load at Conception Bay ports for ship's account for orders. On settling up, I found that my agents, W.B. & Co., had accepted from the consignees of the tallow cargo from Buenos Aires freight at so much per cwt, when my agreement was so much per packet, making a loss to the ship. I refused to accept, and kept the ship waiting several days until the correct freight was paid. The manager of W.B. & Co. was quite huffy about it, which was very foolish of him.

We had a short passage to Conception Bay, a lovely sheet of water. We took cargo at Tomé and Penco and completed at Talcahuano. This last place was a refreshment and meeting place for American South Sea whalers, which was not a good thing for the morals and chastity of the surrounding country.

We had a pleasant passage to Queenstown [Cobh]. After a stay of several days I got orders to proceed to Dublin to discharge. A dispute arose between the shippers W.B. & Co. and the buyers, R.S. & Co. There was arbitration, and for several days I was in attendance with the late Sir Stephen Williamson, and much enjoyed the debates of cultured business men. W.B. & Co. won. The members of this firm abroad were always very kind to me.

Dublin I found a dirty place overrun with vermin. We towed to Liverpool, completing the eleventh voyage.

WINTER SEAS

My Twelfth Voyage
DORIGA
1877

LIVERPOOL – BUENOS AIRES – TOMÉ –
MEJILLONES BAY – HAMBURG – NORTH SHIELDS

This voyage, we had loaded a general cargo for Buenos Aires direct, and had an uneventful passage out of fifty-four days, two days quicker than last voyage. I stayed at an hotel patronized by Yankee skippers in the regular trade. I found them very nice men and enthusiastic patriots. Our stay was during the summer season and I much enjoyed the afternoon visits to the gardens situated on the bank of the river west of the city. I have tasted the best fruits of all countries, but none excelled the peaches of Argentine in flavour; the grapes were also very fine. At this time the city had no striking features and very few buildings of note. The cathedral was only remarkable for the fact that the flags of several British regiments were there, captured when 'Whitlock' capitulated in the plaza owing to bad generalship.

After discharging, we left for Conception Bay. I had to anchor at Indis Point to pick up one of the apprentices, whom I had allowed to visit friends in Montevideo. Smallpox and yellow fever having broken out there, quarantine regulations forbade him to come to Buenos Aires. After picking him up we made an extraordinarily good passage of eighteen days. The Chief Mate was the most timid man I have met at sea as regards carrying sail. It was long before I found out that when I left the deck at night, he would take in the flying jib and fore royal, keeping everything on aft in case I should come on deck. This put the ship out of balance and made the steering harder. The men named him 'Old Stormy'. On this passage the ship was hard pressed and the Mate was often afraid to leave the deck. The *Campana*, a new iron vessel, was sixty-six days on this passage and the Captain of the Pacific Steam Navigation mail steamer came on board to assure himself that the *Doriga* was the same vessel he had passed anchored at Point Indis.

Whilst lying off Tomé, we caught such an abundance of fish that we salted several large casks. They were mostly fine fish. I also purchased from the whalers eighty sea otter skins, for which I paid two shillings each. Such skins are now worth £100 each. I had two beautiful coats for my sisters made out of them at Hamburg, and presented enough skins to the wives of an American and an English Captain to make them coats and caps. I was amused with the way a German ship chandler, in conjunction with the Captain of the Port, tried to squeeze forty dollars out of the ship.

Tomé is an open roadstead. I anchored without the aid of a Pilot in a position suitable for communication with the shore, for I was only here to charter the ship. The ship chandler's father had been appointed Pilot by the Captain of the Port, so I was approached to give him a job to shift my ship. I said 'I am perfectly satisfied with my ship's position; she is out of all traffic and in a safe position.' Then I was offered a bribe. Then I was threatened with the Captain of the Port (who took half the pilotage money); he came to me hectoring and important. I told him I would not allow my ship to be moved. He threatened: I replied by wiring to the Consul General and was let alone. The Germans are enterprising and never miss an opportunity of making dollars.

I had to go to Valparaiso to charter the ship and took passage in the S.S. *Ayacouchas*. We had thick fog all the way up and were detained twelve hours off the port. In conversation, I told the Captain I thought he was unduly timid; having a steamer he could stand in, certain if he got into danger he had the power to stand out. He said, 'Come on the bridge and test your opinion.' He steamed slowly in for fourteen minutes, then stopped and sounded his siren. The sound was echoed, and close on board were the cliffs of Curamilla. I apologised, and thanked the Captain for the lesson which I took to heart and profited by. Soon after two steam launches found us, and with their aid and great care the steamer reached her buoy. The fog was a dense one and very damp.

I chartered to load an odourless guano at Mejillones Bay, Bolivia, at fifty-five shillings per ton, for Hamburg. Waiting for the steamer, I had a good look round Valparaiso and the country. Sansmento[1] is finely situated and enjoys a good climate. There are some fine buildings and plazas and the higher classes are very proud of their pure Castilian blood. The lower classes are not nice; savage little demons with more of the Indian in them than the Spaniard.

The weather was clear on my return passage, and as the steamer made the passage close inshore, the scenery was enjoyed. On arrival I closed my business and left that night, and in five days arrived at Mejillones Bay where I found several ships at anchor. Several of the Masters had their wives and families with them and our spare time was spent pleasantly picnicking and fishing. We supplied the ships with an abundancy of fish, which was a change from the tough beef, our only meat supply. Mejillones Bay is one of the snuggest harbours on the coast. The town a collection of shanty wood erections. The principal, if not the only article of export, was the so-called guano the ships were here to load. The mine was the top of a mountain nearly two thousand feet in height. The guano was run down wood chutes to the lighters. There must have been a tremendous upheaval at some time, for petrified fish and other sea dwellers and innumerable seashells are common at the mine. I was told this guano was not used for manure but that the clever German chemists got many valuable products from it. The Peruvian guano was a bad-smelling cargo: this was without smell, a dull red, earthy substance. All ships had long loading days; we had ninety. If a ship was loaded under that time she had to pay for each day saved an amount stated in the charter party. As this sum only amounted to less than one half of our daily expenses, I did all in my power to save time. This I effected by getting to the loading place at 5 a.m. and getting all the lighters I could seize loaded by the ship's crew. Sometimes by 8 a.m. we would have four or five lighters alongside ready to take in. A whitewashed Yankee ship, i.e. one the *Alabama*[2] had scared into a change of flag, captained by a German who did not want to buy time and whose bucko Mate wanted to be smart,

---

[1] Possibly Santiago, about seventy miles from the coast.

[2] A warship which in 1862 escaped from Liverpool, with a mainly British crew, and attacked Northern ships during the American Civil War for two years. Britain eventually paid damages to the U.S. Government.

came with a boat's crew to take one of our loaded lighters from alongside. I had heard that the Captain had boasted what his Mate was going to do, so took the precaution of running a length of chain through each lighter's ringbolt and padlocking it. The bold Mate came with many of the latest American oaths. I let him get alongside the lighter, then demanded his business. He answered insolently that we had monopolized too many lighters. I pointed out that the way was open to him if he got up at 5 a.m.; then he went too far, and I gave the order and all my crew attacked them with clods of guano and I presented a revolver. They were glad to get away and bothered us no more.

There was much disease and many bad characters in the small town at the head of the bay, so that the Masters of the ships did not permit the crews to go there. One Sunday my men got permission to go fishing: they promised not to go near the town. At sundown they were not in sight so I had the gig manned and went to the town, got the Captain of the Port, and searched the vilest and dirtiest quarters I have seen and picked them all up and drove them to the boats and on board. Some of them were mad with the vile stuff they had drunk and I had quite a job with them. Next morning I fined them three days' pay each and they got no more fishing.

Twenty-eight days from when we arrived we set sail. I was pleased with the work done and gave the crew a gratuity of one pound each on arrival home.

We had good winds and weather until passing the Azores, when the wind and sea increased to a dangerous extent. We ran under lower topsails before one of the highest seas in my experience, the rails level with water all the time. The height of the seas was appalling and there was imminent danger of bursting the hatches, so I determined to heave to. After handing the fore lower topsail and hauling down the fore lower staysail, the fore yards had to be left square as it was impossible to get to the braces, the decks being full level with the rail. The ship staggered along under the weight of water, never freeing herself; some of the men managed to get to the poop, the rest mounted the fore-rigging. The cook, a great strong Belfast man, was demented with fear; he screamed like a hysterical girl and had to be secured to prevent him injuring someone. In bad weather the main braces were worked from the poop. Taking a chance lull, the helm was put down, the main yards braced forward and the ship came to the wind without damage. For twelve hours she lay with her lee sail under water, when the wind took off and the ship was kept on her course. We passed a partly dismantled brig next day with bulwarks gone and decks swept. She was making for Falmouth and did not require assistance.

In the English Channel we met with adverse winds which necessitated much hard work and loss of sleep. We worked up to the South Sound Lightship (off the Goodwin Sands) when the wind fell and the ship drifted back south of Devon. With the change of tide the wind came from the eastward and after making a few tacks I found that the crew were worn out and that my eyes were so affected that I was 'seeing lights', so that I brought up inside the South Foreland, set anchor watch and had a sleep. Next morning at tide time, hove up: the ship cast the wrong way, the anchor jammed, the second anchor fouled the cable, and by the time it was cleared and dropped the ship had drifted close to the rocks on a falling tide. The ship's stern was not ten feet from the shore and the tide falling. Tugs came fussing up and boats from Deal. The ship's position was about one mile south of Deal and many spectators from there were on the beach. The tugs wanted £500 for their assistance. The Deal boatmen would not or could not give me any information as to the rise and fall of the tides at this spot (Kingsdown). A representative of a Deal firm of ships' agents counselled me to slip the cable and anchor and they would provide new ones. I put him over the side. They are as crafty and sharklike between the Forelands as anywhere in the world. My anxiety was allayed by a note in the *Channel Pilot* stating that there was little rise and fall of tide at Kingsdown, and we had six feet of water under us. I offered the tugboat £10 to hold on whilst we got the anchor: he scornfully refused with language a London cabby could not beat, so I made preparations by running a six-inch hawser from the lee quarter to the anchor cable forward and knocked out a shackle pin in the cable abaft the windlass, hove the hawser tight, and when the tide turned set sail. The tug master had been watching our preparations and now offered to take the £10. I offered him £5: this he thought better than nothing and accepted, and I saved the anchor, cable and hawser. Of course my preparations were bluffing ones, for I would have paid £50 sooner than sacrifice the anchor, etc. Three days afterwards we arrived at Hamburg and the receivers of the cargo gave me £20 for their share of G/A, a good business for the Owners. I found no less than three vessels here that had been with us at Mejillones Bay and we all lodged at the same house in Altona. One of the Captains was dubious of the Owners' solvency and drew and kept the freight until he was satisfied. The duel between him and the Owners' representative was amusing to onlookers.

We left Hamburg the 2nd December for the River Tyne. We had much difficulty in clearing the river owing to ice, and we had a hard time in the North Sea. On Christmas Eve we were off the mouth of the Tyne with half a gale from the southeast and snowing. There was neither Pilot or tug to be had and the river must be taken. We ran in under topsails and foresails, crossing the bar; when abreast of the Middens we were close to a brig who was also bound in, and to save running into her our ship was put aground outside North Shields Pier. As the tide was rising I got a tug to pull her off and take us to the tiers. Unfortunately, the ship's bottom had rested on something that had injured a plate and she had to be drydocked again.

I learned with regret of the death of Mr Johnston, the senior partner of the firm. He was a good man, one of the few I have been privileged to meet.

SHIPWRECKED

My Thirteenth Voyage
DORIGA
1878–1879
'AFTER VOYAGE PERILOUS PORT IS PLEASANT'

The superstitious belief that thirteen is an unlucky number was exhibited on this voyage, for the *Doriga* found a resting place on the floor of the Bay of Biscay.

The winter of 1878–9 was remarkable in the North of England for a very heavy fall of snow. For some time the streets in Shields and Newcastle were impassable and it was difficult to get to and from the ship as she lay in Northumberland Dock. Through a Captain Rich of Maryport I engaged Mr T. C. Fearon of Cockermouth as Chief Mate. He was then a refreshingly modest young man of twenty-three years who wanted to go as Second Mate and I had some difficulty in getting him to take the senior position. The Second Mate was also a Cumberland man from Brampton, twenty-six years of age and six feet tall – a contrast to Fearon who did not much exceed five feet, and illustrated Pope's lines 'the mind's the standard of the man'. I soon saw that Fearon was a born sailor who knew his duties and was as active as a cat. The Second Mate was sluggish and snail-like, one whose slow walk said 'Here's my head – the rest of me's coming.'

The day I engaged the crew I was taken ill. The Owners kept the ship with the crew on board at the tiers for several days until I was able to go on board and to sea.

We left the Tyne on the 17th January 1879 with a strong north-east wind and had a rapid run down the North Sea and out of the English Channel. I only left the deck for a few hours whilst the

117

First Mate was on watch from the time we left Shields. On the night of the fourth day I computed we were well past Ushant. We had sighted nothing from the time we passed Beachy Head and neither sun nor stars had been visible. At midnight Mr Fearon took charge; I told him the estimated position and that we were clear of the land, and that I did not want more sail to be made until daylight. The ship was then travelling from eleven to twelve knots under two lower topsails and reefed foresail, the wind ESE with snow squalls and a high heaving sea. I told him that I intended to have a good sleep as we were now in the open sea and clear of all land danger. I left the deck; the steward voluntarily came to pull off my long boots, for I had had them on for four days and my feet had swollen. Whilst he was tugging, the ship gave one heave and went completely over on her broadside. The force was so great that the table, chronometer and stand, and every piece of furniture was sent to leeward together with the steward and I. When I picked myself up the sea was rushing down the companion stairs. I crawled on deck, which was as steep as the side of a house, and with the help of a rope hauled the steward and myself to the rail, where I found the crew. The water was up to the weather side of the main hatch; the sea was finding its way into the hold through the spurling gate pipes, these being under water. Fortunately she lay with her body to the wind and sea: had the deck been exposed to the furious battering of the waves the end of all would have been momentarily impending. Something must be done at once to raise the submerged pipes. There was a eleven inch hawser coiled round the projecting end of the boiler, on top of the engine house: with much labour it was passed along the weather outside and paid over the stern, to pay her off. This had no effect, the rudder was useless, the foresail, topsail and foretopmaststaysail had blown away. Only one thing could be done to raise her more upright and get the chain pipes above the water and that was to cut the masts away. The crew had given themselves up to despair. The big Second Mate was unnerved and unmanned. I even kicked him to get some manhood in him. He lay lashed to the rail crying: nothing could rouse him. Of all the crew, the First Mate and the two apprentices were by far the most courageous. Mr Fearon's conduct was sublime.

In the companion were emergency axes. I secured two and with Fearon's assistance the weather mizzen rigging was cut. We could not get to the lee rigging as it was deeply submerged. The mast, a stout pitch pine spar, would not budge, so in turn we lowered each other and cut away at the mast. We made little impression on it and the precious time was flying with the sea running into the hold. So I decided to cut away the mainmast. With Fearon and the two apprentices this was done, the mainmast in its fall taking the mizzen-mast with it. This raised the immersed deck, freeing the spurling gate pipes and pumps from the sea. Unfortunately the mainmast had broken off under the deck and in falling had ripped the deck; to get the broken place further from the water I cut away the foretop-mast, keeping the lower foremast to run to any port the wind might favour. The lee side of the rigging was so much under water that it was impossible to cut the wreck away from the hull. The most pressing danger was from the broken deck. It was now daylight; the crew for the time had got over their fear, so they worked with a will and got up spare sails which we stuffed into the broken deck, and nailed several parts of sail overall.

When this was done I directed Mr Fearon to take all the crew, with the exception of the carpenter, steward, cook and boys, and start them to trim the coals. There was a way into the hold through the boys' quarters in the monkey poop. They were passed into the hold and given two trimmers' candles each. I directed Fearon, when he got them to work, to slip away, come on deck and lock them in. In the meantime it was discovered that when the large spare spar had broken adrift it had smashed the bollard ventilators, so that water was still running into the hold. The spar before going over-board acted as a battering ram and broke the coamings of the after hatch. With oakum and diving under water, the ventilator leakage was stopped and strong canvas nailed over the broken coamings. When Fearon came up from below he reported that there was a trickling from the broken deck, the broken bollards, and apparently from some broken stanchions so that there was no immediate danger of foundering. So I had hopes of saving the ship, and she would have been saved had even a part of the crew the courage and inclination of the Mate. For some hours we worked elaborating our precautions for keeping the water out of the hold. I never felt the cold although I had constantly to break the icicles congealing on my beard and moustache. Neither did I hear of anyone complaining of hunger or thirst, though no one had broken their fast.

For some time I heard the men who were in the hold trimming the coals, knocking to be let out. I kept them in for a time, for they deserved some correction for their unmanly, cowardly conduct during the night. As evening approached they were let out. They were pitiful objects: terror was written large on their faces. I believe if they had been kept there a short time longer they would have gone mad. If the Second Mate had been a plucky man they might have kept their courage up. The majority of men are lost without a leader. The trimming was of no avail: the ship was so far over that each heave of the sea threw the coal back. The blackness of the hold was only intensified by the glimmering candles; then there were the noises, the grimmest the sound of the large quantity of water that had gained access to the hold, and the constant trickling that was added to it. I had never before seen fear depicted so horribly on the human face.

After they got on deck I directed the pumps to be started: I would leave nothing undone to save the ship. As a young Master, the Board of Trade's vexing enquiry was a thing to be prepared for and the crew would remember the tasks they were put to. As no one could stand on the slanted deck, each man was suspended by ropes, and for an hour we worked the pumps. They would not fetch so I had to conclude they were broken.

By the last glimmer of that winter day a brig hove down on us; when abeam I saw that she was an Italian scudding under lower topsails. I asked him to stand by; he refused to do that and said that if we could get aboard his vessel he would take us. He had lost all his boats excepting the longboat. I told him that I would not abandon: he squared away. Then my brave sailors made a rush for the only boat we had left, making use of much bad language to keep up their courage. Now this boat was in an extremely risky position, keel up on the after skids. If the lashings were taken off she would slide to leeward and get smashed amongst the floating wreckage. In case of having to take to the boat I had planned with the Mate a way to safely launch her over the quarter. So I did the only thing I could do, for I had armed myself with a revolver to keep the men from raiding the spirits. I fired one shot over their heads, and threatened to shoot the first man who attempted to cut the boat lashings. That was enough: they let the boat alone. Then I explained to them my intentions, and told them that for the present the ship was the safest place. Soon after the lights of a steamer were seen bearing down towards us. A lifeboat was lowered from her and came within speaking distance. I informed the officer that I had no thought of abandoning the ship, and asked him to stand by till morning and take us in tow to the nearest port. The crew heard what I said, several of them yelling and shouting for the boat to go forward, and two of them jumped overboard. I saw the boat pick them up and row to the steamer. In the course of an hour the boat came back, with a message from the Captain to me saying that my ship was in a perilous position, there was no reasonable hope of saving her; if I hindered the crew from leaving and anyone was drowned, and I was saved, he would have to give evidence against me for manslaughter. The two men had given a fearful account of our plight. On his own account the officer in the boat called out to hurry up – he could see the ship's keel. I called the crew together, pleaded with them not to abandon the ship, pointed out that the weather was improving and we could soon run to port. Reminded them of the hard time they had before getting in this ship and promised them double pay – and asked them if my life was not as precious to me as theirs to them. I asked them individually to stop. Not one had the pluck to say he would or would not. They slunk away. I told the officer that I would not abandon the ship. I would neither help nor hinder the crew from leaving. The boat rowed forward; in the dim light I saw my men go out on the jib-boom. One after another they slid down a rope. The boat glided along with the sea and grabbed a man each time. In the course of an hour all had gone, and soon the steamer's lights had disappeared.

I now made myself fast to the rail and had rested there some time. My courage unabated, though I was as I thought alone in a slowly sinking ship, when I heard a voice which startled me. I asked, 'Who is that?' 'Fearon.' I said, 'You, why have you not gone with the rest? You know this means death. My stopping is quite different. You ought to have gone.' Fearon said, 'I would not go and leave you here. What would they say in Cumberland if I went home and said I had deserted you?' My reply was, 'You are a brave man; if we are saved, as long as I live I will be your friend.'

We then examined the weak spots and strengthened them against the influx of the water and then returned to our perch. I could not help admiring the perfectly contented and happy resignation

Fearon showed during the next hours. On my remarking that the ship would sink before morning, for we had discovered that water was gaining access to the hold through another bollard ventilator abreast the main hatch that we could not get at owing to the wreckage and water, he said smilingly, 'It is better to die now when we are of good repute than live to disgrace ourselves.' This slowly passing time waiting for death sapped my courage, and as I thought things over I felt I would like to make a bid for life. Fearon looked so bright and happy that it was with diffidence I said, 'We've done all men could do to save the property entrusted to us: I feel now we should try and get taken off.' He consented with the same cheerful alacrity with which he was prepared to die. So I managed to get blue lights and rockets from a locker in the companion that was clear of water and we fired them. To the very last one we saw an answering rocket. We guessed it was about midnight; the wind had dropped to a steady half gale, the sea was smoother and running without breakers. We heard a hail and made out a boat some hundred yards on our weather quarter; the officer shouted that he could not come near us as he was afraid of fouling the wreckage. That being the case, I told him that he might as well go back to his ship as in that sea neither of us could swim the distance. Just then my hand touched the coil of the deep sea leadline, which had been hung to the rail for handiness, and there was also a lifebuoy. With these a passage to the boat was assured. I hailed the boat and told him of our discovery and that I was throwing the lifebuoy with a line attached. When they got the buoy they fastened their line to it, and we could haul it back and the communication was established. I required Fearon to get into the buoy. This he flatly refused to do, saying that I 'must go first; if I had him away I would stop.' I was much moved by his unselfish loyalty, and finally he was persuaded to go on my solemn promise to follow. You can imagine to what a tremendous angle the ship was now tilted by the slow influx of the sea. Fearon walked down the ship's side into the sea. The boat's crew hauled, and I steadied. A shout told me they had him in the boat. I hauled back the buoy; having no steadiment I was as often the wrong as the right side up, and having lost consciousness there was difficulty in getting me into the boat. I was bruised and discoloured for many months afterwards. I did not regain my senses for some time after I was on board the steamer. The boat had to be abandoned.

My first recollection was seeing many people around me. I asked for the Captain. He came, a middle aged Scot with a hard mean face. I told him that I would sign an agreement to pay £3,000 if he would stand by until daylight, and as the wind was rapidly moderating the Mate and I, with volunteers, would go on board and take the hawser. He would then tow to the nearest port. The agreement was signed.

I don't know now what I really thought. I did not want the ship to be picked up by some other steamer, yet even with my knowledge of her sinking condition so many marvellous deliverances had occurred the last thirty hours that a faint hope that the ship might be saved yet lingered in my mind, and if she did sink I wanted to know it.

The Captain had a bed made up for me on the sofa in his room. He occupied the bunk and kept talking of his share of the salvage. I was annoyed and provoked by his ill-advised talk of battening on my misfortune and felt angry enough to whip him. To me the disaster was an overwhelming blow to prosperity in my profession, for I was only twenty-eight years old – only on the threshold of my career, not yet come to those years of philosophic calm that age and experience give.

The Captain apportioned £1,000 as his share of the salvage, and was debating whether to invest it in a house property in Scotland or Birkenhead, when there was an uproar and excitement on deck and news was brought that the *Doriga* had sunk. Fearon, who witnessed it, said she tilted up and slowly sank stern first. The Captain who had delighted himself and annoyed me by so complacently 'counting his chickens before they were hatched' became a very angry, disappointed man. His manner became discourteous bordering on rudeness. At breakfast next morning when I enquired 'Where is my First Mate?' he replied that he did not know. So I left the table saying that 'If he cannot come to your table I will go where he is.' Fearon was sent for.

After breakfast I drew up a concise yet full explanatory statement of the disaster and the causes that had lead to it, and made three copies; called the crew together and requested the Chief Engineer and Chief Mate of the steamer to attend. The statement was read over to the crew and signed by them. The steamer's officers signed as witnesses. The Captain of the steamer was an ill-conditioned, sour-tempered, malignant man; by the sinking of the *Doriga* his castle in Spain had disappeared and at mealtimes his talk was directed covertly at me – tales of Captains' Certificates being suspended, and of Captains and Mates who had stayed on board distressed ships after the crew had left in order to scuttle them, and other things dictated by his spleen.

At last this became unbearable. I called him a paltry coward to speak so to a young Master. I told him he was a liar to insinuate such charges, when he had such ample evidence of the ship's condition; that on arrival at Liverpool I would write to the papers and give them an account of his vile manners and treatment. I left his table, refused to have any further association with him, and sheltered with the engineers.

The engineers told me that on the night they rescued the crew, leaving the Mate and me on board, the Captain rang up 'full steam ahead'; the engineers, backed by the firemen and members of my crew, went and expostulated with him and said they refused to steam away and leave us to drown. He blustered, and said we should have left with the crew. The Engineer pointed out that the disaster had caused a transitory madness in me, but that it was their bounden duty to try and save us. He had to give in. They gave him the character of a nasty, greedy, mean man.

The engineers were exceedingly kind; on arrival in the river the Captain, no doubt afraid of public opinion, attempted to mollify me and made offers of money and clothes. I refused his offers telling him a man of his age ought to have given me his sympathy instead of his malice.

I went ashore wearing the torn and salt-saturated clothes I had been rescued in. At 10 a.m. the Owner after infinite trouble found my lodgings and asked me to promise not to leave the firm: they would buy me a ship. He also dissuaded me from writing to the papers about the steamer Captain. This man called at the Owners' office and Mr T. dismissed him with stinging remarks as to his conduct. The Board of Trade and the Underwriters were perfectly satisfied with the statement drawn up on the steamer and no enquiry was held.

A NEW SHIP

My Fourteenth Voyage
ALPHETA
1879–1880

PORTSMOUTH – CARDIFF – MANILA – SAN FRANCISCO –
SCILLY ISLES – FLEETWOOD

Messrs Johnston Sproule & Co., the Owners, informed me that
Messrs Balfour Williamson & Co., John Belle & Co. and another
firm had called on them and offered a command in their respective
employs for me, and they had told them that they were retaining my
services and I had promised to remain with them. I thought this
was very kind of the firm, and I took the first opportunity of
thanking them for the honour they had done me.

Amongst the vessels considered for purchase were the barques
Andes and *Alpheta*; the former was reported on, then I journeyed to
Portsmouth to examine the latter. The *Alpheta* was a comparatively
new vessel built in Sunderland for Penny of Shoreham. On her
second voyage, when bound from London to Australia, meeting
with strong westerly gales she attempted to take shelter behind the
Isle of Wight and grounded on the Pembroke Ledge. Several
salvage companies became insolvent trying to get her off. Napiers
& Co., the Glasgow shipbuilders, bought up all interests, got her
off and repaired her in Portsmouth town dock. On my report the
ship was bought. Napiers' master rigger was in charge; he was a
great rogue and robbed the ship of blocks and ropes, which he sold
to a fellow townsman in command of a Greenock barque discharging
timber in the dock. I saw a cartload being taken away. He told me
the blocks and ropes were being returned to the Government
dockyard having been borrowed. I was done.

Portsmouth greatly interested me. I lodged at the inn made famous by Captain Marrayat, in the High Street; and visited the house where the Duke of Buckingham was assassinated, the famous old *Victory*, the Dockyard, the Gaol where I saw Arthur Orton the Tichborne claimant, 'Benson' the super-educated rogue and forger, and the ex Police Inspector he had suborned; Southsea Common with the military parades and the memorials of Nelson, the Isle of Wight, and had a trip to the New Forest. I have not seen any place I would prefer to Lymington to live in.

The ship was chartered to load at Cardiff for Manila. It left Portsmouth in tow and was nearly wrecked by the carelessness of the tugboat people on the rocks off the Lizard. Arrived in Cardiff Roads and received orders to enter the Penarth Dock, where she took in her cargo.

We sailed from Penarth on the 20th July with a good crew, Mr Fearon Chief Mate. I was delighted with the prospect of again sailing amongst the enchanted islands of the East. We had favourable winds and weather and arrived off Java Head on the seventy-second day from Penarth. Calm and favourable winds through the Straits, and an anxious passage from there to our destination, this being the dangerous time between monsoons when typhoons prevail. To minimize the danger from these pests I took the route by the Palawan Passage and arrived at Manila on the 115th day from the Bristol Channel, an excellent passage for the time of year.

A few days after arrival I was taken very ill with an enlarged liver and fever. I was taken to a hotel and had a man nurse in constant attendance, and was convalescent in three weeks. I saw little of Manila. Though against the Owners' wishes, I chartered to load dry sugar and hemp for San Francisco at a good rate of freight. A week before we left, a typhoon devastated the north of Luzon. In Manila we had a hard gale with copious rains and a few days afterwards the ship *Thomas Bell*, which had sailed ten days before, put back partly dismasted and much damaged. She had passed through the vortex and had a bad time. We sailed, and as the Northeast Monsoon was now set in we worked up the coast of Luzon as far as Cape Bojeador when we met with the full strength of the monsoon against us. We lost many sails and suffered damage to the rigging before we passed the north end of Formosa. Amongst my many hard sea fights the three weeks of hard striving against the fury of the December monsoon stands pre-eminent: the forces of primary nature are repulsive and brutal.

The ship being deeply laden, and as this was midwinter, I did not take the great circle track across the North Pacific: keeping south of 40° north we had gales of moderate strength. We arrived in San Francisco after a fifty-four day passage; the smart Canadian ship *Alexander Black* was 112 days from Hong Kong and arrived the same day.

San Francisco has, in the Golden Gate, a glorious entrance to as fine a harbour as there is in the world. It has not the fanciful beauty of Sydney or Rio de Janeiro, but is more striking and noble with its range of northern hills. This was the first of my many voyages to this port. I think California an earthly paradise contaminated by man's vileness – for all the vices of the Eastern and Western world flourish there together with some of their own promoting.

My agent was Mr Coleman, a gentleman of Virginia who had fought gallantly in the Confederate ranks. He showed me every kindness; his hospitality was unbounded and he gave me a very pleasant time. I fixed homewards to load a cargo of wheat for orders, and got the Scilly Islands as the port of call, for I had pleasant remembrances of those vanguards of England. The charterer was Mr Henri Lund, the Swiss Consul. One day on board he noticed our fine pigs and said to me in the most pathetic tone, 'Captain, don't give the pigs my good wheat.' I reassured him. He would be glad when he learned we turned out ten tons of wheat more than we had taken in!

The passage home was pleasant and uneventful; anchor was dropped off Hugh Town, St Mary's. A few years before, the *Schiller* had been lost with 331 passengers and crew on the outlying rocks. The Islanders had gruesome tales to tell of the time, and the old graveyard was shunned.

As it was the month of June, the Islands were a delightful resting place. The people are hospitable, and I stayed at the hotel and roamed all over the Islands in pleasant company. Tresco is wonderful – a pretty piece of southern Italy transported to northern shores. The richness of the foliage, the beauty of the flowers and shrubs, the rare plants and delightful climate tempted me to think I was in California. We had lovely weather during our stay and were rather sorry to leave though we were homeward bound.

Having orders to proceed to Fleetwood to discharge, we picked up anchor and sailed round the Scilly Islands, between them and the Seven Stones. We had summer breezes from the westward so scant that we passed between St David's Head and Ramsey Island. Engaged a tug off Bardsey Island and anchored in Morecambe Bay next day, and docked two days afterwards. During our stay here I visited Blackpool and heard Reeves sing his grand old sea songs. No composer has ever approached Dibden for songs that touch the heart of a sailor.

HORRORS OF WAR

My Fifteenth Voyage
ALPHETA
1880–1881

FLEETWOOD – BIRKENHEAD – VALPARAISO – ARICA –
SAN FRANCISCO – VALLEJO – BENECIA – QUEENSTOWN

In summertime I found Fleetwood and Blackpool pleasant places and the five weeks of our stay quickly passed. A cargo of coals was purchased on ship's account and I was given the option of calling at Valparaiso or proceeding direct to California.

The day we left dock was fine with a strong north wind blowing across the channel; we had scarcely got five hundred yards from the pier at the entrance to the River Wyre when the tug had to ease down and stop to avoid running into a schooner who was working down the channel. The ship kept her way, passing the tug to leeward, and before the tug was able to again get into position the wind and current took the ship on the bank where she grounded. When the tide left she was high and dry. A telegram brought an officer of the Liverpool Salvage Corps and a powerful tug; she was towed to Birkenhead, discharged and drydocked. I had a squabble with the Lloyd's Surveyor: he did not come well out of it and apologised next day. It has always been a matter of wonder to me why Consuls, Lloyd's Surveyors, dockmasters, and strange shipowners and their clerks should consider themselves to be at liberty to be rude to shipmasters. I have always hotly resented their pretences: they never again laid themselves open to be 'bitten by the same dog twice'.

My forecastle hands having got a month's advance, deserted. I saw one of them in St Nicholas' churchyard in Liverpool and gave

129

chase, when my old Captain, now retired, brought me up and advised me to let the man go. I asked him since when had he turned philanthropist, for he was a stickler for discipline when in collar: no wonder magistrates and other landlubbers deal so leniently with sailor offenders when such a hard disciplinarian as Captain Can, now that he had done with a sea life, advised condoning the serious offence of desertion.

Whilst reloading the cargo many seamen applied and out of them we picked a splendid crew of young Britishers who made the voyage and resisted the seductions of many crimps and high pay. They were the very best crew I ever had, and I gave them a good gratuity at the end of the voyage.

Ships intending to leave by the next tide enter the dock basin, where they are permitted to rig out their jib-booms. The water is then high; if the dock gate man or berthing master has a grudge against the Master or officers of any ship, for a want of whisky hospitality to him or for not being tipped, he directs the Mate to haul the ship close in the corner. The ship is high above the dock wall when the jib-boom is rigged out and gear set up; on the advent of the coming tide the water in the basin is lowered causing the gear or boom to take the dock wall when it is broken, causing a delay of some days to the ship and much expense and a bad mark against the Chief Mate, who is made the scapegoat. I knew of the outrage, for a former Mate (Dixon) in the *Doriga* had been a victim, nearly getting dismissed for what was not his fault.

The *Alpheta* was in the corner in a position to sustain the same damage when the Owner and I came on the scene; she was hauled out of danger and such a row made that no other vessels have ever been put in the same peril.

The *Alpheta* was a favoured ship; she dropped anchor in Valparaiso Bay just seventy days from Birkenhead Dock. In a few hours I had sold the cargo for seven times the coal price on board, paying a commission of one half of one per cent. The coals had to be discharged at Arica, with liberty to keep enough for ballasting to a loading port. The coals were for the use of Chilean warships and transports. This was the time of the sanguinary war between Chile, Peru and Bolivia. A few days before, Arica had been captured after a hard struggle and the battle of Tacna had decided the ownership of the province of Tarapaca.

We had the usual delightful passage up the coast, dropping anchor on the sixth day from Valparaiso. Two ships were at the anchorage, one of them a coal storeship for the Chilean Navy. On going ashore, reminders of the horrors of war were plentiful and dead bodies of soldiers lying about. Horses and men who had been killed and thrown over had been caught by projecting stones on the cliffside, and the remains of some seven hundred bodies were partly burned with the help of railway sleepers; the smell was very bad. The town was partly in ruins. A brigade of the half-savage Indian Monguls were encamped behind. After their victory at Tacna the triumphant Chilean Army had gone to further victories near Lima. I made the acquaintance of a young Englishman in the Chilean service; his name was Harrington, from a well-known Liverpool family who by commerce had a long connection with Chile. He was a Lieutenant in a cavalry regiment, and had been through all the big battles of the war. He told me such tales of the savagery of the soldiery that they filled me with horror. I asked him how he could bear to be mixed up with such barbarians: he laughed, and said war was war and all men got inured to savagery.

On the invitation of a young London man who held a position under the Chilean Government, I went for a ride to visit the battle-fields. I had the horse belonging to the French Consul; the beast had not been out of its stable for months and had been fed on beans, and my horsemanship was nothing to brag about though I had the sailor's pliancy of body which enabled me to stick on. I had an exciting time before the beast gave up trying to walk on its hind legs, and then trying with the same members to emulate the *corps de ballet* – his high kick was marvellous. I put him at the steep sand-hills: this, with the heavy going, reduced him to order.

I don't want to visit battlefields again. I got the shock of my life, when it was borne to me that Life was not the sanctified thing I had hitherto thought. I saw my companion talking excitedly to a soldier. He came to me, saying hurriedly, 'Gallop back as fast as you can!' The horses went homewards like the wind. When we had gone several miles he told me that the sergeant who was talking to him advised him to get back as soon as possible: the soldiers there were Mongul Chileans and bandits and they would murder us. He belonged to a Santiago regiment and had been left to look after his wounded officer.

On the way back we came to a high-walled whitewashed square. On attempting to ride into the gateway both horses refused, showing every sign of terror and distress. We dismounted, hitching the horses to rings in the wall, and entered a most curious cemetery. The walls were divided into innumerable pigeonholes about two feet square; the coffins were put in, the hole sealed, and an ornate gilded plate set forth the name and virtues of the occupant. Nearly all had been desecrated and the floor was covered with open coffins. The soldiers had done this, looking for loot or for lead coffins in which to send their dead officers to their homes in the South. It was a gruesome sight – death from infancy to old age. The sign of corruption was rare. Something in the dry atmosphere (it never rains) had caused the flesh to have the look of porcelain. However, I got a bellyful of one old gentleman that sent me out vomiting. We found our horses very uneasy; they were apparently glad to leave such a repulsive place. Their olfactory senses must be keener than ours, for outside the gate I could detect no evil smell.

The French Consul was glad to have the too-high spirits taken out of his horse, and announced his intentions of going for a ride.

Men-of-war, transports and tenders came in and were supplied with coal, and any interval was filled by discharging for the store-ships. All the receivers praised my crew for the amount of coal they discharged per day; they were a cheerful, diligent crew and it was a pleasure to see them.

After the shore horrors and the offensive smell when the wind was off shore, I lost my appetite. Then Mr Fearon sickened; very soon he had the worst form of dysentery. As there was no doctor in the port I attended him and gave suppositories as an anodyne. In my lowered state of vitality I took the disease and just managed to do my business. I stopped the discharge of cargo and prepared to beat down the coast to Iquiqui. A few weeks before this Balfour Williamson & Co. wrote asking if I would accept a freight of nitrate of soda for San Francisco, offering a good rate of freight. I closed with the offer, for this freight was so much money found: we were chartered from San Francisco home at a very high figure.

Fearon was very bad. The Second Mate, a very young man, and I were just able, with strong will power, to get about. We left Arica and worked down in the remarkable space of two days: then I collapsed. The doctor was a Londoner, a remarkably nice man. He had Fearon removed to hospital and attended me several times a day and was most attentive and anxious. I got so low that he brought two doctors in consultation; he told me they took the most serious view of my condition. I asked him to tell me the exact truth: were my days numbered? He was moved to tears and said they saw no hope for me, for there was not only the disease but complications. For a moment, when I heard the sentence of death, I felt as an icy hand had been laid on my heart; then came a great wave of joy that I would be done, for ever, with the anxieties and worries of this mortal life, and I felt exalted. I asked him to promise to have me buried at sea, for in this Roman Catholic country (when I was here on my first voyage as Master) I saw on the drear sandy beach the grave of Isaac Cartwell, a Maryport shipmaster, who had not been buried a year. Instead of a mound there was a depression, and out of a burrow I saw a horrible creature emerge, a nightmare land crab. I have always thought the sea the most noble of sepulchres.

The many shipmasters shunned my ship, with the exception of an Irishman, Captain of the *George Crowshaw*. He was an old acquaintance of my Captain Can. He came often and once brought his wife. My steward asked him not to bring her again, for with my illness and natural modesty the presence of a woman was hurtful. I lingered on. Dysentery is quite as loathsome as smallpox. My life was preserved by the more than womanly care and tenderness of my steward, a young German. Night and day did he attend me. At night he slept on the floor of my room: did I move, he was there. He carried out the doctor's prescriptions and drew me back to life. The doctor was surprised at my vitality and told me that his colleagues who had examined me thought that there was now hope of recovery, and so I gradually drew away from death. The Consul had called on board and took my wishes through an open port, he would not venture into my room.

The doctor gave me daily reports of Mr Fearon's progress, and I arranged to have him sent to a Saltuo which would help his convalescence. During this painful six weeks the conduct of my crew was beyond praise, they worked so cheerfully and willingly and were so quiet and content, never asking to go ashore. They kept the ship in such order that the Consul told me the Commander of the British cruiser that lay near us for some time, said he never saw a merchant vessel in such order, nor with such an orderly crew. I was much pleased to hear this and thought what an ideal life we would lead if all crews were so self-respecting and diligent.

For some time my food was the juice of raw beef. The disease had run itself out. What I weighed or looked like at this time I don't know, for three months afterwards at San Francisco I weighed only eighty-five pounds and people said then I was dying.

Three days before the ship left, Mr Fearon returned on board. He had come without the doctor's permission, and I scolded him, for there was some talk of the Consul and agents stopping the ship from proceeding to sea with the Master and First Mate in such a state. I am afraid I hurt Fearon by my too vehement condemnation of his action; I did not mean to, for it was of his good that I was thinking. Poor little chap: he looked like a skull with a skin stretched over it and his eyes were in caverns. When the last lighter with nitrate of soda was alongside on a Saturday afternoon, Captain O'Donnel took me ashore to close up business and clear out, for I thought that the sooner we were out of the port the sooner would health return. Some twenty shipmasters came in a body to congratulate me on my recovery. I told them that I did not wish their acquaintance: they had left me to die, without one of them offering their services to help my business. I had lain there six weeks and only Captain O'Donnel, a Fenian with rebel proclivities, had acted the Good Samaritan – so I left them. They looked surprised and perturbed, but through life I have spoken as I thought, and I don't think the habit has done me harm.

On returning to the ship with my papers in order for sailing, I found the crew still at work although it was 8 p.m., taking in cargo, for good fellows that they were, they thought Fearon and I would get well if only clear of the land. At 5 o'clock next morning the moorings were picked up, and the ship kedged clear of the shipping and sail made ready for the sea breeze. At 10 a.m. we left, Captain O'Donnel and his boat's crew assisting us. With a good breeze we soon sunk Iquiqui out of sight.

We fed on tinned milk, cornflour and rice meal. Our strength did not improve as quickly as expected. I decided to steer for the equatorial rainy zone and fill up with sweet rainwater. One of the tanks was emptied and whitewashed ready. On the edge of the rains we entered the largest and most wonderful river in the world, the great Pacific Equatorial Stream, five times larger than the Atlantic Gulf Stream. One morning I heard excited shouting: on going on deck I found that my handy and fearless steward had seen a large turtle basking in the sun; he jumped overboard, seized it and was struggling to get it near the ship. In a few minutes the dinghy was chucked overboard and both picked up. We had a *real* cook on board who made the most appetising soup for he was learned in the virtues of Calipash and Calipee, and I am sure no London feasts had better soup. We were a week crossing this huge sea river and caught fifteen fine green turtle, plenty of dolphin, and flying fish. We had turtle soup and turtle flesh admirably cooked until the Golden Gate was sighted. Fearon and I picked up strength and felt again something of the *joie de vivre*.

We passed a long night in the Golden Gate. The evening haze prevented the lookout man from seeing the approach of two ships, so no tug came to meet us. With the dawn came a welcome breeze off Black Point as the sun rose, raising the fog like a curtain, when there was disclosed one of the finest sights on earth. San Francisco is a lovely place: Nature has supplied there everything the heart of man could desire.

Before leaving the pier for Vallejo, one evening I dined with Mr and Mrs Sinnot. There was quite a large party and a discussion arose about religion and the general morality of the mixed population of the States. I remarked that I had heard much about the wickedness of San Francisco, yet this was my second visit and I had seen and heard nothing that would offend the most modest and strict moralist. Captain Sinnot whispered to several of the men, then spoke to Mrs Sinnot and proposed to me to visit a theatre for an hour. We took the car to Montgomery Street and walked towards Kearney Street. Captain Sinnot knocked at a door, a wicket opened, there was a conversation carried on in whispers, a rattling of money, and we were admitted to a dim passage and shown into a box. The theatre was quite large, very dimly lighted. Through the gloom I could see the pit was crowded, with only the buzz of whispered voices to be heard. The tiers of boxes were fully occupied. The dim lights were further decreased. Music came from some hidden orchestra, an intense light concentrated on the stage, and a travesty of the scandalous relations and law case then occupying the minds and press of the country was enacted in every detail – the Beecher-Tilton scandal,[1] the most indecent, degraded exhibition of human depravity and the vicious, filthy, conception of a lost soul. The place was a school kept by the Devil and his Demons. Then the hall was over-run by girls dressed in the scanty clothes of the ballet and enticing to drink and sin. I was told the place would hold several hundreds and was filled three times nightly. Such an academy would pollute any community, and give any city the reputation of Sodom and Gomorrah.

We towed to Stans Mills at Vallejo to take homeward cargo. At that time the bags of wheat were loaded by hand by stevedores, a stalwart body of young men. Their wages were fifty cents per hour, equal to one pound and ten pence per day; only the strongest could stand the work. They were driven and dominated by hard-driving foremen; should one falter or straighten his back, causing a momentary stoppage, he was kicked out without pay. In no country have I seen such tyranny practised as in the boasted 'Home of the Brave and Land of the Free'. I was told that, notwithstanding the very high wages, the only possessions of these men were a suit of overalls and a heavy score against them in the whisky shops. They lived in huge shacks in bunks, and were the source from which flowed the wealth of the saloon keepers and their pilots, the overwhelming number of degraded females.

From Vallejo we shifted to Benecia. This place interested me as being the birthplace of Tom Sawyer's opponent, the 'Benecian Boy' – as a boy in the early sixties I heard much of his famous fight.

Our crew had been so uniformly good that we gave them a holiday every afternoon. The people were hospitable, and they had got acquainted with the men at the military encampment who made them very welcome. All enjoyed our stay here.

---

[1] Henry Ward Beecher was a nationally popular preacher and speaker, and for forty years pastor of the Plymouth Church (Congregational) in Brooklyn, addressing congregations of two or three thousand on current matters, social issues and church doctrine. He became editor of the New York weekly *Independant*, whose managing editor Theodore Tilton was an admirer and friend; when Beecher went to England in 1863 to speak against slavery Tilton became editor. In 1870 Elizabeth Tilton told her husband that she had committed adultery with Beecher, but later retracted the admission at Beecher's prompting. However the story was published, and in 1873 Beecher publicly denied it. In 1874 Tilton charged him with gross immorality, but an investigation by the Plymouth Church cleared Beecher. Tilton then filed a complaint for adultery and $100,000 damages, The six month trial in 1875 resulted in wide publicity and a hung jury, said to have been nine to three in Beecher's favour.

After completing the loading we towed to San Francisco and sailed for Queenstown for orders. To 50° south 95° west we had most favourable winds; then for the month of May we had east winds and calms, a most unusual experience in this sea of storms. In standing south we attained the latitude of 61° south and fell in with many icebergs. At last we got favourable winds, and arrived in Ireland on the 118th day from San Francisco.

I put up at the Queen's Hotel and occupied a double-bedded room with Captain Mullen of the ship *Slieve Roe*. After undressing, I knelt and prayed as was my custom. Mullen must have been a good fellow, for with some emotion he said that to say his nightly prayers was his habit; he had got into bed without doing so from cowardice lest I, a stranger, should sneer at him. I liked him for his artlessness. There is much that is childlike amongst true sailors.

Next morning I got a cablegram from the Owners asking me to accept the command of the *Larnaca*, a good ship they had bought from T. B. Royden & Co. I replied, 'Can I promise the command of the *Alpheta* to Fearon, if he passes for Master?' They wired at once that I could.

I was very happy to have such good news to tell Fearon, as he was engaged to a nice girl and eagerly looked forward to promotion as the last step to marriage. When I went on board I noticed that his eyes were bunged up as if from crying. In the cabin I told him the Owners' promise. He burst out crying and said he didn't care for anything, Lizzie had given him up owing to his mother's and sisters' irritating opposition. He showed me several letters and from them no one could blame Lizzie, for the talk of the opposition was unbearable to any self-respecting girl. On going ashore I wrote to Fearon's mother telling her that if she did not do all in her power to bring them together again, her son would go straight to ruin. I also mentioned his remarkably good prospects at so early an age. In London I got a letter from Fearon to say the breach was healed. He made a voyage as Master, then got married.

Captain Flynn relieved me of the command of the *Alpheta* and I left via Liverpool to take command of the *Larnaca*.

THE SINKING OF THE
BRITISH NAVY

My Sixteenth Voyage
LARNACA
1881–1882

LONDON – SYDNEY – NEWCASTLE, N.S.W. – FALMOUTH –
HULL

The *Larnaca* was lying in the Southwest India Dock, London,
nearly finished loading. She was a handsome clipper ship about
two years old with comfortable cabins and a good record for
passages, which had been spent in the Calcutta trade. Her Captain
was a noted dandy with the uneviable reputation of having been a
bad husband to no less than six wives. His present wife was a
fresh-looking girl belonging to a respectable family in New
Brighton. He introduced me when I met them on board; she was
eighteen, he about fifty, but no mean hand at attracting women. He
was snobbishly dressed, with a pompous manner and vulgar
address and pronouncement. I paid him for certain quantities of
tobacco and cigars which he said were under seal, taking his word
as the jerk note was not forthcoming, and found when I got to sea
that he had swindled me. In Calcutta an old gentleman came on
board and told me that the fourth wife was his daughter and how
cruelly my predecessor had behaved to her; he got so excited in his
denouncement of him that I was afraid that he would have a fit. In
after years I learnt that his sixth wife had left him. He sank to earning
a precarious living as a billiard marker, and passed out of knowledge.

The Mate and Second Mate were appointed prior to my arrival,
both young men. I was particularly drawn to the Second Mate by

his bright joyous looks and disposition. He was a nephew of
Colonel F. G. Burnaby[1] and was with me as Chief Mate for several
voyages. Mr Nurule gave him command of the *Glengaber*. After a
few voyages in her he inherited an estate in Cornwall, settled down,
and I have not heard from him for many years.

We left dock early in November in charge of Mr Penton; after
passing Gravesend the wind increased to a furious westerly gale
and we anchored at the Nore. The ship *British Navy*, who had left
the East India Dock at the same time as we left dock, was at anchor.
She also was bound to Sydney, and we were anxious to beat her.
The gale continued for two days; it lulled and shifted to WNW and
both ships hove up and proceeded in tow. The wind fell to a calm;
the weather was gloomy and lowering with a low and falling glass
Bar 28.50. The Downs was full of ships at anchor and we brought
up one mile to the eastward of Deal Pier. Penton, the Pilot, was in
such a hurry to get ashore that he dropped the anchor when the
ship was dead stopped, paid out cable, and gave us a foul anchor
which led us into imminent danger. He had not left half an hour
when the wind came with sudden fury: in a few minutes it was of
hurricane force with blinding rain. We were driven before it among
the shipping. To let go the second anchor would have been fatal to
ourselves and the ships near us, so I let her drive, steering between
the ships, passing some of them within a few feet. After many
narrow escapes of colliding, and by the mercy of God that our
anchor did not foul that of the many ships we drove past, we came
to a clear space, dropped our second anchor and paid out the whole
of the cables on both anchors, and set sea watch. I have only once
on the British coasts experienced a hurricane of similar force; both
times the wind was registered to have a velocity of ninety to a
hundred miles per hour. The wind was now SSW right up Channel;
the sea was running high, flooding the decks. Rockets and blue
lights all around us proclaimed that many ships were in dire distress
and danger. We were riding easily, having such a length of cable out.
At midnight I requested the Mate to have a look at our cables before
being relieved by the Second Mate. He came back spluttering and
vomiting with excitement. I made out that there was a ship driving
down on us, ran forward, and just got on the forecastle head when I

---

[1] Burnaby served with General Gordon in the Sudan, and wrote *Ride to Khiva* in 1875.

was knocked down by the collision (found out afterwards I had broken a small bone in my elbow). On picking myself up, I saw that a large ship had drifted athwart our bows; she rebounded, then struck us again abreast the afterhatch with a crash like squashing a thousand bandboxes. She then slewed round our bows and drifted all along our side, shedding blocks, etc on our decks. When I got on the poop she was just clearing us. The Captain and Channel Pilot hailed to say they were sinking. I said 'May God help you – I can't – we are seriously injured', for before I left forward the ingress of the sea from the broken bow plates was such that it had broken and forced off the forepeak hatches, and at every scend of the sea the water gushed up in tons and seemed like it would burst the forecastlehead deck. The Second Mate and five men of the *British Navy* had scrambled on board our ship. On mustering our crew two Able Seamen were missing; they had jumped on board the colliding ship. The men from the *British Navy* came to me in a great state of excitement asking for drink, which I did not give them: I wanted men of real, not Dutch, courage. I told them that if they did not exert themselves and help my crew who were endeavouring to get a spare anchor over, for the ship was adrift with one cable parted and the other anchor not holding, we should all be drowned. On picking this anchor up two days later we found that one fluke and the stock were broken off. I kept our passengers and the boys firing blue lights and rockets to get assistance for the *British Navy* which had drifted out of sight. The night was too tempestuous and the sea too high for lifeboat or tug to venture out. As we drifted slowly a small stump of a mast came into view, all that was to be seen of the sunken *British Navy*. We could see no sign of life and the tempest roared so loud that no other sound could be heard. By hard work and good fortune the spare anchor was dropped with the steel towing hawser attached and this brought her up within a few feet of the Breaksand Buoy. Had we touched this bank, with the wind, sea and tide all in unison as it was, we would have capsized and all have been drowned. With the tremendous rent in the bows, the enormous force of the sea against the collision bulkhead threatened to break it and let the sea into the hold. To ease the pressure from the sea, I got a sail weighted at the lower end and then with much risk and labour we managed to pass it under the bowsprit, cut the strong lashings we had put round the sail to enable us to handle it in such a storm, and suspended it over the rent. The result was marvellous. The sea no longer gushed out of the forepeak hatch. The water in the peak was dead water and forcible pressure on the bulkhead was removed. I looked down the fore hold and found the cargo compactly stowed against the bulkhead, which no doubt enabled it to bear the enormous pressure before the sail eased it. When day dawned the tempest abated to a gale. With telescopes we searched for signs of life on the stump of the sunken *British Navy*'s foremast (the other masts had gone after colliding with us). A movement in the top showed us there was a living being there. A large Deal wreckers' craft with a score or two of men bore down on us with the intention of boarding: no doubt to them our vessel had a distressed and lame appearance. I told them I did not want their assistance, and asked them to save the marooned men on the sunken ship's mast. They paid no heed and persisted in their efforts to board my ship. I threatened to shoot any man who attempted to board, and presented a small telescope at them; this had the appearance of a pistol barrel and they desisted, then assailed me with language worthy of a 'Frisco boarding master. These fellows are wreckers: once aboard, they would try to get the Captain to do something that would give them a claim to salvage, or make a claim without his help – barefaced robbery of the Underwriters and Owners. I knew these gentry and wanted no truck with them. To me they have a great resemblance to sharks, loafing about waiting for disaster to snap. None of them would venture out when their services could have prevented great loss of life. In the daytime they came for lucre, not to save life, for they ignored my request to save the men on the mast and made for a ship that had dragged near the Goodwins. These fellows have been written up and glorified by several of our nautical writers. I think they are a lazy set, loafing their lives away in a nautical rig and looking for tips from city seaside visitors. They know nothing of the toil of the deep.

After breakfast the tug that had brought us from London steamed round us and noted our injuries, then came for a talk; told of many disasters and ships missing, many of them driven into the North Sea, then demanded £500 to tow us clear of the sands and to a London dock. I told him that I would waste no time talking to him. I would give him £70 for himself and a stern tug to take us (when the gale passed away) to London Docks; if not, when the weather abated I would put a boat out and go to Deal and make arrangements to tow: he accepted my terms. Then I asked him to save the survivors of the *British Navy* and pointed out the mast to him. He went off on his errand of mercy. In an hour he was back and told me he had two men, the only survivors of those on board when the ship sunk. The total loss of lives was twenty-six of the crew, two of mine, together with the Captain and a Channel Pilot. The tug took the two rescued men ashore. It was two days before the weather moderated sufficiently to enable us to leave for London. In passing Gravesend Captain Ewart, the Overlooker, came on board. He was in great trouble. The Captain of the *British Navy* was a life-long friend of his, and had only taken the ship on this voyage to please his old employers who had just purchased her. What lots of Captains I have known who have died or been drowned on what was intended to be their last voyage. It was not in the sense they meant.

On docking in the East India Dock for repairs, thousands of people crowded down to see the huge rent in the bows. The cargo was discharged from the fore hold sufficient to tip her and the repairs were rushed day and night. A few days from the time the ship would be ready to leave an official with subpoenas for the First Mate, Second Mate and myself came on board. I accepted mine, the First Mate his. I took the Second Mate's, gave the official five shillings, and destroyed it. A most unwise thing to do and one that might have had troublesome results for me. I had found the Chief Mate sadly wanting in all that makes a reliable and smart officer. The Second Mate had a Chief Mate's Certificate and had shown himself on that dreadful night in the Downs a smart fellow and one not wanting in resource in an emergency. I wanted to get quit of the Chief Mate and make the Second Chief and this was a good opportunity of effecting my desires. For my part it was arranged that the Agent would accompany me to interview the President of the Board of Trade and get permission to absent myself from the enquiry. This permission was granted. We sailed with Frank Rolleston as Chief Mate, and a new Second. For the month of November the weather was very kind, and we got out of Channel and into summer climes very nicely. I was pleased with the ship, she sailed well and was a comfortable sea home. We had seven nice apprentices. Altogether a nice ship's company.

The anchor was dropped in Sydney Harbour on the eighty-fourth day from London Docks. I was glad to find my friend Lindsey of the *Eaton Hall* here for I much enjoyed his companionship. Sydney, its harbour and surroundings have been so much boomed and photographed that I will spare myself a recital of their beauties; besides, a Jew and prominent auctioneer made me sick of the place and peoples. Among our cargo was a large consignment of iron bedsteads in cases. These were stowed in the fore hold when the cargo was discharged to tip the ship for repair of the damage sustained in the Downs. Several of these cases had been damaged by rolling the discharged cargo on them and at Sydney this was discovered. Only the wood cases were damaged, the contents were perfect: though only a dozen or so of the cases were broken, the Jew refused to accept delivery of any of the consignment of 120 cases. I offered to have new cases made for the dozen broken ones and if there was the slightest damage to the bedsteads to pay for them. He flatly refused to take delivery or to allow the cases to be touched. He claimed full value of £580 on the plea that the bill of lading stated they had to be delivered in the like good order they were received. This was a monstrous proposition and was against law and equity. For the reason that Sydney had built a huge hospital, importers had brought in many thousands of hospital bedsteads more than was required and the warehouses were full of them. They could not be sold, and my Jew with the sliminess of his race had seized on the fact of a few of his cases being damaged to make a profit out of what would be a loss. The surveyors, agents and other sharks all helping to defraud the ship. My agent and surveyor advised holding a survey on the cases, their friends the surveyors getting two guineas each. And then they suggested arbitration, to which the Jew would not agree; like his famous prototype he wanted his pound of flesh, the whole bond. My advisers were all for law: it would be profit to them whoever won. I would have to leave the case in their hands, for the law's delays would be such that several months would elapse before the case was heard. After many fruitless endeavours through my agents to come to terms, the conviction was forced on me they were not working for the ship's benefit so at the last meeting I got so vexed that I told them that Sydney was founded by convicts and they had proved to me the present inhabitants were worthy of them. I informed them that I would manage the affair: I was tired of their useless and expensive surveys. I asked a shipmaster friend to accompany me when I interviewed the Jew. Shylock was very polite and greasy. I asked him to come with me to the warehouse where the merchandise was stored and see if we could not come to some arrangement. He consented. In the cab he boasted of his wealth and said that he had landed in Sydney with only half-a-crown as his capital and asked us to look at him now, with the largest auctioneer's business in Sydney besides his importing connections. I said, 'You must have had many consignments of bedsteads.' That damped him. On examination he could only find twelve damaged cases out of 120, none badly. We adjourned to the cabin for refreshments. After an hour's wrangling I got a note from him that he would accept £100 in full satisfaction for the damage. This was a swindle, but it was much better than leaving the case to be fought out in the law courts, with no chance of justice in the absence of the loyal servants of the Queen. The agents and surveyors were mad at such a plan as the case would have been filched from them.

We had an exciting time towing from Sydney to Newcastle, N.S.W., either on account of a strike or lockout. I had only 300 tons of ballasting coal on board and required 600 tons to be seaworthy if compelled to part company with the tug. The agents urged me to take advantage of an offer from a steam trader to tow to Newcastle, for with 300 tons of stiffening she was safe towing in anything excepting very strong weather, so we started. On clearing the heads the wind freshened and gradually rose to a stiff gale from the dangerous southeast quarter. When off an island near the coast the starboard boiler of the steamer burst, doing damage and scalding several of the hands. With the loss of steam the ship and steamer sagged rapidly to shore, only a short half mile off. The Captain of the steamer signalled he would not cast us off until all hope was gone. I set several fore and aft sails which helped, and by the narrowest margin we crawled to the entrance of Newcastle. The wind was blowing a gale with an angry sea, right into the port. The steamer cast off our hawser and we dragged a Pilot on board through the water when well inside. He told me to steer right into the fairway, and rushed forward and let go both anchors: one cable parted, the other brought her up. When swung round we were a few feet from a large steamer loading at the tips. A most marvellous and fortunate escape.

I did not like Newcastle. It has the worst features of British coal ports and many worse ones of its own. The unimproved land has a melancholy and miserable appearance. I was glad when we left for San Francisco. We had a pleasant passage by Pitcairn Island where a remnant of the descendants of the mutiny of the *Bounty* live a pleasant life. (The majority shifted to Norfolk Island off the coast of New South Wales.) The breeze was too good to spend much time hove to off the island. We gave them books, newspapers and grocery articles, and they gave us fruit and sweet potatoes and fowls. They are a pleasant looking people rather like Spaniards; their speech had an American twang. I think they have the best of this world.

The passage through the Pacific was pleasant and rapid and we arrived off the Golden Gate bar at dusk one evening. A Pilot boat was plainly in sight and we made the usual night signals that we required a Pilot. He took no notice, knowing that the night fog would set in and he would have to stay on deck all night until the rising sun cleared it away and made it possible to enter port. These Pilots are highly paid. In clear weather their work occupies them on each ship they pilot in for not more than two hours. Their knowledge of the currents and soundings are invaluable in a fog, and I was annoyed they should shirk their duty. I kept the deck all night, by soundings and the sound of the foghorns kept in position, and vowed that I would not allow a Pilot to come on board in the morning.

At sunrise the fog lifted, the breeze came, and the Pilot boat made for us. I upbraided them for their conduct and told them that I would rather throw the ship away than accept their services after their scurvy behaviour. I was deaf to their entreaties and blandishments, and took the ship safely in without their help. They offered me great inducements after arrival to sign their pilotage note. I refused to do that, although I promised not to report them.

San Francisco was vastly improved since my first visit and many magnificent stone buildings had taken the place of wooden structures. The Golden Gate Park was growing rapidly in beauty; unsightly sandhills were converted into lovely lawns and flower beds. I have never seen such a variety of variegated hollies – they were as lovely as flowers. Altogether the Park was a dream of beauty, with the blue Pacific at its feet and the crowds of happy people amusing themselves. The seals gamboling fearlessly between the shore and their fastness seemed to know they were chartered libertines protected by law.

Our cargo of wheat was loaded up the river and we left the Golden Gate after a pleasant stay, bound to Queenstown or Falmouth for orders. We had a rapid passage to the chops of the Channel where we encountered strong southeast to northeast gales. We made Mizen Head on the west coast of Ireland; the wind kept to the southeast for several days and we made many tacks before rounding Cape Clear. After beating about for several days in the vain effort to get to Queenstown, I decided to try for Falmouth. We reached there after a weary struggle, well satisfied to have a few days' rest.

Falmouth Harbour is a lovely place; it is surprising more Londoners do not spend their holidays there. A few artists make their homes in the neighbourhood.

There were many 'Frisco ships in Falmouth; all had been over 120 days on the passage. After a stay of five days I received orders to proceed to Hull to discharge. The wind was persistently unfavourable, with inclement weather. For three weeks we battled up the English Channel against cruel east winds, keeping the sea all the time, and got abreast the Goodwin Sands in the Dover Straits.

Then the wind rose to a heavy gale reducing us to lower topsails and compelling a return to the broader waters of the Channel. For several days we lost ground and the crew were disheartened: we seemed to be a sort of Channel *Flying Dutchman*. How we escaped colliding with the many craft crowding the upper part of the Channel has always been a matter of wonder to me. The hazy weather with frequent showers of sleet, and the small show of canvas the storm compelled, hindered us from seeing and manoeuvring. We must have been under the special protection of some good Providence.

At last we managed to work through the Dover Straits, and got into the Haisborough and were driven out by a furious northerly gale. The next day when off Yarmouth the lifeboat came to us. The cowswain said they thought we were in distress: he did not say what made him think so – probably the lifeboat crew got paid each time they launched their boat. I sent letters ashore and offered £100 to any tug that would tow the ship to Hull, a comparatively short distance. I kept the ship hovering in the vicinity for two days, and as no tug appeared I stood round the Kentish Knock and into the North Sea, after a hard sea fight eventually making Flamborough Head, and squared away for the Humber, picking up a tug and Pilot, and anchored in Grimsby Roads after a most trying and harrassing passage of nearly five weeks from Falmouth.

Our ill fortune still remained, for when we got to Hull Roads, a most uneasy anchorage for a large ship, I found we were neaped, and would have to wait several days before there was water to dock.

We entered the William Wright Dock in time, and though we had had unusual detention on the passage home, the voyage was performed in a little over thirteen months, and the financial result was most satisfactory.

LANDSMEN AND SEAMEN

My Seventeenth Voyage

LARNACA

1883–1884

HULL – NORTHFLEET – SAN FRANCISCO – LIVERPOOL

Hull in the months of April and May has a trying climate, and is a depressing place with its very muddy river and unsightly mud banks.

The ship discharged alongside the quay in the Sir William Wright Dock. The Radical shipowning family of Wilson dominated the whole place. The principals are arrogant and domineering; their subordinates verify the old adage 'like Master, like Man'. On going on board one stormy morning Mr Frank Rolleston, the Mate, informed me that one of Wilsons' steamers from Bombay, to expedite the discharge of cargo, had hove out of the wharf into the middle of the dock. The cargo was worked into lighters at both sides. Without asking permission Wilsons' employees had made fast a six-inch hawser to the *Larnaca*'s poop mooring bitts, and as the *Larnaca* was to windward the whole weight of the steamer was borne by her. The hawser had been taken foul of the rail stanchions and the pressure was promising to break them and do other damage. The stevedores also complained that the ship was dragged from the wharf making it difficult for them to work.

Mr Rolleston said he had requested the officer in charge of the steamer to shift the hawser into the fairleads, and so prevent damage, and to run a rope from the steamer to the quay and ease the heavy drag on the *Larnaca*, for it was now blowing hard with squalls. The officer treated his request with offensive rudeness, refusing to do anything. Now Mr Rolleston was the most genial and inoffensive man imaginable, he had a particularly nice manner, so when worked up to such a state of excitement I knew he had met with undeserved and very offensive treatment. The head stevedore also spoke of the over-bearing insolence of those in charge of the steamer. I found that the hawser was likely to do damage at any moment, so hailed the steamer. No one replied. So I asked Mr Rolleston to go on board and ask the officer in charge to speak to me. Shortly a truculent looking middle-aged man appeared.

He demanded, 'What do you want?' I said, 'Are you, Sir, the officer in charge?' 'I am,' he replied. 'Will you give us a rope to hang you, while we shift the hawser before it does harm?' I asked. He said, 'I won't. If there is damage done, Wilsons have money enough to pay for it.' I said, 'You made your rope fast to this ship without permission. You took it round the stanchions instead of through the fairleads, a most unseamanlike thing to do. I want to prevent damage. Please do what I ask.' He was not to be persuaded. A long course of the Wilson haughtiness had killed any civility in him. He said he would do nothing – he would be damned if he would. He was not a sailor, he was a steamboatman. I said 'If in five minutes you don't take steps to ease the strain on my stanchions, I will cut your rope.' He treated my threat with derision. An axe was brought, when the five minutes elapsed the rope was cut. Steamer, lighters, all went with a crash into the dock wall, and the onlookers were amazed that anyone should dare to beard the great Wilsons. The Dockmaster came to me saying that he approved of my action, that the Wilsons were overbearing and tyrannical, but that he durst not say anything or his living would be taken away. They governed the place. Others, the heads of the Dock departments, expressed themselves in a similar manner.

They found another place for their rope; their work was disarranged for some hours.

In the course of a few days I got a letter from Wilsons requesting me to call at their office at 2 p.m. that day. They wanted to enquire into the causes that lead to the cutting of the hawser. My agent, W. Richard Johnston, was a sycophant of the first order. He would have crawled on his stomach to get into the presence of the Wilsons; he begged of me to allow him to accompany me. I said, 'You can come if you want to.' At 2 p.m. prompt we were in Wilsons' office, and as the custom of Radicals and snobs, were kept waiting in the general office for a quarter of an hour. I appeared to be a person of no little interest to the clerks. When the quarter was up I went to the most important looking of the clerks and asked him to see his masters and tell them that if they did not see me at once I would leave. He came back and we were ushered at once into the presence of Mr Arthur Wilson, the Manager, the Marine Superintendent, the officer of the steamer, and a young Wilson. I bowed, announced myself as the Master of the *Larnaca*. My agent grovelled. I told my plain tale, which the one-time truculent officer (now a worm) could not deny. Then the Marine Superintendent drew diagrams and sketches. I suppose this was an accomplishment he wanted to air. I brushed them aside, saying 'Come on board the *Larnaca* then if my tale is not plain enough, you can have it illustrated and hear the evidence of my people.' Mr Arthur Wilson and the Manager copied the manner of the late lamented Queen Victoria, when speaking to a supposed inferior, and spoke through a third person. This third person was my agent W. Richard Johnston whose offensive servility would have sickened men. I turned to them saying, 'Speak to and address me. Johnston has nothing to do with this affair, it is my affair.' After some discussion I said, 'Why do you not summon me, then the magistrate can judge between us? You won't until the ship is ready for sea; then you will put a writ on her. That is mean. I have been told that is what you will do,' and I finished by saying that their 'superior person' tone did not affect me. I wanted nothing from them but that they would appeal at once to the law. The ship was in Hull for several weeks after this. Two days before the time appointed to leave, a writ was put on her. The next day it was taken off. W. Richard Johnston had worked with the Wilsons and written to my Owner who had paid the sum demanded. I never knew what the sum was. I wrote to Mr S., who said he paid it so that I could go in the ship. I was vexed, for the Wilsons wanted showing up in court. By a mean Radical trick they saved their *amour propre*. Mr S. paid the sum out of his private purse. In after years I have been interested in the Wilson fortunes – the baccarat scandal, the Hartopp and Cowley divorce cases, and the ennobling of the head of the house. There is one person of 'no account' who thinks they are a rotten lot.

Mr Giles, the son of a Chester parson and schoolmaster, joined at Hull as Second Mate. He was with me for several years as Second and Chief Mate, and I left him in command of the *Larnaca* when I went home overland to take command of the *Maxwell*. Mr Giles was a gentleman, a good seaman and a very desirable shipmate. I had a very happy time whilst he was with me, for the Chief Mate Rolleston and he suited each other, and there was an absence of those little jars that so much disturb the harmony of life, whether on land or sea.

Having loaded sufficient cargo to ballast her, we left Hull in tow for Northfleet on the Thames where the cargo would be completed; this was the first of many visits to Northfleet, Greenhithe and Gravesend to load cement. I made the acquaintance of a Mr Hoyle who had lately married a remarkably handsome girl. He had then a business as a whiting manufacturer. Some years afterwards he sold this business to Whites and took a position as a department manager, afterwards General Manager. Mr Hoyle was a clever man and invented a process of making cement that gave greater strength to the product and saved 75 per cent of what was, before, waste. I enjoyed for many years the warm friendship of Mr Hoyle, his wife and family. The three sons and three daughters I have seen grow up to man and woman hood – a handsomer set there is not in England, and all of them blessed with equable dispositions and sweet tempers. We had a pleasant time loading at Northfleet. The country was very beautiful in its early summer garb, the woods of Cobham and Rotherville Gardens gave a variety of entertainment; from the ship we viewed the crowds of happy Londoners on their way to and from the different watering places – the traffic to and from London is prodigious.

We sailed for San Francisco early in June and had summer skies and seas until south of the River Plate when we got the commencement of a southern winter. After passing through the Straits of le Maire we had hard gales with snow and very cold weather, all the ropes covered with ice. West of the meridian of Cape Horn we got a strong southeasterly gale – a fair wind to which I was dragging on all the canvas the ship could carry. At 9 p.m. the Second Mate and his watch were rigging mizzen preventer braces when the cry was raised of 'Man overboard!' There is something in that cry that penetrates through a ship in the hardest roaring of a gale. I had taken a star for longitude, for we were nearer the dangerous Tierra del Fuego coast than I liked, and had just finished plotting the position on the chart, when I heard that most portentous cry. I ran on deck and thanked Mr Giles for his presence of mind in 'doing nothing', for a fool would have put the helm down and in doing so the ship in that gale would have been dismasted if not overwhelmed: nothing could be done. The man was miles astern and dead, for the cold was intense; the ship was racing through the water at fourteen to fifteen knots per hour. The night was dark with passing snow and wind squalls. It took all two men could do to steer her. On mustering the watch, we found Jemmy Dux was missing. Poor Jemmy was one of London's strays: when the *Larnaca* had put back to London for repairs the previous voyage, a lad of about sixteen years accosted me in the dock, saying he was starving; he had such a nice face and manner that I took him on board and saw him fed. Both officers asked me to keep him, so I consented and Jemmy turned out well, was a favourite with all and became a fixture in the ship. He was dubbed 'Jemmy Dux': I never knew his right name. Jemmy had no epitaph. A few words in the Logbook, and a few questions asked by the Consul, summed up his exit from a hard world. Perhaps at the last 'muster' Jemmy Dux will not be found wanting.

During my sea life I have seen many killed by falling from aloft and drowned. One of the most affecting tragedies was the fate of an apprentice in the *Alpheta*. This young fellow was the only son of a Captain of the liner *City of Berlin*. Being an only son, his mother would not hear of him going to sea. He would be nothing but a sailor. So at the age of eighteen he was apprenticed. That is far too old, for it needs the body to be pliant to adapt itself to the monkey tricks it is called on to practise at sea in a sailing ship. This lad was willing, and tried to do all his fellows did. One day he was going up the mizzenmast. I told him to be careful: a few minutes afterwards he came tumbling down from aloft, brushing me so closely that he knocked my hat off. Poor lad, he was awfully smashed up; he gained consciousness a few minutes, called on his mother, said he was dying, sank into a coma and died. His father's and mother's grief was poignant to see.

After Jemmy Dux' promotion we made rapid progress and arrived at San Francisco without further untoward occurrence. We kept our crew, a rare event for each man meant much money to the crimps. The only event of our stay here was the passing through of the Princess Louisa and the Duke of Argyle, returning to their Vice

Royalty of Canada, though incognito; they had a warm welcome. On their landing at Market Street a lady commenced the National Anthem, which was taken up by the crowd and sung with fine effect. We loaded a general cargo at the San Francisco wharves for Liverpool. We had a high freight – rates had dropped – and the merchants dribbled the cargo in so that we had long detention. Whilst here we experienced a heavy southeasterly gale. The tugs asked large sums to tow the ships clear of the wharfs, the wind and sea blowing right on. We were one of the few ships that came to no damage.

For the last two voyages I had a Negro steward; he had a most benign expression, a real 'Uncle Tom' face, but was not without guile or the defects of mankind, I found out. On the previous voyage out to Sydney he had done something to seriously offend me, so I told him that I would discharge him on arrival at Sydney. When the time came I told him to come along to the shipping office; he fell on his knees and offered up a prayer to the Deity saying 'tho' his Master persecuted him he would never leave him'. He stuck to that and was my 'old man of the sea' for many years. He professed to have been converted by the Salvation Army, which shortly before had invaded Sydney. He now made it his nightly duty to tuck me in bed, then asked permission to pray, knelt down and prayed fervently, never forgetting a petition that the Almighty would soften his master's hard heart and give him grace to appreciate a good servant. The tears would course down his cheek, and he worked himself up to such a pitch that I could well believe the tales of his ancestors' ju-ju worship in Africa, and the superstitious frenzy of his race at Methodist camp meetings in the Southern States of America. I did not stop him, partially from a natural reverence for all religions and also because I believed he was trying to act up to his professions.

Like all the Jamaican Negroes I have known, he had received a sound education, had a gift for languages, an extraordinary knowledge of the Bible, and I envied him of his really elegant hand writing. I don't know what particularly bad traits he saw in me that he prayed so much for my betterment; so far as he was concerned, my chidings had been for his offensive insolence to the crew, and his neglect to keep his cupboards and drawers in that state of cleanliness that was pleasing to me when I made my periodical examinations. His cooking was excellent and his personal purifications were a part of his religion. According to his lights I think he was earnest in his professions, though he showed nasty tricks of mind that far from accorded with the teachings of Christ. For example, the sail-maker had received Salvation in London, and conducted a Sunday service and Bible readings and prayers amongst the crew on the outward passage. After leaving Sydney the steward started an opposition service and bribed with tit-bits many of the sailmaker's congregation. After a time the steward's 'old Adam' offended all but a few of his disciples, the sailmaker's congregation becoming much enlarged. The demon of envy and jealousy possessed the steward; he enlarged his bribes and blandishments with no avail, for the great majority stuck to the sailmaker. Then after his nightly prayer he proposed that I should issue an order to the effect that anyone neglecting to attend the steward's service would be put in irons and fed on biscuits and water for a day or as long as they were contumonious. This proposition staggered me, and I am afraid that I expressed in violent sea language my opinion of his religion. He was a Negro and had the same perverted sense of Christ's teaching as Pope Innocent the Third and the Grand Inquisitor Torquemada, or the extreme Puritans of the Commonwealth and New England.

I had permitted him to choose his own cook and his choice had fallen on a really amiable little Negro from Martinique. This little fellow was a staunch adherent of the sailmaker's flock; though subservient to the steward in all other matters, in this he was adamant, so the steward, to be revenged, took measures so that the cook's Christmas plum pudding should be spoiled. The crew did not act as the steward thought they would and complain to me: they had gauged his malevolence. This did not come to my know-ledge until the end of the voyage and was the last straw, and I discharged him. He made frantic efforts to keep his job, got the soft side of Mr T. the Owner, who pleaded for him, and pleaded with my mother to use her influence. I did not take him, for both officers expressed the opinion that he was a cause of disturbance. Negroes are better away from white men.

The only episode on the homeward voyage was falling in with a Welsh barque from Coquimbo short of provisions, which we supplied. At this time, when there was practically no penalty for starving or poisoning merchant ship crews, there were certain mean, sordid and contemptible shipmasters and Owners who purposely took their ships to sea on the homeward passage short of provisions, knowing that the trade routes were crowded with sailing ships and they could beg or buy all they required. Even if they had to pay for what they got, the cost would only be a pittance of what they would have paid if they had bought at the port they had left, and many of the decent shipowners made no charge, thinking that a protracted passage had made the shortage. There were far too many pernicious and sordid Owners who really were criminal in their dealings with their crews: shipping legislation was needed.

My old Captain told me he had served an apprenticeship in the *Josephine* of Workington, owned and commanded by Captain Isaac Scott – afterwards a magistrate, who left over £70,000 at his death. He fed his crew on the poorest provisions and tyrannically worked them. One voyage coming home from the West Indies in winter, the main royal mast was carried away. After passing the Western Islands, he kept all hands working in the daytime, shifting the fore-topgallant mast to the main and vice versa; the sails were never set the weather was so stormy. One man was lost overboard, and when paying the crew off he tried to be genial and condescending to a fine old sailor; the old chap turned on him and said he was morally guilty for the loss of the man, and that he had killed him by cruel treatment and useless exposure in shifting the masts. He then solemnly cursed the Captain – and fell down with a seizure: he died within twelve hours.

With steam instead of sail, and Government inspection of seamen's food, the lot of seafarers today is luxurious compared to thirty years ago. It is a pity some of the bad Owners and Masters had not like measure meted out to them.

We arrived at Liverpool in June after a comfortable and quick voyage.

THE CAPTAIN MEETS A BEAR

My Eighteenth Voyage
LARNACA
1884–1885

LIVERPOOL – SAN FRANCISCO – PORT COSTA –
QUEENSTOWN – FLEETWOOD

The ship was fixed to load a general cargo for San Francisco and after discharging she entered the Salthouse Dock. I took a holiday and went for a three weeks' tour through the Lake District with my old Captain Can.

We trained to Harrington, spent the weekend there and left for Keswick by an early train on Monday; we spent that day visiting places of interest, lunched, and arranged for a boat to row us to the head of the Lake. We landed near the Borrowdale Hotel, dismissed our boatman and walked into Rosthwaite. We put up at a hotel there for a week, making long daily excursions into the country, and in the evenings had plenty of amusement chatting to the farmers. In an open air shelter sat the landlady's husband, far gone with consumption. He was cheerful and said he was much better since he adopted the open air treatment. He died shortly after. Two years passed before I visited Rosthwaite again. The landlady had in the meantime married a stalwart dalesman. She kept a good table and a comfortable house and her charges were very reasonable.

On the evening we announced our intention of leaving the following morning, all the people tried to persuade us to prolong our stay. So we promised, if it was convenient and feasible, to return that way. We very much enjoyed a long day on the fells amongst the sheep; it was a delightful picnic. Quite a crowd gave us a send off and two young fellows went with us to Westmorland. We had milk at the farmhouse there, served by a stalwart lassie in short skirts, showing the stoutest pair of legs that Captain Can said he had ever seen.

In June Watendlath and its tarn are dismal and gloomy. It must be a melancholy place in winter. We crossed the fells to Thirlmere, a dreary journey amidst swamps and peat pits, and came out above Daleshead and Armboth. The scenery was very fine. We deplored that for utilitarian motives this beautiful lake had to be converted into a reservoir for Manchester. We crossed by the Roman bridge (or rather Ancient British bridge) which has large boulders for stepping stones and came to the hamlet of Wythburn. In modest quarters at the Inn we spent several days, visiting St John's Vale, Lowthwaite, Wythburn Church and walking along the flank of Helvellyn on the evening before we left.

A spirit merchant's traveller was at the Inn. A glass of spirits was, by his orders, placed before Captain Can and me. This aroused Captain Can's ire. He told the poor man he was taking a great liberty and it was an impertinence, and left the room. It was explained to me that it was a custom for a spirit traveller to treat all the inmates when getting orders, for the good of the house. Captain Can would not be appeased; like all shipmasters of the old school, he was touchy where his dignity was concerned and very independent.

That night we consulted our Ordnance Survey map and plotted a course through Dunmail Raise, Grasmere, Rydal and Windermere, making our headquarters at Grasmere. By breakfast time we had a bright summer's day. We commenced our delightful walk by Thirlmere, through the Raise of Dunmail, adding our stones to the cairn of Dunmail the last King of Cumberland: then such a view was presented that has not its superior in the world, for Captain Can and I have seen most of the beauty spots. The sun was shining in an unclouded sky, the Vale of Grasmere with a glimpse of its Lake, surrounded by mountains, spacious plantations with whitewashed houses peeping from amidst the trees, the tender greens of early summer, the wealth of rhododendron flowers. All sparkling with raindrops in the clear air, it made a picture of beauty that I will never forget. Captain Can said he was glad he had seen such lovely scenery, and never dreamed our island held such beauty.

We left Grasmere with regret, tramped by Elterwater to Hawkes-head and stayed there for two days while visiting all round the shores of Coniston, had a look at Ruskin and his lovely home, and took train for Furness Abbey where we parted, he for Liverpool and I for Harrington to bid farewell, for my ship would be ready to sail in a few days. This tour does, of course, not belong to my sea yarns. I mention it so fully so that you will understand that such pleasant interludes diversified my life, and I returned to my sea life invigorated and full of energy.

Leaving Liverpool in July, we had warm weather and scant winds in the northern hemisphere. After crossing the Equator there was plenty of wind, and south of 50° south bitterly cold weather. One dark night a man reported that one of the apprentices were missing: on searching round the decks we found the body behind the spare spar abreast the main hatch.

This voyage we met with such persistent south winds that we were driven so far to the westward that we passed close to the seldom visited Easter Island, a volcanic island twelve hundred feet high, containing some huge stone figures and other remains of a lost people. Now it is inhabited by a few hundred South Sea Islanders, and white men who have a lease for sheep farming from the Chilean Government, who claim sovereignty.

We arrived at San Francisco early in November; after discharging, the freights were so low that I went into Mission Bay and laid up for a time. I was introduced to a Captain and his wife from White-haven and asked them to spend New Year's Day with me, which they did. During dinner the Captain's conversation was all about how he was Master in his own household – his wife would despise a husband who allowed his wife to dictate to him – and much more to the same effect, Madam modestly assenting to his affirmations. My young officers were duly impressed. I remarked that from what I remembered my mother would not agree to such a creed, and as a bachelor I had observed that wives got their own way either by diplomacy or force of will. He said that he scorned a husband who was under petticoat government. Madam chipped in, to say that if she had such a man she would make him wear petticoats, and a woman's place was to obey. In the evening I went in the boat to land them, and was persuaded to go aboard their ship and spend the night. On getting there I was content to be quiet, but the Captain wanted to go up town and see the New Year's festivities. He told his wife he would not stay an hour and would bring her a bag of

Nagasaki in 1868, the harbour sheltered by low hills. The oar-propelled boats used for towing and lightering can be seen; the Dutch enclave is on the far shore at the head of the harbour.

Yokohama in 1868, with ships lying off the causeway to Kanagawa. (Both pictures are from Signor Beato's *Photographic Views of Japan*, by kind permission of the Victoria and Albert Museum)

A view of Valparaiso, Chile which Fraser visited in the *Alpheta* in 1880 during the war between Chile, Peru and Bolivia. The picture shows the simple wooden buildings and Indians in traditional dress. (Coloured aquatint, *circa* 1840.)

Wool clippers at Sandwich pier, Melbourne (1874). This pier was owned by the Hobson's Bay Railway Co.

The *Larnaca*, 1497 tons, built in iron by Royden of Liverpool in 1878. Her measurements were 234.5 × 38 × 23 ft. Captain Fraser commanded her for four voyages. She was a fast ship, but due to adverse weather once took five weeks from Falmouth to Hull.

Southwest India Dock, London in the 1880s, with foreign-going sailing ships.

Circular Quay, Sydney in 1880. The ship in the foreground was the *Candida*, 1222 tons, built by the Whitehaven Shipbuilding Co. in 1875.

Another view of Circular Quay with the *Cutty Sark* alongside. In 1880 she became an Australian wool clipper and made some of her fastest passages in that trade.

Sierra Miranda seen in Frederickstaad. In 1888 she sailed from Cardiff to Cape Town with a cargo of coal at the same time as the *Maxwell*, taking over fifty days as against the *Maxwell's* passage of forty-six.

The *Umbria*, on which Captain Fraser crossed the Atlantic in the winter of 1887 (the year in which she held the Blue Ribbon of the Atlantic) to take over the *Maxwell* in Liverpool. He evidently found this an interesting trip, and an enjoyable rest from the responsibilities of command. *Umbria* was one of the last two Cunarders to carry sail.

The *Maxwell* proved a well designed and weatherly ship, and a sister ship, the *Grace Harwar*, was commissioned. She is shown here in lieu of a picture of the *Maxwell*. Both were iron; the *Maxwell*, 1865 tons, was built in 1887 and measured 269 × 39 × 23.5 ft, somewhat larger than the *Larnaca*.

Guests at a Captain's reception in Whitehaven in the 1860s. It is probable that at least some of these ladies were connected with shipping, if not Captains' wives.

The *Kircudbrightshire*, which struck the *Maxwell* off the Columbia River, Oregon in 1891.

Langton Graving Dock, Liverpool with a sailing ship inside.

After severe weather, exposed roadsteads such as this often presented scenes of stranded ships blown ashore after dragging anchors or breaking their cables, colliding as they went, or grounding in the shallows. There was seldom any adequate forewarning of such storms at this time, and sailing ships in such circumstances were virtually helpless.

After the *Maxwell* had been salvaged and sold. Fraser's next command (until 1899) was the *Lynton*, a handsome new four-masted barque. Here she is seen leaving Maryport under tow.

oysters, of which she was very fond. On getting up town I saw he was very partial to free drinks and eggnog, a Californian speciality on New Year's Day dispensed freely and gratuitously. I only got him away by threatening to go to a hotel for the night. On the way down I was seized with painful rheumatic pains and had to rest many times before we reached the wharfs: there was no vehicle to be had on this lonely route. On getting on the wharf, a white-robed figure rushed from the gangway and seized hold of the Captain, belabouring and unbraiding him. I have never seen such a fury. I stayed behind until they entered the ship and cabin. I was too ill to walk more than a mile to the nearest decent hotel, so went on board, where I found the two Mates. Then I learned that what I saw was not an uncommon occurrence. She was a termagant and ruled him with an iron hand: perhaps he wanted ruling. In the course of an hour he came on deck to find me. On entering the cabin I found Madam's white dress was a '*robe de nuit*'; she was sipping punch and eating oysters. I declined joining, went to bed, and cleared out before breakfast and dropped their acquaintance. I found it a painful and disgraceful exhibition and never again made acquaintance so freely.

Freights improving, the ship was fixed to load a cargo of wheat. The loading was effected at Port Costa. One evening I had occasion to go to the town to see the chandler who supplied the ship with fresh provisions daily. The town consisted of a few rows of wood shanties, the only light that was thrown by kerosene lamps from the open doors and uncurtained windows. By a shaded corner something big and hairy with a very bad breath jumped on me, hugging tightly. At the first I was naturally startled, then I felt and partially saw that I was in the embrace of a full-grown black bear, more or less tame. I called out to attract the attention of its owner and as I called the beast squeezed me so tightly that I was afraid that my ribs would be broken. I refrained from shouting and the strain was relaxed. On again attempting to get someone to hear, the bear made a vicious snarl and pressed the wind out of me, making my ribs sore. When I was passive the strain relaxed. The last squeeze taught me to be patient, for the beast would do me serious harm if I annoyed it by shouting. I was kept a prisoner for quite a long time, when a railway man came along. I told him my predicament. He called some people who brought lights. They tried to pull the beast off: this enraged it. Fortunately, it was muzzled or it would have used its teeth. As it was, it squeezed me dreadfully and with its hind claws tore my pants to threads and badly scratched my legs. Force, short of killing the beast, would not relieve me. There was quite a crowd and my position was not dignified. When a woman came along with a basin of some sweet stuff which she put to the bear's nose, he relaxed his grip, then released me and went after the tempting bowl. I was glad to be relieved and felt sore for days. My scratches were well washed with diluted carbolic acid and dressed. They mended with little trouble. The scars are there to remind me of a dangerous, humorous episode. In Britain I would have had damages from the owner, in America I was thankful to get off so well – the beast had broken its chains.

For the first time I had dealings with the 'Frisco boarding masters. The sailors were terrorized and have no say in their disposal – the worst form of slavery. I engaged Tommy Challown, a famous ex prize fighter, as my shipping master or go-between the boarding masters and myself. I always found that he did his part fairly and honestly.

We left in company of several ships; off the Horn we fell in with the American clippers *Kennebec* and *Iroquois*; in a very strong westerly gale these ships carried an enormous press of sail, not to be beaten. I was foolish enough to drive my ship and we kept ahead of them. Wellington never wished more fervently for night and Blucher than I did for 'night or less wind'. When night shut down I reduced sail to topsails without losing anything. Next morning we had thick weather and got among the ice, which caused us some anxiety. We pressed on taking great risks and cleared the ice region. We arrived in Queenstown five days before the *Kennebec*, and passed the *Iroquois* bound to Liverpool on our passage from Queenstown to Fleetwood.

In Queenstown I stayed at a small hotel which was infested with many nice-looking Irish girls. These girls captured many seafarers and were not particular as to the nationality of their husbands; their charms enmeshed many Scandinavians, I heard.

Getting orders for Fleetwood, we were favoured with gentle winds and anchored in Morecambe Bay on the fourth day from Queenstown. There were several American and British ships there so I had a pleasant time discharging.

A VOYAGE BEGUN ON A FRIDAY

My Nineteenth Voyage
LARNACA
1885–1886

SAN FRANCISCO – PORT COSTA – QUEENSTOWN –
HAVRE DE GRACE

After ballasting, we left Fleetwood in tow for Cardiff where we drydocked to paint, then entered the Roath Basin to discharge ballast and load a cargo of steel blooms (ingots) and coke.

We left Cardiff Docks late in the afternoon. Early next morning, before daylight, we were making sail off Lundy Island, prior to discharging the Pilot and tow boat, when I noticed something like an oilskin coat falling from the main topsail yard. There was a sickening thud: it was the body of one of the men. He was dead. From enquiries I learned that he was subject to epileptic fits: of course he should not have come to sea. I suppose he had no other way of earning his living. The tugboat master refused to take his body ashore, saying 'The man was dead. To take him ashore would give useless trouble and cause expense. Better by far to bury him at sea.' I thought so too. The Pilot and tug left and as soon as sail was set and the ship ten miles from land the body was decently committed to the deep. He was a native of Austria, twenty-two years of age. Someone would wait in vain for his return home.

We had rather a harrassing time before we reached the region of the Northeast Trades and I was reminded that no luck attended a ship that sailed from port on a Friday. A few degrees north of the Equator we had severe shocks of earthquake, which frightened the crew, broke crockery and glass, and made all think the ship had struck a sunken reef. At 2 p.m. the ship was slipping through the water at about six knots, the sky was almost cloudless and the sea smooth, when the first shock set everything dancing, there was a rumbling sound as if both cables were running out, or the ship driving over a coral reef; this was followed by a more severe shock, making the ship tremble and masts quiver and jerk. There was a horrible noise; a mile away on the lee quarter the sea was agitated and clouds of vapour or smoke arose; this last shock appeared to last for several minutes. The crew were frightened and all the watch below hurried on deck thinking the ship was ashore. The carpenter I caught sounding the pumps. Submarine earthquakes are quite as startling as land quakes. I have experienced both.

On the polar edge of the Southeast Trades one of the men and an apprentice named Pearson were with the grains and harpoon spearing dolphin from the martingale back ropes, the ship travelling seven knots, when Pearson while making a cast slipped from his bowline and fell into the sea. The dividing water from the bow threw him clear of the stem and I caught a glimpse of him on the quarter. I threw a lifebuoy in his direction and put the helm down, throwing the ship aback, and sent hands aloft to keep him in view and direct the boat. The boat was got over and manned in quick time, and directed by the lookout aloft picked him up after he had been half an hour in shark-infested waters. He could swim a very little, sufficient to enable him to get to the lifebuoy that luckily had fallen near him. After a good sleep he was quite well again. Pearson was eighteen years old at the time. He was intelligent and bright, his face was nice to look on, though from its serious cast and formation it was more fitted to adorn a man of forty-five or fifty than a boy. His father, now dead, had been a prominent doctor with a large practice in Leeds. After finishing his apprenticeship and passing for Second Mate, I lost sight of him for some years, then I received a letter from him. He was then an officer in the P & O mail boats. Some time afterwards I met a Leeds lady who was a friend of his family. She told me that he had taken his life, through a love disappointment, and sent me the newspaper with a full account of the inquest. A romantic story was told there.

Off the Horn we had a severe time; we were driven back by tremendous gales and lost sails. The lower foretopsail yard gave lots of trouble. The crane and sling broke, and the crew suffered much in securing the yard and rigging jury slings and crane. The weather was bitterly cold, ice and snow with gales of hurricane force and tremendous seas. At one time we could not show a thread of canvas for five days. The absence of observations, for the sky was obscured all the time, made me anxious to get on the other tack as the sea and wind was driving the ship near the coast of Tierra del Fuego. The sea was so high that to attempt wearing under bare poles would have swamped the ship, neither could we make sail in such a hurricane. At dawn on the sixth day the wind took off and there on the lee beam not three miles off were the glacious and snow-covered cliffs of Desolation Island, with another ship, also under bare poles, in company. This was a thrilling escape. We now were able to make sail and were forced to again stand far south; in latitude 60° we got a favourable wind and got away from the most inclement and dismal portion of the seas. After such an experience the balmy Southeast Trades gave us the greatest pleasure and enjoyment. During the cruel six weeks of misery unutterable, the crew had got despondent. Their superstitious belief in unlucky Friday's sailing demoralized them and they moved about like damned men. The officers and apprentices bore their suffering well and did their best to liven up the men. From this experience I, for the future, avoided sailing on Friday. I was free from the silly superstition, yet I took into consideration the beliefs of my crew.

Through the Pacific we had delightful weather, which we fully appreciated as none could do as those who had gone through six weeks of the hardships found in a mid-winter passage south of Cape Horn.

We arrived at San Francisco at the end of September and found that with all our detention we had made the best passage from Europe for the last six months. Ships arriving after us reported similar miserable experiences to ours off the Horn.

After the ship anchored in the Bay and all sail was unbent, the crimps were allowed on board. To stop them would indeed be seeking for trouble for they have the power to harrass a shipmaster. The law in the 'home of the brave and the land of the free' gives poor protection. Dollars and dollars' worth rule in the United States. Before going to the wharf we had to lie at anchor in the Bay for five days. For the first day the crew resisted all the efforts of the crimps to get them to leave. The second day, with the help of rye whisky, promises and blandishments, and in a few cases terrorism (for no one knows better than crimps the foibles of human nature), they netted eight men. The other ten ABs could not be moved. On the evening of the third day several of the crimps gave up, or pretended to; then a notorious member, who had killed several men, addressed them to the effect that they had a good ship. Captain F. always fed his crews well and he advised them to stop and not be led away by men who wanted to make a pile out of them. He shook them all by the hand and left a bottle of whisky: he knew that if he had offered them a drink they would have refused, being suspicious of his motives, and leaving the bottle was a master stroke. Next morning this same crimp called on board at breakfast time and chatted cheerfully with them, giving them a basket of eggs, fruit and soft bread – never mentioning desertion. At dinner time he called again, and gave them cigars and left another bottle. That evening when I returned on board Mr Giles told me that five men had gone. I was surprised, for the five were all hard old shellbacks who were notorious stickers (i.e. indifferent sailors and workers, but who stuck to a good ship; the officers would sooner be without them). As they knocked off work at 6 p.m. the crimp came alongside with two runners, came on board and addressed the men as follows:

'Now boys, hav'n't I always advised you to stick to your good ship? Now I didn't want to see nice fellows like you in the hands of fellows who would "shanghai" you. Now I have something good to offer you: see this telegram – it's from a friend of mine. He wants five live men to go up the Sacramento River to catch salmon. Your pay will be twenty dollars a week, everything found, doughnuts for morning coffee and a nigger to wait on ye – and I now advise you to take my offer. Here is to your good luck – have a drink on the head of it boys, and see here, I am to give you each a gold double eagle.' He handed to each one of the five a massive coin. 'On that you will have a good time for two or three days. My friend comes for you in his launch on Saturday.' Then he turns to his two satellites – 'Give 'em a hand to pack up.' 'Which is your bunk?' 'Which your's?' – bundled their things together, and had them in the boat alongside before the poor fellows gathered their wits together. When in the boat, and before starting, the crimp emptied his pockets, turned over his money, and with much lamenting bewailed the loss of something. On his henchman enquiring the cause of his trouble, he said 'You know that marked double eagle my poor dead wife gave me for luck on her deathbed? Well I've lost it. My God, I would have sooner lost my head.' Then quickly turning to one of his entrapped victims, 'Let me look at the $20 piece I gave you.' The man handed it to him 'No, that is not it . . . yours, yours, yours,' until he had all he had given on board in his possession. He put the five gold pieces in his pocket, gave Mr Giles a knowing wink, and gave orders to pull away. Those five men were shipped the next day, with three months' advance to work up and of which they had not received a cent. Each man was worth £20 to the crimps. If they dared to say anything they would get beaten cruelly, perhaps killed.

The five men left on board were young men waiting to go up for the Second Mate's examination. The crimps did not bother them. My permission was asked to allow a young Scotsman to be hidden on board. He had been persuaded to leave his ship by his chum, a much older man; they were in the clutch of Smith, the most infamous of all the Barbary coast (a 'Frisco waterside Ratcliffe Highway) boarding masters. The man had demurred at being shipped on board a Yankee ship notorious for the cruelty practised on the crew by her bucko mates; as he could not be persuaded, the bullies called 'runners' employed by Smith beat him so cruelly, gouging out one of his eyes and crippling him, that the young fellow fled from the house. After hiding for some days he made his way to the Longbridge Wharf where the *Larnaca* was discharging, which is miles away from the City wharfs, and enlisted the sympathy of my young men and officers. I cautioned them to carefully keep the story he had told them and the fact that he was on board a dead secret, for if it was known the crimps would not allow a man to be shipped on board my vessel and would give me much trouble whilst lying at Lowbridge.

I had to travel to town daily. For the first mile I had to walk among the sandhills, then take the tram where civilization commenced. The sandhills were infested by criminals who stealthily crept behind belated shipfolk on their way to the vessels at Lowbridge, sandbagged and robbed them. Many shipmasters were robbed and maltreated. I had a narrow escape, only eluding them by my swift running.

One morning on my way to town I was accosted on the tram by a Welshman who told me he was Master of a barque lying in Mission Bay. I expressed my admiration for a fine new ship lying there which he said was the *Pengwern*, owned by Caernarvon people, acquaintances of his. He then told of the delinquencies of the Captain, a dissolute, drunken, worthless man; he thought it his duty to write to the Owners and acquaint them with the Captain's doings and how he was spending their money. Only two nights before he was so helplessly drunk that the driver and conductor of the tram we were now on, on arrival at the sandhill terminus had dumped him out on the sand, and there he spent the night; and a lot more of the man's sins. He showed spite, envy and jealousy and I gathered he had been a candidate for the command of the *Pengwern*. I put the most of his detractions down to the envious strain in the Welsh character.

A week after this I had occasion to call at the stevedores' office. In the vestibule there were two doors, one leading to a common room where some shipmasters, and the loafing hangers-on always to be found there waiting for free drinks, or to act as pilots to shady places, congregated round the stove, smoking and talking. The other door opened into the private office, where I went. Out of this office was a door into the common room. After I had done my business, I was leaving when the stevedore called my attention to a conversation going on in the common room. (Listeners never hear good of themselves.) I recognized the voice as that of my Welsh fellow traveller on the tram. He was decrying myself and Lindsay of the *Eaton Hall* as being arrogant, proud and unsociable, keeping aloof, etc. I slipped into the room, slapped him on the back, turned to the man he was sitting next to and asked him if he was Captain of the *Pengwern*: he said he was. I said 'I am Fraser of the *Larnaca* – this man I heard speaking disparagingly of Lindsay and myself, well, he introduced himself to me on the tram the other morning, and told me you were a dissolute drunken man, unfit for your trust, that you had been thrown out of the tramcar on to the sand and were so helplessly drunk that you spent the night there. Also, that he felt it his duty to write to Wales to your Owners, to let them know how you were behaving and wasting their money.' Then I turned to my Welsh tram acquaintance, saying 'Lindsay and I are too proud to vilify a man we pretend friendship for: I leave you now to explain matters to the Captain of the *Pengwern*.' There was quite a sensation. It would take more than the sliminess of a Lloyd George to get him out of the mire.

After discharging the ship towed to Port Costa to load wheat for Europe. To pass the time I went duck shooting. I had not much success, though there were plenty of wildfowl. I was surprised to see the large number of sturgeon caught by Italian fishermen: the flesh is very good and they ought to compete with Russia in the supply of caviare.

I learned that the bear that caused me no little pain last voyage had badly mauled his owner, so he had been killed and eaten last fall. Those who partook of him said his flesh was tender and of fine flavour. His cured skin I offered ten dollars for: the owner would not part with it and said it was an elegant rug for his kids to roll about on, and they would break their hearts if he sold it.

Having finished loading, we towed to San Francisco to finish necessary business and procure a crew for the homeward passage. Seamen were scarce; there was a demand for the seal, whale and haddock fisheries. Ships were detained, the boarding master demanded a bonus (blood money) though they were more reasonable than was expected, owing to the scarcity. The men were picked up and put on board one or two at a time, and to prevent them being stolen or deserting the ships employed big burly men who had a constable's licence to see that no one tampered with them. Each man represented over $100 paid by the ship when he was put on board. These constables were armed with large revolvers, and if occasion called did not hesitate to use them. Every ship got a percentage of landsmen shanghaied on board, drugged and drunk. Poor chaps, I've heard many pitiful tales from them how by hocus-pocus tricks they had been lured into the net of the crimps. I, of course, having paid for them made them take the passage to Europe.

One night I was taking boat at Valley Street Wharf for the ship, when I saw the crimps and runners taking several men to the steps to convey them on board. The men were unwilling and resisting their efforts; there was much excited and waterfront language, then blows and the sound of a pistol shot; I saw a man fall. He was shot through the heart, quite dead. A notorious boarding master, slain by a young Swedish sailor in revenge for shanghaing his brother, who was lost. He was convicted of murder and, a rare thing in

California, hanged. The brotherhood of boarding masters having such power, they doubtless thought, did this man get off it would form a dangerous precedent and life for no crimp would be safe.

During my enforced stay to procure a crew I learned of a sad tragedy, the outcome of a senile passion and drink. A Liverpool ship had laid at the same wharf as the *Larnaca* when discharging and I had a nodding acquaintance with the Captain, apparently a man of sixty. I heard that he had been a man of good reputation who for a generation had commanded Liverpool ships. A year or so ago his wife had died. It was said that since then he had taken more drink, and his conduct was peccant; he had a grown-up family. San Francisco is a place where the nationalities that make its population have a yearly custom of pleasure picnics. The Bay is full of lovely resorts; a steamer is chartered, and with a band a joyous company travel to the place and have a very good time. This Captain accepted an invitation from the stewards of the Canadian picnic. He was introduced to the very young widow of a doctor and in three days married her; in a week her money requirements had been so much that the agents got frightened at the amounts he was drawing and wired the Owners, who instructed them not to advance beyond a certain sum. She ran up bills for jewellery, etc and things came to a climax when the agents were forced to advertise that as agents of the Owners they would not be responsible for any debts contracted by the Master. Next day the Captain's dead body was found alongside the ship. I heard afterwards that the widow went to Liverpool and very much troubled the Owners and his family.

After a wait of eight days I got the number required to complete my crew, and sailed to Queenstown for orders. By the time our ship was off the Horn our scratch crew was got into order. We had an uneventful passage, arriving at Queenstown 104 days from San Francisco, and I received orders to proceed to Le Havre, where we arrived in five days. Mr Sproule with his wife came over and stayed at the splendid hotel facing the sea, and Mr Giles and I went home for a fortnight's holiday. This completed my nineteenth voyage.

PASSENGER BY TRAIN AND SHIP

My Twentieth Voyage
LARNACA
1887

LE HAVRE – NEWPORT – SAN FRANCISCO. OVERLAND
TO LIVERPOOL

On the eleventh day at home I got a telegram from Mr Sproule to rejoin the ship at Le Havre, as she would be ready for sea in a few days. Mr Giles joined my train at Crewe and we had a pleasant journey via Newhaven and Dieppe. In passing Rouen we decided to stop for a few hours to visit the fine Gothic cathedral, the old church of St Ouen which is quite splendid, and the interesting stone carvings depicting the Field of the Cloth of Gold. We were both much impressed with the cathedral, though we thought the iron central spire was a monstrosity. Carved stone is wanted there. I don't think the artistic French nation will be satisfied until the cheap-looking deformity is supplanted by something more in harmony with the original beautiful conception. The interior is grand; the pillars, roof, paintings and carvings exquisite. The relics of Joan of Arc and Richard Cœur de Lion should make this cathedral a place of pilgrimage for both the French and British. The ancient church of St Ouen we thought quite as beautiful as the cathedral. We had not as much time as we would have liked, and only viewed hurriedly the lovely chapels and paintings, promising ourselves a longer visit to this interesting historical place at some future time. I regret that time for me has not yet arrived.

On arrival at Le Havre the ship was found ready to tow away.

We left in tow for Newport, Monmouthshire where we were to load a cargo of steel and coke for San Francisco. We had a pleasant passage and caught quite a lot of mackerel. The English coast looked lovely; I was much struck with the beauties of the north coast of Cornwall, Devon and Somersetshire. We arrived at Newport and drydocked there, then went into the Alexandra Dock to load. There was nothing interesting about Newport, and I had not time to visit the many beautiful places in the neighbourhood.

Visiting Le Havre reminded me of a curious experience I had had there on my first visit, when Third Mate of the *Carricks*. The talk at the hotel was all about a play at the Theatre. It hinged on the execution of Charles I at Whitehall, so we went to see it. The trial in Westminster Hall, the King's farewell to his children, the execution outside Whitehall, the scene on the scaffold were so realistic that I have not ceased wondering how the actors managed such a clever deception. Of course I have seen Indian jugglers perform most wonderful feats, and have witnessed Maskelyne and Cook's phenomenal legerdemain, yet nothing else has left me with such a feeling of puzzled wonderment. The staging of the scaffold was perfectly in accord with tradition and history: there was Bishop Juxon; the King, dressed in black velvet, his face and figure like Van Dyke's paintings; the Executioner and assistants, and the Commonwealth guards. The slight preparation for the beheading – the handing by the King of a book to the Bishop – the King's last word – his head on the block – with one blow severed – then the head with blood streaming from it exhibited by an assistant. People were invited on the scaffold to view the head and body. I went and saw the severed head and trunk. The throat, windpipe, flesh and bones of the severed part were dripping with blood. I touched the forehead, which was clammy to the touch and had the pallor and appearance of death, and came away sickened and fully convinced of the reality of what I saw. I was told that the play was not allowed in England. How was it done? The living man who talked on the scaffold to the people and to Bishop Juxon – when was he changed for the artistically made dummy? The dummy was a perfect copy in every particular of the anatomy of the human neck, so the elder men declared; there was endless discussion. The thing was a mystery, and with me remained so. The cleverest managed jugglery conceivable. It is now forty-five years since and I am still perplexed.

We left Newport in the latter end of August bound for San Francisco and had a pleasant and uneventful passage, arriving at our destination the middle of December. Immediately on reporting at the agents I was handed a cablegram requesting me to return to Liverpool to assume command of the *Maxwell*, a fine new ship of 1,900 tons registration. She would load a general cargo for Australia and would not be loaded for some five weeks, so I need not hurry on my journey, and I could appoint who I wished as Captain of the *Larnaca*. With much pleasure, I acquainted my Chief Mate of his promotion to the command. Mr Giles was an exceedingly nice fellow, a good seaman and a man of the highest character. We had spent four years very happily together and I was delighted that this step would enable him to marry, for he had long been engaged to a girl of good family in Chester. Mr Giles was highly pleased with this stroke of unexpected luck, and I may mention now that he made an ideal ship's Master and gave the Owners every satisfaction. His first passage as Master was a notable one: ninety-two days from Portland, Oregon to Queenstown. This has only been exceeded once by, I believe, a passage of ninety-one days. Captain Giles married; his wife sailed with him and two children were born on board the *Larnaca*. When the *Larnaca* was sold he retired from the sea, and I think engaged in farming pursuits in the South of England. Giles was one of the real good men I had the good fortune to meet; he was *suaviter in modo, fortiter in re*. He lives in my remembrances.

For several days I was engaged with Captain Giles for the transfer of the command. My chronometers and nautical instruments, etc and charts were of the best, and better for a young Master than quite new ones for the chronometers had 'found themselves' and the charts, all 'blueback',[1] had my tracks and notes, a good guidance with useful information, and all the *Sailing Directions* were up to date including the last magnificent work of the U.S. Hydrographic Bureau. Captain Giles empowered me to refit myself with similar instruments, charts and nautical books. I presented him with my library and copies of several useful works, and also offered that should we meet at any time, I would if he wished exchange the new for my former possessions.

---

[1] Published by one of several private firms in England, rather than by the Admiralty.

Several kind acquaintances gave a dinner at the Baldwin Hotel the night before I left, and quite a lot of champagne was drunk. The next day I left San Francisco, joining the Union Pacific Railway at Oakland. I now parted with Giles and the nice fellows who had accompanied me over the Bay and started on my week's voyage across the continent, then a rare experience.

I had only six fellow through passengers. I suppose the time of the year (mid-December) accounted for the small number going East. Among them was a lady and her husband who tenanted the private portion of the car. He was a Drexel, a member of the famous millionaire banking family of Philadelphia. His wife had been staying in California for her health for several months and was returning to her home to undergo an operation. She was a nice woman and sociable. The others were rich Californians returning to their homes in the Eastern States to spend Christmas. Nowhere in the world can kinder or more hospitable people be found than among Americans. I have had much kindness shown me by them. Their absolute freedom from snobbery and ostentation, their cheery goodwill and generosity make them most charming companions. During my many visits to American cities I always came away with an overwhelming sense of gratitude for hospitality that had been extended to me. Several of my fellow travellers to San Francisco always came to see me and made my stay there very pleasant.

Before describing my journey across the continent I will relate an amusing episode in connection with a Saint Andrew's Banquet I attended at the Palace Hotel, San Francisco, the previous voyage. No one would credit the appalling heights, depths and lengths to which a dour and sedate Scotsman will go on these festive occasions, in boasting and glorification of his race and country. I have been a guest at Saint Andrew's and 'Nights with Burns' in all parts of the world, and I have often blushed for the absolute absence of modesty in the speeches made on these occasions. No American orator on the Fourth of July, or Irishman on Saint Patrick's Day, depicting the glories of his race could approach the Scot on these anniversaries.

On this occasion everything was done to give *éclat* to the proceedings. It was a super banquet in honour of the election to the Presidency of the Saint Andrew's Society of a young Scotsman who was hailed as a financial genius and referred to by the papers as the Napoleon of Finance. He was the head of the Nevada Bank and the many commercial and mining undertakings controlled by that corporation. Unfortunately, the belief in his infallibility and genius received a rude shock some time afterwards. His schemes went all amiss, and another pseudo-Napoleon sank into oblivion.

We met at 7 p.m., some three hundred of us, in the parlours of the Palace Hotel (no ladies!) with the stewards notable by huge blue rosettes. One of them mounted a chair and requested the company to follow the pipers two by two into the dining hall. The seats were numbered corresponding with the tickets and we marched round and round the tables until all were seated in their proper places. My friend Lindsay was next to the British Vice Consul and I next to him. Amongst the guests were the Governor of the State, the General commanding at the Presidio, the Admiral from Mare Island, the Mayor of San Francisco and many other lesser lights. And all the Scotsmen of the State from mine managers to merchants.

All the Scottish dishes from cock-a-leekie soup to haggis were served – the last-named dish being brought in headed by pipers in the full Highland garb – and all the dishes in season, so that all tastes were catered to. Champagne and other wines accompanied the meal. Then strong whisky punch was dispensed during the speeches by men in Highland dress; the usual toasts were proposed in pompous speeches, and honoured – 'The land of our fathers', 'Bonnie Scotland', etc.

The orator claimed everyone of note from Adam to the present time to be a Scotsman or at least married to a Scottish lassie. Amongst others, he claimed that the ruling President of the United States was a Scotsman, saying that his father had been a captain in the Black Watch. (The Americans did not like this and there were many hisses and shouts of disapproval.) Then speaker after speaker rose and declaimed on the supergreatness of all things Scottish, so that I was annoyed at their vainglory and impertinent assurance in daring to boast so when they had so many aliens as guests. When the toast to the Press was proposed, the proposer was answered by a dapper little man with a strong voice and a vibrating Yankee accent. He commenced his speech by apologizing for the absence of his friend Macdonald, a journalist on the *Chronicle* who, being called away, had asked him to attend the banquet and reply to the toast of 'the Press'. He said that he was glad of the chance of assisting in the disposal of so many good things: he had tasted haggis for the first time and did not like it, and he thought that when Burns wrote in such glowing terms of it he must have been pretty full of that other Scottish dainty, whisky. He said he was amazed to hear gentleman after gentleman hour after hour declaiming the beauties of Scotland – their men, lassies, scenery, heroic deeds, virtues and inventions. They told how all the nations on earth were indebted for all they had of good to Scotsmen. They were the chosen bankers and financial magnates of the world; all the notable soldiers and sailors of the world they said were of that race; they even claimed President Arthur as one. Then their lassies were the most lovely and the scenery of Scotland the most beautiful – though he had read that a certain Dr Johnson of *Dictionary* fame had said that a Scotsman first saw the finest scenery of his country when he was leaving it for good. In their speeches two gentlemen had quoted the venerable dictionary maker, who defined oats as the 'food of horses in England and of men in Scotland', and each of them had voiced the old chestnut 'and where do you see such horses as the horses of England or such men as the men of Scotland?' (Both utterances had provoked a storm of applause.)

He continued: 'Among the great and noble men claimed by the speaker tonight, I noticed many people of distinction and of undoubted Scottish nationality that they never mentioned. There was Macbeth and his wife, stamped by the genius of that mere Englishman, Shakespeare, for all time as the personification of the worst of crimes. Then, when they spoke of Sir William Wallace they never mentioned Sir John Monteith who sold him to King Edward, nor of the perfidy of the great Bruce who stabbed the unarmed Red Comyn in Dumfries Abbey; nor Queen Mary's murder of her husband; nor those brave Scottish knights who, clad in armour, stabbed to death in the presence of their Queen, David Rizzio; nor James the Sixth of Scotland who connived at the beheading of his mother so that the way was clear for him to succeed to the English Crown. Nor that when Charles Stuart, their own King and countryman, sought shelter with them, they 'sold' him to Cromwell for 30,000 pounds Scots – and I am told that a pound Scots is equal to ten cents. Nor did they speak of the Scottish noblemen and their tool, Captain Campbell, who by the foulest treachery enacted the massacre of Glencoe. Nor of Johnie Law, whose schemes brought death and disaster to thousands and who has a present-day prototype in Jamie Balfour. And lastly, of Sawney Bean.

'It is a singular thing that I have asked innumerable Scotsmen about this worthy, and they all put on that stolid wooden face that only a Scotsman can make and deny all knowledge of him. Well, when I was last in Europe I went to the British Museum, for I was told the story of his incredible crimes were embalmed in the ancient volume of the *Edinburgh Journal Transactions*. So after a long search I found the true and authentic history of Sawney Bean . . .

'This miscreant and his wife had left Edinburgh to escape punishment for atrocious crimes. They were searched for in vain. Fifty years afterwards, in consequence of a close search for the reason why so many travellers disappeared on the high road from Edinburgh to the South, a cave was discovered off the main road. No less than fifty-six brutalized men and women and children were found inhabiting it. The roof was hung with human hams and cured sides. The oldest couple were proved to be Sawney Bean and his wife and their offspring.'

All the time the intrepid little Yankee was speaking he was subject to interruptions and loud cries of disapproval. He persevered; his loud voice dominated the room and he would not be put down. When the Sawney Bean climax was reached, the Scots, full of whisky, made for the little chap. Nothing but his gore would satisfy them. The glass and furniture was smashed; pandemonium reigned. Lindsay and I and others sought safety under the tables. The uproar was awful. It was 4 a.m. before we reached our ships. The damages to the room and furniture ran into thousands of dollars, which the Society had to pay, and the papers revelled in a paying scandal. The Saint Andrew Banquets were either omitted or very very quietly celebrated after this. No Scotsman in 'Frisco would discuss the affair. That is the best way to smother anything disagreeable: silly folk talk and keep it wick.

Now to return to our mutton (as Johnnie Croper would say). The railway track from the lowlands of the Sacramento Valley to the passes of the Rocky Mountains gave many interesting and surprising views, from snowy ridges to the foliage of perpetual summer. I enjoyed to the full the beautiful sights and only the setting of the sun made me leave the observation platform for the smoking car. I slept comfortably and well for the first time in a Pullman sleeping car. The motion and the noise did not disturb me; they were like those on board ship.

At this time the Union Pacific Railway had no dining cars on their overland trains until the Missouri River at Council Bluffs, Iowa. So meals were served at wayside stations on the route, and very decent meals they were, trout and game in perfection. Sometimes when the engine was taking in wood and water (no coal), we wandered about the Indian settlements. The women collected the wood to supply the locomotives; the bucks stalked about doing nothing. When they wanted to they had free rides on the trains. The encampments were foul and dirty, the Indians disgusting animals: my ideas from Fenimore Cooper's novels shattered for ever.

In the Rockies the scenery was grand. Fantastic mountain peaks covered with snow, the wooded valleys, now and then a glimpse of a mining village, a band of miserable-looking Indians and desolate stretches of marsh. As the train passed through Nevada large tracts covered with sagebrush were the outstanding features until we came to the prairies, like unto the sea, though to my eyes much more monotonous. An ugly unsatisfying land, only fit to breed cattle and ox-like men.

The weather had turned very cold with much fine snow and there was no amusement to be derived from the observation car. A dead level of ugly land. So we found our amusement in the smoking car. I heard many tales of the great Civil War of some twenty years before. Two of our fellow travellers had served through it, fighting on different sides, one with Lee in a Virginian regiment, the other under McAllan and Grant in a Massachusetts regiment. My sympathies were with the South, though I could not but admire the courtesy and nice bearing of the Northern man to his Southern adversary.

At one of the wayside stopping places we took on a Cattle King, for we were now in the cowboy country. This Cattle King was a dictatorial nasty man and we were glad when he got off. That night during a terrific blizzard the train ran into a mob of cattle and was nearly derailed. My fellow travellers at once demanded that the train return as near the place of the disaster as possible, and that the wounded beasts be put out of their agony. This was done. The conductor and train men went with revolvers and poleaxes on their mission of mercy. The night was a dreadful one: a blizzard on the prairies is worse than a gale at sea. The thermometer was far below zero and the hurricane drove the fine particles of snow with such force that it was not bearable to face the wind. The cold was stupefying in its intensity. None of the passengers dared the adventure until one of the trainmen returned for help, when all volunteered. The few hundred yards we had to traverse to get to the scene of the slaughter was a passage of pain and danger, which we overcame by linking ourselves together. We found the work done; two of the men had been overcome by the dreadful cold, and were lying as if dead. We had very hard work to get them borne to the train when restorative measures were taken which proved so far successful that they regained sensibility and were put to bed.

Some thirty hours after this the two men were taken off the train at Cheyenne, the capital of Wyoming, suffering badly from frostbite and shock. A collection was made for them. From Cheyenne we passed through the State of Nebraska, our principal occupation to try and get warm. When we arrived at Council Bluffs we had some time to wait, and my companions wanted a drink to warm them. Iowa was a prohibition state and this was managed by going into a druggist's store near the station. The doctor, as druggists are called in the States, diagnosed our complaints and prescribed a jorum of hot rye whisky with plenty of sugar. We found it most palatable medicine. Nothing like it to relieve the effects of severe cold. We re-entered our train and next day arrived at Chicago, the capital of Illinois, where I had to wait for the Lakeshore Express to take me to New York. It is said there are two bad payers: the one who pays too soon and the one who pays not at all. I paid a nigger porter a dollar to get my luggage to the depot. Something made me go back to look after him. The rascal had cleared off leaving my things unprotected by the side of the track. I hired a white man for half a dollar and got them in safely. Then I drove to a hotel and had a square meal, and afterwards hired a carriage to have a look at the town and a sight of Lake Michigan. On reaching the shores of the Lake, the cold was so severe that I drove back to the hotel and got into bed for a few hours. I hate cold weather, and love the tropics. Heat is only discomfort, cold is misery and the worst sort of pain. It is much easier to be brave in warm than in cold weather. The only impression Chicago left on my mind was the deathly cold picture of

Lake Michigan, the miserable out-of-place appearance of sun-loving niggers, and the enormous charges of the hackney coachman.

I joined the Lakeshore Express, which on this trip for the first time was made up of vestibule cars. Acting on advice, on each section of my journey I had wired ahead to secure a bed in the sleeping cars. The train was overcrowded and many had to spend the long cold night in the day and smoking cars. On this section good meals at a reasonable price were served in dining cars.

I struck up a train acquaintance with a St Louis drygoods merchant; he was loaded up with humorous stories, many of them of a 'high flavour'. He wore a shining broadcloth frock suit with spotless linen and had the face of a well-to-do local dissenting minister. On this gentleman's advice, as the train would arrive after midnight, I decided to put up at the Murray Hill Hotel, which I found to my cost and discomfort was the latest swell thing in New York hotels (in American talk). I was located in a magnificent bedroom with bathroom *en suite*. I slept well, had a bath and breakfast, then went downtown to present my letter of introduction and renew my acquaintance with Mr Hogan, the head of the stevedoring firm which had discharged the *Corea*'s cargo of Japanese tea on my last voyage as Chief Mate, and who was present when the marshal fired at me for resisting arrest. Though twenty years nearly had elapsed since then, Mr Hogan knew me at once. He was now a large shipowner as well as head of the stevedoring firm. He was most hospitable and pressed me to stay at his house, which I refused, though I went to lunch with him. Through his good offices I obtained a First Class passage with a good room to myself in the Cunarder *Umbria*, then in her first year, with her sister ship the wonder and pride of the nautical world.

In the evening I returned to the Murray Hill Hotel. On entering the dining room, such a show of bare necks with glistening diamonds, spotless shirtfronts and immaculate costumes met my gaze that I decided not to spoil the show with my travelling rig, so made my way out and enquired for the restaurant, where I satisfied my wants. Next morning after breakfast I called for my bill – and survived the shock – then after running the gauntlet of the hotel gentlemen and lady helps, I drove down to the Cunard Pier and boarded the *Umbria*. As this was Christmas Eve there was not a large number of passengers. I stayed on deck until we passed Sandy

Hook. At dinner time I had a seat at the Doctor's table. My neighbour on one side was a superintendent for a Glasgow firm of shipowners; on the other I had a cheeky, offensive Yankee drummer. Opposite were several females, a few of whom would have been happier in more homely surroundings.

Then there was only salmon or sturgeon: now there is excellent Second Class and intermediate accommodation, which supplies all wants. On going on deck for a walk before turning in, I was surprised to see one of the Continental ships overtaking us. An officer told me the reason was that the *Umbria*'s stokehold hands were drunk and fighting and steam was not kept up. Next morning we had run into a gale; the weather on deck was too bad for anyone to stay there, unless they were paid for doing so. There was plenty of amusement to be had from observing folks in the smoking room and saloon. My drummer neighbour had found his like and they were discussing in strident tones the shortcomings of the Cunard Company. This drummer made himself so obnoxious at table – denying everything and rating the stewards – that everyone was relieved when my Glasgow neighbour tackled him that his 'grumbling about the food was nothing but vulgar snobbery, and said to make people think that he was used to much better things. The food was good and well served: much better catering than was to be had in any American hotel.' This and a few more home truths sufficed to make the drummer seek the Chief Steward and get his seat at another table.

We arrived in the Mersey early on a Sunday morning, having been delayed by fog and hard easterly gales. I was surprised that with the tremendous racing of the screw the ship did not break. The Captain and officers of the Atlantic mailboats are brave, skilled and careful men. It has always been a matter of wonder to me that they perform their hazardous duties with so few disasters. On their stormy route there are many dangers.

So I completed my twentieth voyage.

A NEW COMMAND AND A MONSTER

My Twenty-first Voyage
MAXWELL
1887–1888

LIVERPOOL – SYDNEY – SAN FRANCISCO –
QUEENSTOWN – DUBLIN

My new command, the *Maxwell*, I found in Princes Drydock, getting painted and coated with antifouling composition. She was a fine vessel, a medium clipper of some 1,900 tons register, built by T. B. Royden & Co. and designed by a popular naval architect. I was much pleased by her rig and accommodation. The crew were most comfortably housed and lavatories were provided for their use. After making all arrangements in Liverpool I took a short holiday in Cumberland and joined the ship ten days before sailing. The officers, apprentices and petty officers were all strangers, so different from my experience of the last six or seven years where I was surrounded by tried friends and the ship was a home. The Chief Mate was a man of about twenty-six years with a good face; the Second Mate, on his first voyage as an officer, was in his twenty-first year, a smart, energetic, bright young fellow with tact and prudence; six apprentices were all well-grown lads of decent parentage.

Before leaving Liverpool I was introduced to a Mr William Montgomery, a London merchant, who was so pleased with the *Maxwell* that he arranged with the designer to have a duplicate of her, which was built by W. Hamilton & Co. of Port Glasgow and named the *Grace Harwar*.

We left in tow and had thick rainy weather down St George's

Channel, cast off in the neighbourhood of Tuskar Rock at 3 a.m. one dirty morning and faced a southwest gale. We had hard work to hold our own for the first day. Fortunately the *Maxwell* was a scientifically designed ship, and proved herself a very weatherly vessel under the low sail the stormy weather forced us under, or I would have been compelled to run back to Holyhead for shelter. We gradually gained an offing with much trying work for all hands, and cleared the land on the third day from casting off the tug.

We had adverse winds with much stormy weather until the Canary Islands were sighted, when we got the belated Northeast Trade Winds: the ship had done all it was possible for a ship to do, yet the prospect of making a record passage to Sydney had vanished. On reaching the Equator, so many of the crew had not crossed the Line that Neptune had a joyous time; the ceremonies were well carried out and all enjoyed themselves in a sober, decent manner. The *Maxwell* did not sail so well as the *Larnaca*, though none of the many ships we sighted could pass her. Among them was a new four-masted ship of Brocklebanks, named the *Scindia*. As we drew away from her, the Captain signalled, 'Does your ship sail well?' to which I could only reply 'Yes', as we were beating his ship.

As the weather was fine on approaching the Tristan da Cunha Islands, I hove to and soon had two whaleboats alongside, with potatoes, vegetables, fish and some joints of meat, which they traded for clothing, sugar, flour, biscuits, etc. They had most of the necessaries of life on the islands, and had communication with Cape Town, 1,700 miles away, every three or four months. Some of their young people emigrated to the Cape, where they got work. On the whole the inhabitants of the Island lived a happy life; they were a healthy people and free from the cares that soured the lives of people in larger communities. There were then nearly one hundred inhabitants of mixed blood. The original people were British soldiers, who took coloured wives and settled there after Napolean's death at St Helena. During his lifetime a detachment of soldiers were kept there to prevent the islands from becoming a base for an attempt against St Helena.

From Tristan da Cunha to Sydney we had the usual brave winds, and arrived there in eighty-six days from Liverpool. The *Thermopylae* was ninety-six days from London and eighty-one from the Lizard, having had the same storms and adverse winds to contend with as we had.

During the discharge of the cargo the Chief Mate was so anxious that the stevedores should not damage the many bales with their hooks, nor broach the spirit and wine cases, that he was continually going up and down the hold, though I had requested him not to do so as he had several of the apprentices stationed in the hold to watch that nothing peccant was done.

One morning when the hold in way of the main hatch was clear of cargo, he swung himself carelessly over the coamings, lost his hold and fell some twenty-six feet to the ceiling. When I got to him I thought he was dead for he showed no sign of life for some time. With the measures we took he regained consciousness. On examination his injuries were found to be serious: a fractured thigh, broken ankles and wrist, and a very bad wound on the head. We put on temporary splints and conveyed him to hospital, where he was well attended to. It was pitiful to see his anxious care that things should be attended to on board the ship. During my daily visits that was his constant theme. I doubt if any employers have such earnest loyal servants as shipowners have. Here was a man all smashed to pieces, not thinking of himself; all his thoughts given to what had been his work.

I had to leave him in hospital and made careful arrangements for his comfort and transportation home, and wrote the Owners in his favour. When he arrived home he was nearly recovered. The Owners behaved very generously with him and kept him until he was fit to take a berth.

Sydney at that time was a bad place for young men. Girls of the flapper age were immodest and forward and haunted the wharfs. The apprentices in their smart uniforms were a great attraction to them. The lads got led away, and many deserted their ships to the grief of their parents and sank to a debased life. Amongst our apprentices were two seventeen or eighteen years of age. One was a relative of the man the ship was named after, the other was the son of Major Want, R.E. who had taken his life in Morley's Hotel, London in a fit of chagrin at the chaffing he got for some very stupid mistake he had made in designing a Rajah's palace in India. These two lads were missing.

I employed a private detective to find where they were, and told him not to arrest them until I gave him further instructions. In a few days he reported that they were kept in a small sweet and confectionery shop. The proprietors were two young women who had tempted them.

Acting on the detective's advice I sought an interview with the magistrate of the Division. He received me most kindly and sympathetically, and said he would have them arrested and commit them to custody until the ship was ready for sea. I was much disturbed with the idea that they would be put in gaol; he kindly reassured me by saying they would not be put in gaol but in charge of the sergeant and would be kept in his house. They were arrested, the young women soundly rated and warned that they would be proceeded against for harbouring, and keeping an immoral house. The lads were dealt with as proposed. And many years afterwards one of them, then Chief Mate of a mail steamer, called on me in London and thanked me for, as he put it, saving him body and soul. I have deep feelings of gratitude for that good Sydney magistrate.

We loaded a cargo of shale for San Francisco in Sydney harbour, which was much better than shifting to Newcastle, N.S.W. for coals. Being now nearly loaded I had to arrange for a Chief Mate; by Australian law I could not proceed to sea without a Chief Officer holding at least a First Mate's certificate. All the applications I had were from men whose evil, dissipated faces showed the sort of men they were. I could not stomach having such men for the rest of the voyage, probably lasting a year. Then I had one from a man of some thirty-five years. He had not a prepossessing appearance, though neither the look of a drunken man. He was very importunate and told me he had left the ship *Aristophane* at Newcastle, and owned that he had a bad discharge. I told him to call again. Shortly after he left the Captain of the *British Merchant*, with several other shipmasters, called on me to say they had heard that the ex Mate of the *Aristophane* was a candidate for the First Mate's position on board my ship. They said that he was one of the greatest blackguards in the world; that among other delinquencies he had set fire to the *Aristophane* to spite the steward and get him blamed, and though the Court had acquitted him for want of sufficient evidence yet everyone believed he was guilty, and that for six months all shipmasters had combined to prevent him getting a berth as an officer. I asked them what could I do. Would any of them that had a Second Mate with a First Mate's

Certificate loan him to me until we reached San Francisco, for they well knew that I could not leave Sydney without a First Mate. I knew they all had such officers, but none of them would help me, so I would not promise not to take the arson-suspected Mate. Having exhausted every channel, even writing to neighbouring ports, I had the choice between drunken wastrels and the man from the *Aristophane*. So I told the last-named that I was acquainted with his character and did not want to hear his protestations of innocence: what I wanted was his promise to do his best when on board my ship, to sign on to be discharged on arrival at San Francisco, for Mr Beasley, the Second Mate, though so young, would be quite competent to act as First Mate on the passage from San Francisco home, and one of my Boatswain's Mates had a Second's Certificate. On these terms he signed on, and for the first month attended to his duties and whenever he got the chance praised me for my goodness to him, and with coarse flattery said he would be a different man if all his Captains had been like me, and much more insincere and distasteful talk of the same sort. I bore with him until one morning at daybreak I heard him tell the bo'sun that when the decks were washed he would trim the yards. That startled me, for the first duty of an officer is to push the ship: besides, we were in company with the ship *British Merchant* and any sailor would try to keep ahead. Also we were among the islands near Tahiti. I ran on deck and found the ship in the wind, off her course, and the competing ship abeam.

After the yards were trimmed I spoke seriously to him. He promised amendment. Having lost faith in him, I took little rest during his watch. When within a few weeks' sail of our destination I left the deck at 1 a.m. during his watch and returned at 2.30 a.m., no Mate was to be found on the poop or round the decks, and neither wheel nor lookout had been relieved. In searching round I found him fast asleep in the W.C. and locked him in, called all hands, appointed the Second Mate Chief and made one of the assistants Second Mate. After breakfast I released the ex Mate from his durance and told him I relieved him from his duties. He was a prisoner at large with the only restriction that he had to keep to his room and the quarterdeck. On arrival at San Francisco I discharged him and found that my young officers were splendid.

After a pleasant stay in California we left with a cargo of wheat, bound to Queenstown for orders. In latitude 5° north we entered the Great Pacific Stream and had a high temperature. One morning I heard a great commotion on deck and a great thud against the ship's side, as if it had bumped against a well-fendered wharf. The Second Mate, much excited, came to ask me to come on deck as a huge creature nearly as long as the ship was alongside. When I went on deck I saw a great whale or sunfish hard against the ship's side. After getting over my first surprise, I examined it closely. Apparently the head, a great boa-like structure somewhat resembling the head of the sperm whale, was to our stern, abreast the after bumpkin; the body as high as our rail extended to the fore royal backstay above the water then tapered gradually out of sight. The back was as broad as half the ship's beam, without fin – a broad smooth back of a bluish grey colour. The length from the head to where it dipped in the water by the fore rigging was 152 feet; it probably had from ten to twenty feet under water. The flat of the back would exceed twenty feet.

Though the head had some semblance to the sperm whale, it was different. The lower jaw was quite as deep as the upper, and there was no blowhole. The ship was gliding through the oily-looking sea at the rate of five knots per hour the monster braced so tightly alongside going along with her without effort. There were several large sharks swimming about; they looked like flies on a prize bullock. In my sea life I have seen many times all the known sea monsters. Never before did I behold such a mountain of living matter. The oceans, I am convinced, contain wonders unknown to science. Perhaps one day an expedition will be sent to observe the enormous sea-life abounding in the great Pacific Current from 10° north to 10° south and longitude 100° to 130° west.

For several hours the great creature kept in the same position. Its presence got on the nerves. I fired several times from a bulldog revolver into its head: it took no notice, though several good-sized fish appeared to come from its mouth. The breeze freshened and the creature sank bodily out of sight, which gave us no little relief.

On arrival home I was appealed to by newspapermen who had heard the crew's stories to give my version. I refused, as I did not want to be pilloried as another Münchausen, as are all the men who have testified to seeing that other wonder of the deep, the sea-serpent. We arrived at Queenstown without further adventure and received orders to proceed to Dublin to discharge, where we duly arrived at Sir John Rogerson Quay.

I do not admire blarney in the Irish – or in any other folk – yet I was amused with the finesse of a female Queenstown vegetable peddler. On coming to the wharf, she accosted me to buy her wares – 'Captain, will ye not buy my pretty basketful?' – and kept importuning with wiles and flattery. I said, 'Why do you bother me? How do you know I'm a Captain?' Quickly she answered, 'Sure you're too good-looking to be anything else!' After that I bought her wares.

It was on this voyage to Dublin that I observed in Phoenix Park that the old peddler women kept the ground plucked bare of grass where the victims of the murders of 1882 were struck down.

I do not admire Dublin. I thought it a very dirty place, with people as keen after money as Asiatics.

A DIFFICULT PASSAGE

My Twenty-second Voyage
MAXWELL
1888–1889
DUBLIN – CARDIFF – CAPE TOWN – CALCUTTA – DUNDEE

The ship was chartered to proceed in tow to Cardiff and load a cargo of coals for Cape Town. The passage from Dublin to Cardiff was most enjoyable being summer time. As is the case in all coal ports our stay there was unpleasant, and I was glad to get to sea and get the coaldust washed off. Several fine ships had left for Cardiff during the preceding week: the *Sierra Miranda, Knight of Saint Michael, British Sceptre, Sierra Pedrosa* and two others, all first class ships, so the *Maxwell* had her work cut out to compete with them.

For the first part of the passage we were hampered with light westerly winds, then the trade winds in the northern hemisphere were far to the north and it took twenty-six days to reach the Equator; from there we had the strongest Southeast Trades in my experience. We passed to the eastward of the Martin Vaz Islands. These rocks I have imagined are the place where Morgan Kidd or other famous pirates have buried treasure. No safe hiding place could be found, for the great South Atlantic swell prevents an anchorage or landing excepting in the height of the fine season. After clearing the Trades, we made a sweep to the southward as far as Inaccessible Island [in the Tristan da Cunha Group] and arrived in Table Bay on the forty-sixth day from Cardiff. We anchored at midnight, and owing to the white paint of the *Ticua Miranda* I miscalculated my distance from her and had to call on her people to give me more cable to avoid damage. Her crew were very dilatory in obeying her officers; by making use of our sails we kept from fouling her, and at daylight I towed to a better berth. The port was congested and there were many ships in the Bay awaiting a berth in the dock. Amongst them the *Knight of Saint Michael* who had made the passage in one day less than our ship. The *Sierra Miranda* was over fifty days, the rest of the Cardiff ships were over sixty on the passage. The *Sierra Pedrosa* was high and dry ashore having parted her cables during a furious southeaster the day before we arrived.

We were detained in the Bay for fifteen days awaiting a berth in the dock to discharge. A few days before we got in we had an experience of the dangers of Table Bay. For some hours the 'table-cloth' was spread over Table Mountain: it is a large white cloud that settles on the flat top of the mountain, reaching halfway down – an infallible sign of the early approach of a southeaster. The wind came in furious gusts, stretching the cable to the utmost. The gusts fell suddenly to a calm, the tension on the cables became relaxed and pulled the ship to the anchor, then the gust came again, driving the ship before it, causing a tremendous strain on the windlass and cables. To ease the strain on the windlass I had the towing spring, fifteen fathoms of fifteen-inch manilla cable, lashed on the cable forward of the windlass with a five-inch tackle attached, and taken to the quarterdeck bitts. This saved the windlass, but the demon southerner would not be denied: it parted the cable and drove the ship with rapidity towards the shore. Fortunately we were on the lookout and dropped the second anchor. It was several days before the harbour authorities recovered the lost anchor. Fully half the ships anchoring in Table Bay suffer either the loss of anchors or cables, or break their windlass.

The *Sierra Pedrosa* was got off the beach principally owing to the fine seamanship and knowledge of Captain Williams of the *Knight of Saint Michael*. The officer sent out by the Liverpool Salvage Co. was an amiable nonentity, a Scotsman and a snob, and knew nothing of his job. The Captain of the *Sierra Pedrosa* and his wife had lost all their effects, as the ship had been looted by the many bad characters on the beach, so a number of us subscribed, and I was deputed to hand McWhinnie £100.

The Captain of the *Sierro Miranda* was a Jerseyman, a prim elderly man who stayed at a hotel during his ship's stay in port. I generally met him at the agents each morning. He was very polite and fulsome and asked me on several occasions to dine with him at his hotel. Circumstances did not permit until one day when I accepted. After dinner when I was leaving, a waiter came to me and politely asked me to pay for my dinner. I was quite taken aback and asked him if Captain Mesuard had not told him I was his guest. He said that Captain Mesuard had told him I would pay, which I did, and learned from several shipmasters that they had had the same experience of Captain Mesuard's hospitality. We meet very queer people on our pilgrimage of life.

The authorities at Cape Town were very good in helping Masters to maintain order and discipline during their stay in the docks. My crew gave me no trouble after I had the first offender arrested.

On the new dock works many convicts were working, quite a big percentage illicit diamond buyers. Perhaps some of them blossomed out as Park Lane millionaires.

While lying at anchor in the Bay, my crew caught quantities of fine fish and an abundance of crayfish. A fortune could be made by anyone starting a fish-canning factory. I was surprised at the high price of vegetables – potatoes were at famine price – and was told the reason was that the Dutch descendants of the early settlers owned the land: they restricted the output and would neither sell nor let their land.

My patriotism got many shocks from the Afrikaners I met, and I was not surprised ten years afterwards when Kruger's diplomacy led to war, for nothing but the price of war could clear South Africa of the hatred and racial suspicion that possessed the Dutch community. Majuba and Gladstone's clemency had given them swelled heads.[1]

We sailed from Cape Town bound to the Bay of Bengal and the Sandheads [off the Hooghly River] for orders. The ship being in ballast gave a good opportunity to get the hold thoroughly cleaned and painted. We were favoured with pleasant weather and arrived off the Sandhead Lightship the last day of October, communicated with the Pilot brig (there were no orders), spoke a Calcutta tug and

---

[1] A reference to the defeat of British soldiers at Majuba Hill by the Boers, in 1881. Gladstone then made the Transvaal independent again. A gold rush then led to an unwelcome influx of foreigners, mainly British. The Second Boer War began in 1899 and lasted until 1902.

engaged her to steam up to Saugor Island to find out the agents and get their instructions. Much against my will, I came to anchor practically in the open sea in the hurricane season. After two days the tug came back to say the agents were Thompson Anderson & Co., and that we had to proceed to Calcutta. The weather was threatening and foul and the barometer falling, so the tugmaster said he could not get a Pilot and would return in the morning, and away he steamed to Saugor and safety.

That night the barometer fell to 28 inches; the wind rose to a strong gale and we had a high confused sea. Both anchors were down with all the cable out. The Pilot brigs had stood to sea (they were hardy vessels); we could not, for the wind was from a quarter that would not allow us to clear the sandbanks. We passed an anxious and busy night, getting the royal and topgallant yards on deck and marling the sails on the yards, doing everything that seamanship taught would work for the safety of the ship. During this night and the following day I had a most anxious time, for should the cyclone's track cross the head of the Bay there would be no hope for the *Maxwell* or her crew. At noon the barometer stood at 27.98. The wind blowing in gusts never exceeded the force of a land gale; the rain was heavy and the sea running in high confused masses. The ship lay very uneasy on the ebb tide. Towards night the barometer began to rise and kept on doing so. No one, excepting a seaman in a like situation, can imagine the awful depression and nameless dread the falling of the barometer in such an appalling manner causes, nor the feelings of hope and exhilaration when it commences to rise.

By midnight the rain stopped. Patches of heavenly blue sky showed, and the stars peeped out. To the southwest a heavy bank of clouds with vivid flashes of lightning showed the direction the awful scourge was travelling. The sea did not go down. Towards evening the tug came within speaking distance, congratulated me on riding out the storm, and said a heavy cyclone had passed south of us, causing great devastation on the Madras coast with much loss of life. The Pilot was still off the station. He would come along in the morning and if possible take us in tow. It was a thoughtless and reckless thing for the Owners and agents to do, to have the ship anchored at Sandheads in the hurricane months: even the Mutlah Lightship and one of the Pilot brigs came to grief.

Next morning we got a Pilot and the trip hawser. Heaving up the anchor both cables parted, and we lost fifty fathoms of cable on the port and forty on the starboard, with both anchors entailing loss of £800 to the Owners (the Underwriters not being responsible for such a loss) besides the cost of having the ship detained at Calcutta while new anchors and cables were sent out from home.

On arrival at Calcutta, owing to our loss of anchor cables we had to moor with wire until such time as mooring cables could be hired. At this time the Harbour Master was a big German, a pronounced type of all that is objectionable in his countrymen. His abusive hectoring manner to his subordinate who had charge of the *Maxwell* was so offensive that I was driven to express my view of his conduct. The subordinate was a smart young Englishman holding an Extra Master's Certificate, who had to bear the insulting bullying or leave the service. There is no other nationality who promotes foreigners to positions of trust in the public services, and it jars to hear tyrannical and uncalled-for language from foreigners who have been placed over our countrymen. Englishmen are sadly wanting in clannishness.

My agents were a branch of the Liverpool firm of Thompson, Anderson & Co., who had neglected their duty in not having instructions for me on board the lightship or Pilot brig at Sandheads. It was owing to their neglect that the ship was in such peril, and that the Owners suffered the loss of quite £1,000. On receiving my letters I found that one of them contained a letter of credit for £1,200 for disbursements on the Bank of Bengal. I requested the clerk to direct me to the Bank: he asked if he could not present the letter of credit. I said he could, for I would only credit his firm as my agents for the sum and draw on them; to finish this yarn, when six weeks afterwards I came to settle up with my agents I found they had debited me with $2\frac{1}{2}$ per cent for supplying funds and was told the clerk had forgotten to lodge the letter of credit in the Bank. I refused in any way to allow such a charge. In Liverpool they made a claim, and I went from Dundee to refute it; when they found that J.S. & Co. took the same view as I did of their monstrous demand, they dropped it.

Their Principal in Calcutta had brushed past me for three weeks, daily, in his office and had not deigned me the slightest recognition, then through the clerk he expressed an intention of being introduced to me – by the clerk. I said I had been daily in his office for three weeks, the only ship consigned to them, and he had ignored me. I now refused to meet him. The clerk was the one I would do business with. How very silly some of our countrymen are in their snobbishness: Scotsmen are the worst.

For the first and last time in my life I attended a race meeting. Calcutta has a fine course and the leading spirit at this time was Lord William Beresford; the Marquis of Lansdowne was Viceroy, and there were many visitors from Europe. I got on the grandstand through the instrumentality of an Irish soldier on guard and had a good view, but saw nothing in the races to tempt me to go again. Amongst the Viceregal party were many nice-looking ladies.

I chartered to load a cargo of jute for Dundee, and through the miscalculation of the designer of the ship I found I had not ballasted sufficiently; canting the yards would list the ship a couple of feet and I was afraid the crew would refuse to proceed. As we proceeded I found there was no danger of capsizing: the trouble was she would not sail, drifted to leeward like a haystack, and took 135 days to reach Dundee. I was thankful that I had not to put into some port, for I never expected to get her home. I was glad when the voyage was ended for it was heartbreaking work.

VOYAGE TO OREGON

My Twenty-third Voyage
MAXWELL
1889–1890

DUNDEE – LONDON – GREENHITHE – SAN FRANCISCO –
ASTORIA – PORTLAND – DUNKIRK

Dundee is a nice town. I found good quarters in a famous Temperance Hotel in Reform Street, a favourite resort of commercial tourists who told me it was the best Temperance Hotel in Britain. I was amused on Sunday: the commercial gentlemen mustered a great force at dinner – a President was chosen and a Vice. The dinner was conducted with much dignity and politeness: no function at the Guildhall could have had a more exalted pose, and no Lord Mayor more pomposity; the dinner was excellent and the company amusing.

I took a holiday for a week, leaving Flynn in charge. Before the week was up Flynn sent urgent telegrams for me to return. When I reached Dundee I found that he was at loggerheads with the stevedores who were stowing iron and steel plates, part of the outward cargo for San Francisco. His excuse for shortening my holiday was that the men would not work for him and that Mr S., the Owner, should see they did not work for me. I saw the men: their grievance was the hectoring language used by Flynn. They went to work and Flynn had a holiday for the rest of his stay in Dundee.

I ran over one Sunday to St Andrews, so famous in Scottish history for its University and golf. A grey old town with some picturesque old ruins framed by a cold green sea.

The ship was chartered to load 600 tons of iron and steel plates at Dundee, then tow to London for drydocking, afterwards proceeding to Greenhithe to complete loading with cement.

At this time Havelock Wilson was coming into prominence as a seamen's agitator. His methods were some fifteen or twenty years before their time, for his policy was to force all the members of a crew excepting the officers and apprentices to become members of his Union and pay an immediate levy. My carpenter, bo'sun, cook and sailmaker were old hands, had been two voyages in the ship, and strongly objected to paying this blackmail. Then the Union boycotted the ship and I could not get runners. Then I arranged that the bo'sun and sails should pay the levy. The carpenter showed that he belonged to the Shipwrights' Union, and the cook and the steward were free.

I shipped the runners to take the ship from the dock at Dundee to London Docks. The Union officials came and informed me that their men, the runners, would not move the ship from her berth to the dock basin: that, they said, was the work of the Riggers' Union. This was heaping up the expense of the ship with a vengeance. I put the delegate ashore and moved the ship to the basin with my own petty officers and apprentices, the riggers and their allies using offensive language and throwing stones at the ship. I have never heard such very nasty swearing and beastly language in any port as I have in Scottish ports, Dundee, Glasgow and Leith. Dundee was the worst.

At the pierhead the runners came on board and we proceeded in tow for London. They and their delegates had been so arrogantly offensive that I studied how, with behaving to them with strict justice, I could teach them that it was the better policy and more to their profit for them to behave with more decorum and civility. I gave them their exact allowance of food; the apprentices and petty officers kept watch and the runners were kept working all day, and the holds were got ready for cargo, sails bent and ship cleaned. On arrival in the London drydock I paid them their due at once and did not allow them to sleep on board, which put them to the expense of a night's lodging and several meals, for the Scottish passenger boat did not leave until the next night. I told them I treated them so as a lesson that the whip is not always in the same hands. I also took on one runner less than I would have done under former circumstances, and repaid the blackmail extorted from bos'un and sails.

After finishing the painting in drydock we towed to Greenhithe and moored to the buoy near the *Worcester* and lay there comfortably for a month. I renewed my acquaintance with Mr Hoyle, his family and other nice people, and as it was in the months of June and July I and all the crew on board the *Maxwell* had a pleasant time. In fact the times I spent at Greenhithe are amongst the 'Red letter days' of my life.

On the 16th July we towed away. The country round Greenhithe looked lovely and we left regretfully.

We had a passage through summer seas until we reached the latitude of Cape Frio in Brazil. There we were buffetted by exceptionally heavy gales and lost many of our summer suit of sails, and from this time till we crossed the Tropic of Capricorn in the Pacific we had hard weather and severe gales to contend with. Off Cape Pilar[1] we lost a seaman overboard during a heavy northwest gale. We were not able to pick him up, for with our heavy cargo the ship laboured so much, then the lifeboat was smashed in trying to put it out. Perhaps this was a fortunate happening, for had the boat got away probably we would have lost her and her crew. There was a faint chance of picking up the man, who was a strong swimmer, but an attempt was in the nature of a forlorn hope. With the cold and high sea the lost one would soon give up the struggle, and like thousands of his fellow Britons his bones would pave the ocean.

We arrived at San Francisco early in November having made a good passage, and found the *Larnaca* with my former Chief Mate and his wife who had arrived from Australia, and we were mutually pleased to meet again. Mrs Giles was an amiable little lady. She presented her husband with a son whilst lying at the wharf. Captain Giles, with a Briton's patriotism, had his ship decked with British flags whilst the doctor and nurse were relieving Mrs Giles of her burden, so that though born in foreign waters he came into the world on British territory with the flag waving over him.

Having been chartered to load a cargo of wheat at Portland, Oregon when quit of the outward cargo and ballasted, we proceeded for the Columbia River. When two days out, the ship was travelling at the rate of seven knots with the patent log over the stern; a school

---

[1] A notable landmark for sailing ships at the seaward end of Desolation Island which forms the southern side of the approaches to the Magellan Strait from the Pacific. It is in about 53° south latitude.

of whales raced past the ship, and after getting half a mile away a large one turned back, attracted by the bright brass rotator of the patent log, and swallowed it, breaking the line. The rotator did not agree with the whale, for the monster threw itself out of the water and thrashed the sea for many hours until we had sailed it out of sight. I am afraid the poor animal would have a painful death.

We had dirty weather off the Columbia River bar which retained several days; then one morning out of the mist came a tug with a Pilot on board who soon transferred to us. The tug got hold and away we went for the bar, and although the *Maxwell* was a large ship quite twenty feet out of the water the sea broke over the stern, breaking the skylight and deluging the saloon, breaking over the ship's sheerline. The next wave filled the main deck. The tug straightened her up and she slipped into smooth water and soon anchored off Astoria, where the notorious Columbia River boarding masters came on board and cleared out the seamen shipped at San Francisco. No one living in a law-abiding country could imagine how these rascals set law and order at defiance. They behaved as if the men were their chattels. I am afraid that under the aegis of Lloyd George and his Radical admirers we will see something like it in our country, for when a country is governed by professional politicians corruption and anarchy will surely follow.

The British Vice Consul at Astoria was a man called Cherry, said to have been an officer in the British Indian Army. What any educated man of good character could find to make life bearable in that rough wooden town stuck in a clearing of the woods at the mouth of the Columbia, with a population of roughs and crimps, was hard to understand. One thing was certain, he was (as the Yankees say) out for making the dollars. He was a suave, oily-spoken gentleman with a curtseying voice, a sort of Pooh Bah, for in addition to his services to Britain he was agent for all the firms in Portland to a degree. Those rascals of crimps demanded very large sums as blood money in addition to several months' advance and other charges, and compelled shipmasters to carry to their office these large sums in gold before they would put a seaman on board. Shipmasters had to submit to this degradation – they got no help from the Vice Consul at Astoria or his conferee the Consul at Portland – or ruin their Owners by keeping the ship waiting.

It always appeared to me that in these Pacific States everyone took the line of least resistance: Vice Consul Cherry refused to witness this paying of the blood money, a virtuous resolve that did not blind anyone to the good understanding that existed between the crimps and himself. One bluff old Liverpool shipmaster asked me to go with him whilst he paid this blackmail (I was waiting for a tug to take my ship up to Portland), for he said his Owners were a hard, suspicious lot and as the Consul would not witness his transactions with the crimps he would be obliged if I would. I went with him. He was a most indignant, proud old man. He refused the proffered handshake of the crimps, paid his money, and only by an effort suppressed his feelings. The crimps were arrogant and rude; they wore much jewellery (diamonds and chains) and bore themselves with an overbearing insolence it was hard to endure.

In due time the *Maxwell* was taken in tow by one of the Palace passenger boats that ply on the Columbia River. The crews were highly paid and extremely well fed; the ambition of deep-sea Jack was to get a berth in these boats. I never heard that their desires were realized, for I could imagine there seldom would be a vacancy. The passage from Astoria up the Columbia River was a delightful one. The banks were clothed to the water's edge with primeval forest with a small clearing now and again where some brave pioneer was making himself a home. About ten miles from Portland we entered the Willamette River, whose muddy waters contrasted with the clear Columbia, and soon got moored to a wharf. Portland was a duplicate of a section of San Francisco as to the buildings; outside the few business streets, the roads were almost impassable during the winter months; the rain is constant and roads a mess of deep mud in many places, from four to six inches deep to get to and from the town. I had to adopt the general wear of rubber boots reaching to the thigh. The telephone, electric light and trolley cars were installed, the streets and roadways were abominable. There was nothing of interest to be seen: the city was in the making. There was abundance of food and constant rain. Had the season been summer I would have taken a trip up the Columbia River as far as the famous Cascades.

One day two Germans came on board desirous of shipping. They had been working ashore and had saved several hundred dollars. I consented to take them and engaged them before the British Consul. They gave into my keeping nearly $500. As the *Maxwell* could not load her full cargo at Portland owing to want of water over several bars in the channel of the Columbia, some 500 tons had to be taken on at Astoria, the mouth of the river. To do this the ship had to go to a wharf; when the last of the cargo was alongside I went to Portland where all business was transacted, to clear out and settle up accounts. When I returned the Mate told me that forty or fifty men, some of them armed with revolvers, had raided the ship, held up the officers, and forcibly taken the two Germans I had lawfully engaged out of the ship. This was an act of piracy. I called on Vice Consul Cherry, who shrugged his shoulders and refused to do anything and told me to let the thing go, for if I provoked the crimps they would make me suffer and I could not get any redress. That advice did not appeal to me. So after anchoring my ship in the roads several miles from the town, I went up to Portland and saw my agents Balfour Guthrie & Co., who took the matter up, and I stated the case to several Senators. These gentlemen did what they could, and I learned afterwards they had got a Bill through the State Legislature making it penal for anyone to board a ship or entice a seaman to desert. This was a move in the right direction, but owing to the crimps having the power to prevent a ship getting a crew, and in other ways persecuting a shipmaster, it was a weapon that was seldom or ever used.

On my return I was interviewed by an attorney who demanded the money I was bailee for, belonging to the two abducted German sailors. He showed me an order purporting to be signed by them. I refused to hand the money over to him: I would give it to the men in the presence of the Vice Consul. He threatened to have me arrested. I finely stuck to my resolve, so next day, in the presence of the Consul, the two cowed and terrified men were handed their money. Poor fellows, they must have endured much to make them so abjectly servile and terrified of the crimp who accompanied them. That money was divided amongst the unholy band of partners who governed the town. So much for 'the powers that be' in their boasted 'God's own country'.

For a large ship the difficulties and dangers of crossing the Columbia River bar were very great. Many ships have been detained for several months. Whilst I was detained the Pilot informed me that there was a good opportunity of crossing as such a channel might not happen for months, so after consulting with my agents I sent the ship out in charge of the Pilot to cruise off the river until

I was free to join her. She crossed the bar in safety, as I saw from the Pilot's lookout. In two days I had finished my business, receiving orders to proceed to Dunkirk direct, and went on board a tug chartered to find the ship. The weather had been strong since she crossed the bar and the way that tug behaved was astonishing. She stood on her head, then on her stern, jumped like a porpoise and rolled horribly. I was more sick and ill than I have ever been; the ten hours I was on board of her was abject misery. I did not know how the crew can stand it; their life was seafaring at its worst.

We did not find the ship before late at night. I had arranged that the second night after leaving a blue light should be shown every two hours, and that was how we picked her up out of the mist and darkness. It was a risky job boarding the ship in the tug's skiff, for a bad sea was running, and for some time the tugmaster would not risk it. However, the ship made a lee, and as she was rather crank with a wheat cargo she laid down quietly and I boarded. I was so glad in getting on board, that over and above the agreed remuneration I gave $100 between the Pilot and tugmaster. The Pilot got safely on board the tug, which left for port and we proceeded on our voyage.

We had a fine run through the Pacific, passing Pitcairn Island the twenty-fifth day from the Columbia River bar. We had just finished bending our best suit of sails when the wind came away strongly from the northward, with thick rainy weather, and for fifteen days neither the sun by day nor the stars by night were to be seen, and the ship was navigated by dead reckoning – and by a fact I learned from my old Master, that 'the next best thing to knowing where you are, is to know where you are not'. This paradox I will explain.

By careful dead reckoning a track was projected on the chart; a parallel line was drawn to the north or south of that line. When passing the Horn and the dangerous islands to the south of it, the course was laid so that there was no possibility of the ship running foul of those dangers, and the course from the same data also kept the ship from a too far southerly course. In passing from the Pacific to the Atlantic the course is from southeasterly to easterly then northeasterly. So well did the formula work that when I got sights after fifteen days of blind sailing we were only some twelve miles of latitude and forty miles of longitude out in the dead reckoning, and that was on the side of safety, a very human error.

Many ships heave-to at night under such circumstances and proceed under short sail. We drove along comfortably, our only fears collision with ice or some other ship. I have always found something to hinder me making a record passage. We were into the Atlantic well north of Rio de la Plata on the fifty-first day out when we met with light headwinds and calms until we reached the latitude of the Martin Vaz Islands, when we got the trades. From there until we anchored in the Downs we had good winds, making the passage in the good time of 102 days. In the Horse Latitudes we fell in with a Liverpool barque with a Welsh Master, and supplied him with provisions. Another mendicant of the seas.

From the Downs I engaged a tug to tow to Dunkirk, as the winds were unfavourable, arriving there all in good health and so finishing my voyage.

COLLISION

My Twenty-fourth Voyage
MAXWELL
1891–1892

DUNKIRK – GREENHITHE – SAN FRANCISCO – ASTORIA –
DUNKIRK

My admiration has always been excited in French seaports by the magnificent manner in which the docks, piers and lighthouses are designed, and the pleasing architecture of the powerhouses, warehouses and houses for officers and officials. The massing looks so good, and the stone so bright, and the quays are kept so clean.

Dunkirk has many interesting attractions for a Briton for it was long under our flag and has many historic associations. From Dunkirk came many privateers who preyed on our merchant ships, and the notorious Jean Bart, who shares with Paul Jones the distinction of having been the most dreaded scourge and bugbear of our narrow seas and ports, was a native and made this port his base. He was the most successful of privateers. Squares and streets are named after him, and a large monument occupies the principal site in the town. He is a national hero.

The cathedral is a fine building, the tower separated from the main structure by the width of the street. The interior is beautiful, the chapels have much fine carving and paintings. The altarpiece is much like the work of Flemish artists. Dunkirk, being near the Belgian border, is strongly fortified; the earthworks are not unsightly and I often wandered amongst them without question or hindrance from the sentries. The French have little of the suspicious outlook of Germans. I often went along the seacoast to Malo les

Bains, the watering place of the district. The amusements were after the style of Blackpool, with the addition of the casinos where *rouge et noir* and other games were played and quite a lot of money changed hands. On market days I made a point of attending the mart, which was held in the principal square; the country people were chiefly fair-haired with a Dutch cast. The supplies were cheaper than similar articles in an English market town and there was a larger variety of fine vegetables.

After discharging, we ballasted and drydocked, then towed to Greenhithe to load for San Francisco. I had a delightful time whilst loading, and visited Rochester and all the churches within a reasonable distance. Kent is a lovely county with nice people.

From Greenhithe to the Straits of Le Maire we had favourable winds and weather, passing Cape Horn on the fifty-second day from Beachy Head, the point where we cast off the tug and made sail. The day after passing the Horn the wind settled from the WSW quarter and under reefed canvas, topsails and storm staysails, we had a heavy drag up the dangerous coast until we sighted the land to the south of Cape Pilar. We wore round and kept on the starboard tack for twenty-four hours, then wore onto the port tack, working up the Chilean coast as far as Valdivia, when the winds kept from WNW to WSW, very light. We sighted the Juan Fernandez Islands on the sixtieth day out, and had Robinson Crusoe's Island [Más a Tierra] in sight for thirteen days. We passed between it and Más Afuera [Alexandra Selkirk Island]. For three weeks we had calms and faint airs until at last we got the Southeast Trades. Such an experience is unique. We had every prospect of making an exceptionally quick passage, but our hopes were blighted by the persistent west winds which prevented us getting to the westward and drifted us into calm latitudes.

From the time we got the Trade Winds until arrival in San Francisco we did very well, making the passage, after all the detention, in 123 days; and I had the mortification of finding that the *Larnaca* had arrived three days before, beating the *Maxwell* by five days. On comparing logs, the *Larnaca* was north of Staten Island the day the *Maxwell* sighted Juan de Fernandez. She rounded the Cape and made good westing with the northing, passing the *Maxwell*, then became becalmed 10° to the westward. This was hard luck and I did not at all like being beaten. Giles, like the good chap he was, sympathized with me, and I believe would have been pleased had the *Maxwell* got in first.

Captain Giles had with him his wife and child and sister-in-law, a handsome young lady of some twenty years, and I had a pleasant time during my stay. We spent ten days at Monterey, a famous tourist centre 125 miles south of San Francisco. We put up at the Hotel del Monte, a comfortable hotel with gardens, grounds and parks enriched by skilful landscape artists and trees, plants and flowers of such beauty and profusion that I have not seen equalled. There were long drives in the hotel grounds of from ten to thirty miles, an encampment of Indians, and a zoo containing specimens of the aboriginal fauna of the country. From the beach drive the Pacific Ocean showed a deep blue with magnificent foamy breakers. On the rocks and small islands near the coast were rookeries of seals and sea elephants, whose antics were amusing to watch. There was also provision made for guests who desired the sport of hunting the deer, bear and other wild beasts and birds. Chalets were erected in the woods and hills where, with a skilled hunter, parties spent weeks enjoying sport without discomfort and at the minimum of risk.

The hotel and surrounding country, to the extent of some English counties, was owned by the Southern Pacific Railway Co., and I doubt if there is such a complete and luxurious holiday resort in any other part of the world. The climate is perfection, there was luxurious provision for the amusement of stay-at-home guests and invalids, concerts were held daily, and every night balls and conversaziones. There were excellent baths and sea bathing. We visited the old Mission buildings of Monterey and the remains of the Spanish town and agreed that life in such a country and climate offered the quintessence of existence.

On returning to San Francisco both ships chartered to proceed to Portland, Oregon to load wheat for Europe. The *Larnaca* sailed a few days before us and got into the Columbia River a week before, as we were detained outside owing to the bar being impassible.

For three days we were beating about waiting for a chance to cross, in company with the ship *Kirkcudbrightshire*. At midnight we tacked ship and soon after were run into by the *Kirkcudbrightshire*, breaking our spanker boom lift. The boom fell on the wheel and smashed it, and the anchor broke the halfround plate and the plate below it, and the rail and stanchions. Our ship was on the starboard tack; the colliding ship refused to answer her helm as she was six feet by the head, having discharged part of her cargo to an even keel. She was manned by a crew of Pacific Union runners, an unruly set of men who did as they liked. Some minutes before the collision we heard someone, presumably the Captain, storming and swearing at the man at the wheel and the officer for not giving way sooner. To my mind nothing could be clearer than that the *Kirkcudbrightshire* was to blame. We were on the starboard tack and had been for quite ten minutes before the collision, and had the right of way, and my crew had raised a shout to warn the oncoming ship when we saw a collision was possible. Yet, as I will relate later, my belief in the omniscient wisdom of men who administer justice was for ever shaken.

We made temporary repairs, thankful that we had escaped greater danger and that the man at the wheel was not killed when the heavy boom smashed the wheel. Early next morning we got the tug and Pilot, crossed the bar and came to anchor off Astoria, when those pests the crimps surrounded the ship tempting the men to desert. They daren't come on board, for the law was now in force. (I mentioned in my last voyage's narrative that the State Legislature was making an attempt to protect ships from the lawlessness and piratical practices of crimps.) They did not succeed in getting any of my men that day. Next day was Sunday, a stormy day with heavy squalls. During one of these, in a violent gust our windlass was torn from its bed and the ship was driven near the shore. No doubt the bedplate of the windlass was broken (cracked) during the cyclone at the Sandheads the previous voyage. Now the crimps came along-side. Several of them, I found, smuggled themselves on board. My officers were too much afraid of them to bundle them out, so I went to them and soon had them ashore. Every vituperative epithet was applied to me, and threats to shoot me should I go ashore, for daring to interfere between them and what they considered their legitimate prey. I went ashore, found the marshal deputed by the Legislature to protect shipping, and had two of the worst offenders arrested. They were fined and cautioned and openly boasted they would be revenged on me. This I did not heed, for I had many times proved that threatened men rarely come to grief.

The *Kirkcudbrightshire* came in next day. I called on her Master to examine my ship's damages, and commiserated with him on the careless and reckless conduct of his officer in causing the damage. He said that he had had much trouble with his runners. He had his wife on board, and was roused up by my crew's warning shout. I agreed to have only temporary repairs done to my ship and leave our respective Owners to settle the payment when permanent repairs were carried out, then dismissed the affair from my mind and went into the more important matter of recovering my anchor and chain, and getting in tenders for the repair to the windlass. I was afraid that I would not get such a large casting as the bedplate executed outside of San Francisco. I hired a barge with a powerful windlass and in two days recovered the anchor and cable, got one side of the ship's windlass to work, then towed to Portland where I found a bright young fellow who undertook for £100 to cast and fit a new bedplate, binding himself to time. In due course he completed his contract to Lloyd's Surveyor's and my satisfaction. I was well pleased to get so well out of a situation that promised at one time to cause much delay and expense.

The ship was nearly loaded when Vice Consul Laidlaw sent a note requesting to see me. When I called on him, he after much shuffling said that he had decided to hold an enquiry into the collision between the *Kirkcudbrightshire* and the *Maxwell*. I said, 'This is a monstrous act of injustice to me, for I have been here for six weeks and you have not moved in the matter, and now when I am about ready for leaving you spring this on me! What is your reason for acting so?' He could give no reason. Lloyd's Surveyor, Captain Pope, told me that the Vice Consul was also agent for S. Law, the Owner of the *Kirkcudbrightshire*, and that he had received a letter from Law to try and relieve the pressure of blame now resting on the *Kirkcudbrightshire*.

For three days the enquiry went on. Our evidence was simple and to the point. On the arrival of the *Kirkcudbrightshire* Captain Pope had taken her draft: this was important as it proved why the ship would not readily answer her helm when under sail, being no less than six feet by the head. The Pilot who brought the *Kirkcudbright-shire* over the bar and the Pilot who took her up the river stated that she steered very badly. Then the other side had their innings. I was astounded at the lies sworn to – my crew got indignant and the Court was like a bear garden. As I cross-examined, Captain

Giles rapidly drew diagrams of the position they put the ship in, with which I confuted their evidence. Lloyd's Surveyor told the Consul that he was trying to screen the *Kirkcudbrightshire* and accused him of having 'packed the jury'. One of his assessors was a drunken frequenter of brothels, the other a young man he had suborned by having him to dine with him.

There never was such a travesty of a Court. It was the laughing stock of Portland, for it was openly said that an enormous bill had been run up by the *Kirkcudbrightshire*'s Master and agent for repairs allegedly occasioned by the collision. I was never asked to examine any damage, and the conspirators had little knowledge of the way such things were managed if they thought by such action to get damages from me. The closing day was a bad one for Vice Consul Laidlaw. He was a mean fellow both in looks and character, and was no ornament to British prestige. He never had the pluck to personally acquaint me with the findings of the Court – though one of the assessors came to me with tears in his eyes saying that whatever I thought of the finding of the Court he assured me that he had tried to act justly. I said, 'Oh I see you have whitewashed the *Kirkcudbrightshire*. I do not think you a knave, only a soft fool Laidlaw has hoodwinked.'

On the day I was clearing for sea the Consul sent his clerk to hand me the finding of the Court, which was to the effect that the *Maxwell* was to blame for tacking under the *Kirkcudbrightshire*'s bows, not giving her room to keep away. And the *Kirkcudbrightshire* was guilty of contributing negligence in not doing anything to assist the ship in paying off and so clearing the *Maxwell*. A false finding: one they had been forced into. I did not accept their ruling and demanded a full transcript of the evidence. This the Consul refused to give me. I threatened to have the case re-opened at home. This frightened him, and I found on arrival home that he had sent a garbled partial and partisan account to the shipping papers in London. He believed in getting his blow in first.

When I arrived at Queenstown some hundred days afterwards I went to Liverpool and with the Owner saw a member of the great firm of shipping lawyers Grey, Hill & Dickinson, who heard my statement and said they were perfectly satisfied to let the finding stand. The Underwriters were content. On my exclaiming on the injustice of the Consul's Court, he asked me if I was prepared to put down £500 to commence an action in the Admiralty Court. I shook my head, then he asked the Owner if he was. Mr T. emphatically declared he was not. Then the lawyer said, 'This world is full of injustice – we all have to put up with it. It is not worth risking £500 or more in defence of your *amour propre*. What will the collision cost you?' I said, 'Probably sixty pounds.' 'And what the cost to the *Kirkcudbrightshire*?' I said I was informed £1,200.

'There you are: they have to pay for all their own damages and a bad conscience, you suffer a little in your self esteem.'

I left the lawyer and have always bracketed this with the Wilson affair (as told in my seventeenth voyage) as a great miscarriage of justice. Laidlaw the Consul is now dead. I cannot say any good of him.

The *Larnaca* left Portland and cleared the bar a week before the *Maxwell* left Astoria, both ships cleared for Queenstown or Falmouth for orders. When the *Maxwell* was ready to leave the Pilot reported that the bar was feasible, so in great glee that we had not to have a weary wait bar-bound, we left the wharf at Astoria. Night had closed in when we approached the bar, and I noticed as we neared the dangerous zone that the waves were running high and there was an ominous booming sound that was not reassuring. The Pilot looked anxious and was fidgety. I asked him was there not a high sea running on the bar: he said there was, and it often happened in the winter season when only moderate winds were blowing on the coast that the high seas from a storm thousands of miles away broke on the bar. He said that now was the height of the highest spring tide, we had the most powerful tug, and he had every confidence we should cross in safety. With this assurance I tried to be at ease, though I did not like the roaring on the bar, nor the phosphorescent glow on the surf which was now all round us and cast a baleful light in the blackness of the night. Suddenly we got into broken water, the ship was hove up and down by huge waves, then she bumped heavily again and again. The seas filled the main deck, washing away movables and getting the running gear and braces into disorder. For a time she stuck. The Pilot lost his nerve, got excited and said he would jump overboard. I got hold of him and told him not to be a fool, to wait a bit and then he would have company, for if the hawser parted, or the tug slipped it, the ship would broach to the sea, capsize, and destruction and death would be inevitable. (Danger always stiffened and brightened me.)

After another and lighter bump the ship dropped down the flank of a big wave and was on the seaward side of the bar. The tug was ordered to tow slowly seawards. The pumps were sounded carefully for three hours, and the second officer was sent down the pump well and reported dry timbers. So sail was set, and the Pilot and tug dismissed. Both Pilot and tugmaster were very much shaken with the experiences of the last four hours.

For two days we had moderate winds and then a heavy gale from the SSE to southwest set in and rose to the force of a hurricane, blowing away our best lower topsails; then the battering of the beam sea, for she would not keep to the wind, shifted, or rather settled, the cargo of wheat to leeward, causing the ship to take such a list that the main deck was half under water. We were helpless to do anything to help her and fast drifting to the west coast of Vancouver Island, which amongst North Pacific sailors goes by the name of 'the graveyard', so many ships get lost there. When the tempest stayed its fury and we were able to take the hatches off and get to work to trim the ship upright, at the end of the first four hours' work, when part of the hands were called up to dinner, the men shipped at Astoria came to me in a body saying that the ship was unseaworthy and wanted to know what I was going to do. Was I going to put into San Francisco? I said, 'You want to know what I am going to do? Well, I am just now going for my dinner.' I left them. Three months' advance had been paid for these men, which they had to work up. They would have very little if any balance on arrival home, and for the ship to put into San Francisco would suit them very well, for they would desert there in the hope of bettering themselves – which hope, experience never taught them, would never be realized.

After I had dinner I called all hands, saying that I had been asked by the men engaged at Astoria if I intended putting into port to get the cargo re-stowed. The object of those men was plain for all to understand, and it was a waste of precious time to discuss that matter for the ship was in imminent danger: she was now not under control. Providence had given us a few hours of moderate weather in which we must do our part manfully, for we were only seventy miles from the dangerous shore of Vancouver Island. The barometer was falling again, and if everyone did not exert themselves the ship and all on board would be lost, for she in her crippled state would drift ashore or get capsized.

All hands then got to work with a will, some to bend the topsails and get sail set, the majority to trim cargo. At midnight the topsails were set, the ship fairly upright and pumps manned. After four hours' strenuous pumping a suck was had and assurance given that the ship had no leak, which I feared from the bumping on the bar. The water had got into the hold through the pumps, the lee pump having been many hours under water. The wind rose rapidly to a hard northerly gale which soon drove us into more genial latitudes.

The seamen from Astoria, still thinking to make something from the disaster, were seeking a backing from the old members of the crew: I again called all hands together and told them we were now in fine weather; I was perfectly satisfied the cargo would not shift again, explaining that it was only the mischance of meeting so soon with an exceptional gale, before the cargo had shaken down, that had caused the dangerous situation that we had so narrowly escaped from. I explained the system by which the cargo was secured by shifting boards, that my duty was to take measures to save the ship's cargo and lives from justly apprehended dangers and that if I had the least suspicion that the cargo would again shift I would put into a port of Southern Chile. We had a four thousand mile run through fine weather before entering the southern bad weather latitudes: when we got there, if they were still in fear I would again discuss the position with them. With my proposition there was no cavil; it was a case of 'molasses being better than vinegar'. Out of my crew of thirty, twelve were new hands who had everything to gain by the ship putting into port. They were ready to strike and would have had adherents, for sailors much resemble sheep and follow a leader. Hectoring, overbearing conduct on my part would have precipitated a row, which at the best would not have benefited the ship. They never again occasioned any fears for her seaworthiness and I heard no more mutinous talk.

We arrived at Queenstown 102 days from Astoria, a good passage; the *Larnaca* got in three days afterwards, the *Maxwell* beating her by ten days and getting revenged for the outward passage. We were ordered to Dunkirk to discharge and had a rapid passage there, so ending my twenty-fourth voyage.

DISASTER ON THE
LIVERPOOL BAR:
MAXWELL CHANGES HANDS
My Twenty-fifth Voyage

1892
DUNKIRK – LIVERPOOL BAR

We had a very good dispatch discharging our cargo, and left Dunkirk in tow for Liverpool. On arrival in the Mersey I could not secure the services of a stern tug, and in docking during a severe squall the ship's head was driven against the pierhead, damaging a plate and a cathead and increasing the damages to be repaired. I would have gladly taken a holiday, and an arrangement was made with the Marine Superintendent to superintend the repairs. Unfortunately, he was unexpectedly called on to look after one of the ships of his permanent employ and I was kept in Liverpool. In due time repairs were executed, and *Maxwell* drydocked and taken across the river to load for San Francisco. I then ran down to Cumberland for a weekend. On returning I engaged the crew, and the loading being completed we left Birkenhead Dock on a lovely summer morning, the 18th July 1892, in tow of the paddle tug *Great Western*.

As we approached the Rock, the sky became overcast and a thick haze came in from the sea, which gradually thickened into a dense fog. The tug kept slowly on her way, passing the bar ship about noon. Soon after, the Pilot boat was seen and the Pilot dismissed, the fog having lifted and the wind a faint air from the west. An hour after passing the Northwest Lightship, without any warning the wind burst on us like the shot from a gun and blew with extraordinary fury. The tug could do nothing against the wind and tried to hold her own by zig-zagging; to help her we attempted to set the lower staysails. Each one was blown away. The storm was now of hurricane force. In pulling the ship's head round from the west shore the hawser parted; to anchor would have ensured the loss of ship and all on board, for with such a wind and high sea the cables would have parted the moment the weight of the ship came on them. The helm was kept hard down, the mizzen yards backed and foreyards run square to keep the ship's head as near the wind as possible and retard the drift towards the banks.

The broken hawser was the tug's; we had a new five inch steel hawser. This we passed through the towing pipe, and with much labour along on the lee side to the quarter. The tug was manoeuvred under shelter of the ship, and after many fruitless endeavours and narrow escapes from collision at last succeeded in getting her heaving line on board the ship, as we could not run any risk of the hauling line parting by having the heavy wire hawser entrusted to it. We bent on a long length of new three inch manilla rope, and were gladdened by being once more attached to our only hope, the tug. In such a position, in narrow waters bounded by an iron-bound coast and banks, with a hurricane from seaward the force of which precluded the idea of help from our motive power, the sails, a sailing ship is indeed a helpless machine.

The tug resumed her zig-zag tactics. Hour after hour was consumed in striving against the wind and sea. We were losing ground, for the sea had risen to an exceptional height and power. The tug, being a paddle boat, lost much of her power by the sea throwing the paddles out of the water, and to keep on meant inevitable destruction for we were now not far from the banks. As a last resort the tugmaster I saw was resolved to try to re-cross the bar. It was now 10 p.m., the tide ebbing, no abatement in the force of the wind, its direction unchanged. When before the wind, the sea was so high the *Maxwell* pooped twice, a thing she had never done in the heaviest gales in the open ocean.

We passed close to the bar ship, hugging the buoys on our port side where the deepest water was; I had hopes we should cross in safety until, after one heave on the crest of a high wave, the ship sunk in the trough and I felt a peculiar undescribable tremor. This happened again and again, then she struck with such force that spars were broken and everyone shaken off their feet; the hawser parted, the seas overwhelmed the ship, and standing aft I now felt and heard a great crash. Then the ship settled down and lay quiet, with the sea washing over her.

On the first crash I had all hands mustered at the extreme end of the poop, as being the place most free from the force of the waves breaking over the bridge. Very little of the ascribed traditional courage of our race was in evidence: many were crying and lamenting like hysterical children. I was forced to use some suitable sea language to them. Our children should be taught that death is not the end but the beginning: death should not be feared.

At midnight the wind had jumped to the northward and fallen in force. A schooner under small canvas ran into our quarter, dismasting herself, drifted away and sank with the loss of her crew. Soon after this a lifeboat attempting to come near was capsized by the raging cross-sea and drifted out of sight. Then the New Brighton lifeboat, after much difficulty, succeeded in reaching the lee side of the ship. This boat was managed in a masterly manner; one by one the crew were rescued until all had left. I alone was on board in the mizzen rigging, for now even the poop was under water. I was silly enough to refuse to leave the ship, not from any foolish sentiment but from feelings that only those who have been in a similar position can appreciate. No entreaties could move me: then the coxswain and one of the lifeboat's crew, at considerable peril, got in the rigging and proceeded from supplication to intimidation. At a hint of the latter I showed fight, then they entreated me to leave the ship for they said they would not leave without me. The lifeboat had twice nearly capsized. The crew were all married men, and their loss would plunge their families into distress and poverty. With that I promised to leave, so after they had got safely into the lifeboat when she was on the crest of a wave I jumped into her, bruising myself severely and being stunned. The next thing that I remember was someone putting into my mouth something that had a strong taste of Stockholm tar, which I was told was rum. The lifeboat landed me at New Brighton Pier, a kindly policeman took me in his care and got a cab in which I reached my brother's son's house. The rest of the crew were taken to the Liverpool side and duly cared for by the humane and benevolent societies seafarers are so much indebted to.

I learned that the lifeboat that was capsized in endeavouring to get near us was the Number Two Mersey Dock and Harbour Lifeboat launched from Princes Stage upon the *Great Western* giving notice of the disaster to the *Maxwell*. This pulling boat was manned and taken in tow by the tug *Kingfisher* proceeding down channel to the wreck. With such a heavy sea, the lifeboat was filled many times but the water left the boat automatically by the two valves in the bottom.

After more than an hour's towing, the lifeboat was cast off some three hundred yards to the windward of the *Maxwell*. She was pulled [rowed] toward the sunken ship through the heavy breaking sea, striving to get to the lee side. She had crossed the stern to take up the best position to rescue the crew, when suddenly a high cross-sea struck her and threw her clean over and her crew into the water. The crew managed to scramble onto the boat's bottom, and clung to the keel. They were driven before the gale for five hours, across the banks, clinging to the overturned boat as best they could. More than once, benumbed with cold and tired of being buffeted by the sea, one or other of the poor chaps let go his hold and fell back in the sea, only grabbed in time by one of his mates and hauled back on the boat. When lifted on top of a wave they could see the New Brighton lifeboat which had followed them down channel. The roar of the gale, the noise of the waves and the darkness prevented the men on the half-submerged boat attracting their attention.

About seven o'clock in the morning, the lifeboat to which the men were still clinging was seen by some fishermen who were on the lookout on the beach close to Hoylake, as is the custom of fishermen after a stormy night. They saw the boat drifting towards the beach near Leasowe Lighthouse. Assistance was obtained and the men brought ashore. A little while before the boat grounded all the men were alive, but when they landed two were dead and a third was in a critical state and died a few hours after being taken to the Hoylake Hospital.

Amongst my many hazardous adventures this wild night in the Mersey estuary holds a prominent place in my memories. It was really a tropical hurricane that strayed far north that July night. The force of the wind was registered at Bidston Hill Observatory at from eighty to one hundred miles per hour. Though we old seamen of the long voyage sentimentally deplore the passing of the white-winged clippers, yet when I think of this and other wild nights, the painful and abominable sufferings off Cape Horn and on the eastward run to Australia and the Far East, I am thankful that Science and Steam have so much lessened acute and undeserved suffering and death amongst our successors who carry on the seaborne trade of the world.

A Government enquiry was held to enquire into the loss of life from the lifeboat. This enquiry covered the mishap to the *Maxwell*. I was not called on to attend and there was no Board of Trade inquisition. The *Maxwell* wreck was abandoned to the Underwriters, who handed her over for salvage to the Liverpool Salvage Co. Very few, if any, ships had ever been recovered from the tideswept banks of the Mersey estuary, and little hopes were entertained of the *Maxwell*. Singular to say, however, the tides had swept her up a hard sound bank, instead of what was expected, that she would sink in the quicksands. Salvage was possible, and all the appliances to that end were made use of. I went down with one of the ex Owners and was amused: the clever, rather conceited salvage officer in charge had large relays of men at high wages busy discharging cargo out of the forehold to get the pumps to work when, without effort, at his hand there was a roomy and clear way for the pumps to reach the limbers by putting them down the chain locker. I pointed that out to Mr T. who asked me not to point out such an obvious way to the officer as he had no desire to have the salvaged wreck. It was entertaining to listen to the boasting glorification of himself by the salvage officer when explaining to some Underwriting swell the need for the discharging out of the forehatch when there was already an ample way for his pumps without trouble. So I left him to his own devices.

Next day when I went down I found the pumps working; the divers had partially blocked the rents and the pumps could master the water. There were many tugs in attendance and at high water with a pull together and much shrieking of sirens, the *Maxwell* was drawn out of the maw that had never before released its prey.

The ship was docked in the Great Float, Birkenhead and I was put in charge of her. Discharging of the cargo was pushed on from dawn to dark, the steam pumps kept going all the time, with the salvage company's engineers in charge. I was lodged at the Seacombe Hotel, a short distance from the berth.

One night I was called up at one in the morning by the ship's watchman to say the ship had capsized onto the dock. I hurriedly dressed and went to the ship and found her lying at a dangerous angle. I got all the men available and had the heavy staging used for the discharge thrown off the ship, and got the steam pumps going. As the sun rose a strong offshore gale sprang up, which greatly helped to upright the ship; by breakfast time all danger was passed. I wired to Liverpool for a gang of riggers and had yards and masts sent down, which would do much to prevent another such danger. The pumping engineer was in fault. He had partaken of too much liquid refreshment with his supper and fallen asleep while the pumps stopped. The ship had a slight inshore list from the weight of the stages, which the constant ingress of the water increased until the ship fell over. The pumping staff, after my report, were relieved of their duties in a satisfactory manner and the cargo was discharged. The hold was cleanswept and the leaks stopped by a lavish use of cement. The pumps were taken away and an examination made of the damages sustained from the inside.

One hundred and twenty-six floor frames and reverse frames on the port side and forty on the starboard side were broken. The rudder was broken off by the closing plate and the sternpost from the second pintle, and the plates from a line from there to some fifteen feet of keel. The after run of the ship was constructed in the old-fashioned way by having large pockets from a twenty foot base filled with cement carried up decreasing in size as far as the 'tween decks. This made it possible to salve her, for the cement in great measure held in place, and the influx of water was not beyond the power of the steam pumps. A more modern built ship would have been a total loss.

What loose ideas reputable men have of their duty to their neighbours where Underwriters are concerned. Several foremen boilermakers and riveters were sent from one of the oldest and most respected shipbuilding firms in Liverpool, to test the rivets in the beam knees and make a thorough examination of the floors, etc. After they had been down the hold several hours I went down to see how they were getting on, and found two asleep. I roused them up and asked had they finished? They said 'Not quite.' I made them show me what they had done and found that they had not done five minutes' work. I dismissed them, then found that their mate had spent his time in a public house. He was fuddled, and in answer to my remonstrances said, 'It's an insurance job – we always make such jobs last.'

I dismissed him, reported the three. Next morning the yard manager came over and was surprised that I should have made such a fuss and bother when it was an insurance job. I said, 'Don't care who pays – anyone who comes to work whilst I am here has to do his work or I send him away.' After this, men sent from that yard did their work diligently. The ship was taken into the drydock in the Great Float, and underwent the usual examination by Lloyd's Surveyors, shipbuilders and others, and estimates were made of the cost of repairs. After several days' delay I got instructions to see she was fit to be taken over the river to be repaired by S. B. Royden & Co. who had built her. After using more cement to choke the leaks and taking other precautions, I got my rigger on board and left the drydock and towed to the basin, waiting there until such time as the dock gates would be opened. Just on the point of leaving, a red-faced old chap in broadcloth and a silk hat came on board in a great state of excitement, handing me a note which instructed me to hand over the ship to Captain . . ., the representative of Clover & Clayton, ship repairers. This I did, with a sarcastic comment on his want of repose.

Gregory, J. S. & Co.'s clerk, explained the reason for such a change in the ship's disposal. Mr S. had made a lucrative bargain (for him) with the Underwriters; he was to receive the sum of £12,000 and the ship. The repairs by Royden's estimate would not exceed £6,000, giving the Owners a ship with a very small capital value and a large sum into pocket. At the meeting on the day I had been in the basin, this agreement was to be ratified. Mr S. got up and expatiated on his own generosity in not demanding his full pound of flesh, as he might have, he said, claimed his full insurance, and rubbed in his magnanimous conduct. The Underwriter who had the matter in charge (I think he was called Mr Wallace) jumped up and replied: they were obliged to Mr S., they did not want his generosity, they had taken the risk and would abide by it. Let the matter stand over for an hour, then he would settle it. In less than an hour he informed his colleagues and Mr S. that he had sold the ship to Clover & Clayton, which transaction would largely benefit the Underwriters and they would pay Mr S. the full insurance on the *Maxwell*. Gregory said that Mr S. was much chagrined and regretted his generosity speech.

After an interview with the Owners I agreed to put £2,000 or so into a new ship they proposed building. I went to Cumberland for a time, and now and again went up to Liverpool to see the Naval Architect who had the designing of the new ship in hand. I was also to undertake Marine Superintendence duties.

The *Maxwell* was repaired and managed for a time by Nicholson & Co. and then by John Edgar & Co. After a few years' sailing she was sunk by a collision off Dover. There was not a great loss of life.

My twenty-fifth voyage and the twenty-seventh year of my sea life ended in July 1892.

ACKNOWLEDGEMENTS

D. S. Stonham AMA, BA   Assistant Keeper Historic Photographs, National Maritime Museum, Greenwich

Mrs Holmes   Information Retrieval Department, National Maritime Museum, Greenwich

H. Fancy AMA   The Curator, Whitehaven Museum

D. Hays Esq   Whitehaven

E. R. Wilkinson Esq   Local History Librarian, Carlisle Library

D. Perriam Esq   Assistant Custodian, Carlisle Museum Collection

T. Stephens MA   Director Walker Art Gallery, Liverpool

A. P. Nute Esq   Assistant Secretary, Mersey Docks and Harbour Co.

Nancy Eaglesham MA, PHD   Carlisle

R. D. Johnson MIPR   Port of London Authority

R. Brown Esq   Archivist, Port of London Authority

D. Wilson Esq   Photographic Library, Australian High Commission

M. K. Stammers AMA, BA   Keeper of Maritime History, Merseyside County Museum

The Parker Gallery   2 Albemarle Street, London W1

D. G. Wright Esq   Victoria and Albert Museum, London